ACKNOWLEDGMENTS

A special thanks to all those who have contributed to my knowledge and brought this book together. My parents, for teaching and encouraging me to appreciate boutique alcohol instead of abusing it. My sister Charlie, who introduced me to the hospitality industry. Sam and Josh, who taught me so much foundational knowledge about the world of mixology and spirits. Fleur, for designing and creating the book and brand. Madison, for her writing and editing.

A huge thank you to Mike, Bruce and Emma for all their help.

Another thank you to Charles, Trish and Jess for all their hard work, passion, and knowledge that helped bring the book together.

And of course, to Mike, for encouraging me to create the book and bringing it to life!

Authors: George Grbich and Madison Fisher
Contributor: Jessica Clayfield
Design: Fleur Curac
Website: worldginguides.com
Instagram: @australianginguide
Facebook: The Guide to Australian Gin

PUBLISHED BY
People Media Group
Newmarket, Auckland, New Zealand
peoplemediagroup.co.nz

© People Media Group 2022
ISBN 978-0-473-64665-3

CONTENTS

6	The Team	40	Bathurst Grange Distillery
8	Australian Botanicals	41	Battery Point Distillery
12	**GIN DISTILLERIES**	42	Beachtree Distilling Co.
14	7K Distillery	43	Bellarine Distillery
15	78 Degrees Distillery	44	Big River Distilling Co.
16	100 Souls Distillery	45	Big Tree Distillery
17	Adams Distillery	46	Billson's
18	Alfred Wiley Distillery	48	Blackmans Bay Distillery
19	AmberChes Spirits Distillery	49	Blackwood Valley Distillery
20	Ambleside Distillers	49	Blend Etiquette Craft Distillery
21	Ambra Spirits	51	Blue Mountains Gin Company
23	Ambrosia Distillery	52	Boatrocker Brewers & Distillers
23	Animus Distillery	53	Bombak Distillery
25	Antagonist Spirits	54	Bond Store Wallaroo
26	Anther Spirits Distillery	56	Bondi Liquor Co.
28	Apollo Bay Distillery	57	Brogan's Way Distillery
29	Applewood Distillery	59	Brunswick Aces
30	Archie Rose Distilling Co.	60	Bruny Island House of Whisky
31	Artemis Winery & Distillery	61	Buffalo Vale Distillery
33	Artillery Artisan Distillery	62	Camden Valley Distilling Company
34	Australian Distilling Co.	63	Cape Byron Distillery
35	BABY Pink Gin	64	Capricorn Distilling Co.
36	Backwoods Distilling Co.	65	Castle Glen Distillery
37	Baker Williams Distillery	66	Cedar Fox Distilling Co.
38	Banks & Solander Distillery	67	Clarence Distillery
39	Barossa Distilling Co.	68	Clark & Kealey Distilling

2

THE GUIDE TO AUSTRALIAN GIN

69	Critters Distillery	99	Headlands Distilling Company
69	Cuprum Distillery	100	Heathcote Gin
70	Darling Distillery	102	Hellfire Bluff Distillery
71	Darwin Distilling Co.	103	Hepburn Distillery
72	Distil on the Hill	104	HG Hemp Gin
73	Distillery Botanica	104	HHH Distill
74	Diviners Distillery	106	Hickson House Distilling Co
75	Dunalley Bay Distillery	107	HillsCrest Distillery
77	Dune Distilling Co.	107	Hurdle Creek Still
78	Earp Distilling Co.	109	Husk Distillers
79	Echuca Distillery	110	Imbue Distillery
80	Emerald Island Distillery	111	Imperial Measures Distilling
81	Envy Distilling	112	Impression Spirits
82	Esperance Distillery Co	112	IronHouse Distillery
83	Ester Spirits	113	Joadja Distillery
84	Eventide Hills Distillery	114	Kalki Moon
84	Farmer's Wife Distillery	116	Kangaroo Island Spirits
85	Finders Distillery	117	Karu Distillery
86	Flowstate Brewers and Distillers	118	Kilderkin Distillery
86	Fonzie Abbott	119	Kings Cross Distillery
87	Fossey's Distillery	120	Knocklofty Spirits
88	Four Pillars	121	Ladbroken Distilling Co.
90	Gindu	122	Lark Distillery
91	GinFinity	124	Lawrenny Estate Distillery
92	Ginny Pig Distillery	125	Legacy Spirit Distilling Co.
94	Ginworth	126	Libation Liquor
94	Gold Emotion Australia	126	Little Juniper Distilling Co.
95	Goodradigbee Distillers	127	Little Lon Distilling Co.
96	Grower's Own Distillery	128	Loaded Barrel Distillery
97	Hang 10 Distillery	129	LOBO Spirits
98	Happenstance Distillery	130	Loch Brewery & Distillery
99	Hartshorn Distillery		

131	Lord Howe Island Distilling Co.	159	Puss & Mew Distillery
131	Luxe Brew	160	Queenscliff Distillery
132	Manly Spirits Co. Distillery	161	Red Hen Spirits
133	Maria River Distillery	162	Republic of Fremantle
134	Mountain Distilling Company	163	Riverbourne Distillery
134	Mt Uncle Distillery	163	Ruby Wednesday Distillery
136	Murray's Craft Brewing Co - Distillery	165	S.A. Distilling Co.
137	Naught Distilling	166	Saint Felix Distillery
138	Needle and Pin Spirits	166	Sandy Gray Whisky Company
139	Never Never Distilling Co.	167	Seabourne Distillery
140	New Norfolk Distillery	167	Seppeltsfield Rd Distillers
141	Newcastle Distilling Co.	169	Settlers Spirits
143	Newy Distillery	170	Seven Seasons
144	Noble Bootleggers Distilling Co	171	Sin Gin Distillery
145	North of Eden	172	SIP Distillers - TROGIN
147	Nosferatu Distillery	172	SoHi Spirits
148	Old Kempton Distillery	173	South Coast Distillery
149	Original Spirit Co.	174	Southern Wild Distillery
150	Otways Distillery	175	Spirit of Little Things
151	Paradise Distillers	176	Spring Bay Distillery
152	Pietro Gallus Estate	177	St Agnes Distillery
152	Plan B Distillery	178	Stableviews Distillery
154	Pokolbin Distillery	178	Strait Distillery
155	Poor Toms Distillery	180	Styx Brewery and Distillery
156	Portia Valley Wines	181	Summerleas Distillery
157	Prohibition Liquor Co.	182	Sunny Hill Distillery
		183	Sunset Gin

183	Sunshine & Sons	214	Wildbrumby Distillery
184	Taka Gin Co	215	Willing Distillery
185	Tamborine Mountain Distillery	216	Winding Road Distilling Co.
186	Tar Barrel Brewery & Distillery	217	Winston Quinn Handcrafted Gin
187	That Spirited Lot Distillers		
188	The Abel Gin Co.	218	Wolf Lane Distillery
189	The Aisling Distillery	219	Yack Creek Distillery
190	The Antipodes Gin Co.	221	Young Henrys Brewing and Distilling
192	The Craft & Co		
194	The Derwent Distilling Co.	**222**	**FEVER-TREE**
195	The Melbourne Gin Company	223	A Short History of Tonic
196	The Splendid Gin	224	How to Create the Perfect Gin & Tonic
197	The Still Co.		
198	The West Winds Distillery	226	Tonics
199	Three Little Birds Distillery	228	Gingers & Cola
200	Threefold Distilling	229	Sodas
202	Tinberry Distilling Co.		
202	Tiny Bear Distillery		
203	Tread Softly		
204	Turner Stillhouse		
205	Twenty Third Street Distillery		
207	Underground Spirits		
208	Unexpected Guest Distillery		
209	Wandering Distillery		
210	Wild Flower Gin Distillery		
211	Wild Hibiscus Distilling Co		
212	Wild Road Spirits		
213	Wild Wombat Spirits		

THE TEAM

GEORGE GRBICH - TASTER & AUTHOR

George is a New Zealand based spirits writer and judge with many years of experience working in the hospitality industry. A passionate gin advocate whose love for spirits sprung from his father's love for a good gin and tonic. He has extensive knowledge of the New Zealand and Australian Gin industries, comprehensively tasting just under 1000 Australasian gins over the past two years. Deeply intrigued by the variety of styles and distillation techniques being used in the modern world of gin, he is a strong supporter of the ever growing boutique and artisanal spirits scene. He also obtained the WSET Level 2 Award in Spirits qualification in 2021.

JESSICA CLAYFIELD - TASTER & CONTRIBUTOR

Jess was brought up in the kitchens of some of Adelaide's old-world fine dining restaurants before moving to bar work via festivals and cocktail bars. Fuelled by a love of gin and tonic, she eventually landed at Melbourne's institution of juniper, Gin Palace. During her long tenure there, stirring martinis and creating contemporary cocktails, she was given the unofficial title of 'The Lady of Botanicals'. Her knowledge of all things gin has been built with a focus on the scientific reasons certain botanicals have made their way into gin. Diving into the history and compositional analysis of Australia's most prolific indigenous botanicals, she continues to push her understanding of Australian flavours and champion their qualities.

TRISH BREW - TASTER

Trish is a prominent figure in the Australian hospitality scene as an award-winning bartender, spirit competition judge, hobbyist distiller, and liquor enthusiast. She managed Gin Palace, the oldest and most prestigious gin bar in the country for almost nine years, preceding the local gin boom and contributing significantly to the awareness of the category. She is also the first ever Australian ambassador of Fever-Tree mixers. A role centred on spirits and mixing education, which includes working with bartenders and local spirit producers to upskill staff and enhance their venue offerings.

CHARLES CASBIN - TASTER

Charles was schooled in classic cocktails at a relatively young age by an enthusiastic father and continued a dedicated education in spirituous drinks whilst studying Physics and Mathematics at the University of Sydney. Moving on from academia, he worked his way around Sydney's hospitality scene, eventually pursuing a serious education in wine and becoming certified as a sommelier by the Court of Master Sommeliers in 2011. He has since opened his own cocktail bar, Moya's Juniper Lounge, in Sydney in 2016 (recognized as Australia's Best Gin Bar in the Australian Bar Awards – 2022) and judges at the Australian Gin Awards.

Our tasters have selected a range of highly commended gins.

NATIVE AUSTRALIAN BOTANICALS

- Jessica Clayfield, The Lady of Botanicals

TASMANIAN PEPPERBERRY:
Tasmanian Mountain Pepperberry is one of the most popular Australian gin botanicals. Not actually a pepper, the berries and leaves of the plant boast oily, camphoraceous notes with distinct eucalypt oils and hints of candied fruit. Often used as an alternative to traditional peppery botanicals, pepperberry maintains its sweet and spice characteristics throughout the distillation process, and creates a bold and warming lift in a gin.

STRAWBERRY GUM:
One of Australia's most intriguing botanicals, named for its intense jammy strawberry aroma. The sweet, pungent gum leaf also has notes of balsamic vinegar, tea tree, and almond. In addition to its unmistakable aroma, it is also prized for its synergistic properties in gin, much like orris root, creating harmony between botanicals.

LEMON ASPEN:
Lemon Aspen is an Australian citrus with two varieties sharing the name, True Lemon Aspen has a more intense in flavour, while White Lemon Aspen is more widely grown. These small star shaped fruits are packed full of bright, fresh lemon sherbet flavour, and can be quite astringent and intense. Distillation in gin helps to release its more complex characteristics of eucalypt resin, honey, myrrh, and green apples.

LEMON MYRTLE:
Widely used in Australian gin as an alternative to lemons, Lemon Myrtle is the most widely cultivated native gum in Australia. Prized for its fresh lemon aroma, it contains the highest quantity of citral of any natural plant, the compound responsible for giving citrus peel its scent and flavour. Also containing notes of bay leaf, rose, and geranium, lemon myrtle gives off a cooling, intense citrus aroma with a sweet, candied lemon taste.

BOOBIALLA:
Often called 'Native Juniper', Boobialla is a type of widespread shrub found throughout the southern Australian coast. Originally planted as windbreaks and hedges, much like blackthorn berries, boobialla berries are too astringent to be consumed raw. Distilling helps to break down the astringency and brings forth more woody, fruit flavours.

SEA PARSLEY:
A small leafy plant that grows widely along the southern coasts of Australia, variances in specific coastal landscapes significantly alter the appearance and taste of different varieties. It carries a distinctive fresh, bitter flavour, with a distinguished oceanic saltiness.

ANISEED MYRTLE:

Aniseed Myrtle contains the highest concentration of anethole of any natural plant, the compound which gives aniseed flavours to plants. Its cooling sweetness has made it a popular botanical in Australian gins, in place of more traditional anise botanicals such as liquorice root or star anise. It has the same synergistic effect on other botanicals, helping to bond flavours together, with added notes of eucalypt, chestnut, and fennel. The leaves, whether dried or fresh, contain a lot of oil, and anethol in particular is prone to louching (clouding) in alcohol when chilled or mixed.

QUANDONG:

Quandong is one of Australia's widest growing fruit trees, growing in all arid parts of the continent. Often nicknamed 'native' or 'wild' peach, the tart quandong is a member of the sandalwood family. The fruit often varies in sweetness and astringency, and therefore its complex composition gives it a unique and difficult to define flavour, largely comprised of tropical stone fruit qualities, fermented dry eucalypt aromas, and hints of floral and green spice.

RIBERRY:

Riberry is one of 60 varieties of Lilly Pilly. Typically an ornamental plant, riberry is favoured above other varieties for its abundant fruits which are high in vitamins, antioxidants, and minerals, making it a 'superfood'. Growing in clusters, the small pear-shaped fruit has an astringent cranberry flavour, with hints of musky floral, conifer, and spiced tea. In distillation, the spiced notes become more pronounced without the bitter acidity. Clove, cinnamon, rich honey, refreshing menthol, and conifer notes carry through.

SALTBUSH:

Saltbush is one of Australia's most versatile plants. With 52 Australian varieties, the most commonly used are Old Man and Bluegreen. As its name suggests, Saltbush is a distinctly salty, arid shrub. The leaves are the most commonly used part in distillation, offering a strong salty, grassy flavour, bringing a lot of umami. However, it also carries notes of oaky root, rose, honeysuckle, and a touch of lemon verbena.

GERALDTON WAX:
A popular floristry shrub, often used in place of lemongrass or lime leaf, Geraldton Wax has a dominating grassy pine note that comes through strongly in distillation, with a heavy backbone of citrus oil and lemon-scented gum, and more delicate, woody floral undertones.

RIVER MINT:
An important medicinal herb to Aboriginal Australians for the treatment of colds and headaches, River Mint is the most popular of seven mints native to Australia. Complex sweet citrus and bright herbaceous notes come through when used in distillation. It lifts the overall flavour of a gin and gives it a burst of freshness which is often lost when distilling with more common mint varieties.

FINGER LIME:
One of Australia's most unique citruses, named for its oblong shape. They are one of Australia's most prized native foods globally. The flesh of the limes has the appearance of caviar or 'pearls', and a bright zesty flavour with a hint of astringent mint. In distillation, the flesh can be used either fresh, to bring acidic citrus notes, or freeze-dried, to get some sweeter citrus flavours. The peels cannot be used, as they are incredibly bitter.

NATIVE THYME:
Native thyme is more closely related to mint than thyme, a member of an Australian genus called Prostanthera in the mint bush family. It has many other names, including cut-leaf mint-bush and native sage. The strong, pungent aroma from the leaves is caused by high levels of essential oils and special glands on the leaves that release the oil aroma when bruised or disturbed. Use in distillation creates strong characteristics of musky menthol and earthy tones. It can be used dried or fresh, depending on preference for more woody notes or stronger mint and citrus.

DESERT LIME:
One of Australia's 'true citruses', desert lime is a small grape sized fruit that can be eaten whole, skin, seeds and all. The bright zesty flavour has long been enjoyed as a summer snack, both fresh and cooked into sweets, sauces, and cordials. The fruits contain very little sugar and have a sharp-sherbet, grassy flavour. They are not as tart as lime and have a slight herbaceous twang when cooked with other flavours.

BLOOD LIME:
Blood Limes are a hybrid of red finger lime and Ellendale mandarin. The mandarin is high in sugars and acids, while red finger limes are the sweeter variety available. They have a flavour similar to blood oranges, highly perfumed with a hint of bitterness and a distinctly sharp, spiced oil quality. Typically, only the flesh is used in distillation, to prevent too much oily bitterness from the skin and maintain its acidic, crisp quality.

DAVIDSON PLUM/OORAY:
Like most Australian fruits, they are incredibly low in sugar and are very tart and astringent. They are macerated in gin to make an Australian version of sloe gin. There are three types available. Two grow naturally in northern New South Wales' rainforests, offering fresh beetroot and slightly bitter plum aroma and flavour. Whilst the third variant, grows in northern Queensland's rainforests and has a musky rhubarb, rosella note with lolly-like acidity.

WATTLESEED:
Growing throughout most of Australia, particularly in arid desert climates, the seeds are roasted and ground before use to remove the hard shell. Different roasting levels heavily impact the overall flavour and intensity, with the seeds becoming more than nine times more flavourful through the roast. While the flavours of different seeds can vary widely due to different location and climate, Wattleseed often has a strong bitter coffee and chocolate characteristic. It can also help to dry out a gin and add an interesting mouthfeel.

BUSH TOMATO:
Closely related to tomatoes and eggplants, the small fruits are often dried after harvesting to develop their flavours and caramel sugar characteristics. They add a sweet raisin and sun-dried tomato quality in distillation that creates depth and umami sweetness.

ROSELLA:
Rosella is an Australian hibiscus, naturalised over thousands of years, that is believed to have been first brought to Australia by Indonesian fishermen. All parts of the flower are edible, but it is the calyxes, which support the large flower, that are most prized. The calyxes must be hand-harvested, as they are incredibly delicate, and then stored immediately to preserve the flavours. Rosella has a distinct rhubarb and hibiscus flavour that is tart and a little bitter when eaten fresh. When distilled or stewed into sweets, it releases notes of strawberry, cardamom, gardenia, and floral anise.

MUNTRIES:
A short, ground hugging tree, which only fruits for a short time during February and March. The berries have a crisp, crunchy texture, similar to an under-ripe pear, and a strong minced fruit flavour, most commonly associated with stewed apples. Through distillation, flavours of muntrie can be identified through notes of apple, light sweet juniper, and mild bush honey.

GIN DISTILLERIES OF AUSTRALIA

7K Distillery
Hobart, TAS

Situated in Derwent Park that borders the Derwent River on the northern end of Hobart, 7K Distillery specialises in spirits made with fresh ingredients and is so named because all Tasmanian postcodes are 7000 numbers. They source as many ingredients as possible from farms close to their location, with an ethos of environmental consciousness and waste minimisation, and believe that everyone should enjoy a good drop.

Tasmanian Modern Gin 43.0%

BOTANICALS: Juniper, Imperial Mandarin, Lemon, Lime, Tasmanian Eucalyptus Regnans, Lemon Myrtle, Lavender, Chamomile, Cardamom, Angelica Root, Coriander Seed, Orris Root & Rose Petal

TASTING NOTES: Eucalyptus, sweet chamomile, and bright citrus on the nose, peppery cardamom and coriander seed on the palate, a bright fresh finish.

SERVING SUGGESTION: Enjoy with Fever-Tree Refreshingly Light Indian Tonic Water.

Dry Chilli Gin 53.0%

BOTANICALS: Juniper, Fresh Orange Peel, Dried Orange Peel & Carolina Reaper Chilli

TASTING NOTES: Earthy savoury spice with wheat tones on the nose, bright citrus and coriander on the palate, warm smoky chilli heat to finish.

SERVING SUGGESTION: Enjoy with Fever-Tree Premium Indian Tonic Water.

Tasmanian Raspberry Gin 30.0%

BOTANICALS: : Juniper & Raspberry

TASTING NOTES: Raspberry jam on the nose, tart raspberry and a tea-like dryness on the palate, Pinot Noir character to finish.

SERVING SUGGESTION: Enjoy with Fever-Tree Wild Raspberry Tonic Water.

78 Degrees Distillery
Hay Valley, SA

Sequestered in the small locality of Hay Valley just east of the picturesque Adelaide Hills, 78 Degrees Distillery was founded by an Australian winemaker after working 13 vintages around the world and being inspired to start a distillery, taking its name from the boiling point of alcohol. They also extract their botanicals at 78 degrees, which is much lower than standard, using water from on-site bores that is then fully recycled as part of their 'Purveyor of Better' quality and sustainability initiative.

Classic Gin 42.0%

BOTANICALS: Juniper, Coriander Seed, Orange, Lemon, Lime, Clove, Cinnamon, Black Peppercorn, Nutmeg, Star Anise, Orris Root & Angelica Root

TASTING NOTES: Juniper, orange peel, and a hint of woody spice on the nose, orange and warming woody spice continue on the palate, with strong orange and a touch of angelica to finish.

SERVING SUGGESTION: Enjoy with Fever-Tree Premium Indian Tonic Water.

Better Gin 40.0%

BOTANICALS: Juniper, Coriander Seed, Lemon Myrtle, Blood Lime & Native Pepperberry

TASTING NOTES: Fragrant lemon myrtle and tart lime on the nose, dry lemon myrtle and lime with a touch of pepper warmth on the palate, dried lemon with pepper spice on the finish.

SERVING SUGGESTION: Enjoy with Fever-Tree Premium Indian Tonic Water.

Sunset Gin 42.0%

BOTANICALS: Juniper, Strawberry Gum, Bush Apple & Rosella

TASTING NOTES: Rosella, river mint and strawberry gum on the nose, sweet blossoms and light citrus with creamy strawberries on the palate, light spice and floral blossoms to finish.

SERVING SUGGESTION: Enjoy with Fever-Tree Elderflower Tonic Water.

100 Souls Distillery
Woodlands, NSW

Founded in the cool climate of the Southern Highlands of NSW by the team at Artemis Wines, 100 Souls Distillery was born from the desire to create Australia's finest spirits using the most renowned ingredients from around the world. Driven by a love of discovery and exploration, they focus on blending old-world distillation methods with modern techniques in hybrid pot stills.

Hinterland Dry Gin 40.0%

BOTANICALS: Juniper (Himalayan), Juniper (Hungarian), Sichuan Pepper & Mandarin

TASTING NOTES: Strong juniper with green pepper and clean citrus on the nose, Sichuan heat, mandarin zest and warming baking spice on the palate, fresh lingering spearmint to finish.

SERVING SUGGESTION: Enjoy with Fever-Tree Mediterranean Tonic Water.

Artisan Pink Gin 40.0%

BOTANICALS: Juniper, Sichuan Pepper, Lemon Thyme, Mandarin, Rose & Hibiscus

TASTING NOTES: Dried rose with mandarin oil and lemon-thyme on the nose, light pine alongside Sichuan spice and lemon-thyme on the palate, lingering mandarin to finish.

SERVING SUGGESTION: Enjoy with Fever-Tree Mediterranean Tonic Water.

Adams Distillery
Perth, TAS

Located at Glen Ireh Estate just south of Perth on the route between Launceston and Hobart in Tasmania, Adams Distillery was founded as a partnership between two best mates who shared a dream and the name Adam, later joined by Berni 'The Prof'. With an approach that they call "controlled-madness", they aren't afraid to have epic failures on the way to creating exciting products.

Dry Gin 45.0%

BOTANICALS: Juniper, Coriander Seed, Angelica Root, Liquorice, Orange Peel, Cardamom, Chamomile, Native Pepperberry, Rose Petals, Hibiscus, Lemon Myrtle, Elderflower, Cassia, Orris Root, Almond & Black Peppercorn

TASTING NOTES: Rosemary and pine resin on the nose, cardamom with pine needle and sweet herbs on the palate, dry bitter finish.

SERVING SUGGESTION: Enjoy with Fever-Tree Mediterranean Tonic Water.

Barrel Aged - Pinot Cask 40.0%

BOTANICALS: Juniper, Angelica Root, Chamomile, Cardamom, Cassia, Coriander Seed, Elderflower, Lemon Myrtle, Orange Peel & Orris Root (aged in Pinot Noir Casks)

TASTING NOTES: Rum, toffee and hazelnut notes on the nose, light florals with honey on the palate, honey continues and lingers to finish.

SERVING SUGGESTION: Enjoy neat or with Fever-Tree Ginger Ale.

Blueberry & Lavender Gin 32.0%

BOTANICALS: Juniper, Angelica Root, Chamomile, Cardamom, Cassia, Coriander Seed, Elderflower, Lemon Myrtle, Orange Peel, Orris Root, Blueberry, Blueberry Juice & Lavender

TASTING NOTES: Prominent lavender and blueberry lead the nose, jam-like blueberry with bursting lavender on the palate, drying with a hint of tannin and mint to finish.

SERVING SUGGESTION: Enjoy with Fever-Tree Elderflower Tonic Water.

Sloe Gin 32.0%

BOTANICALS: Juniper, Angelica Root, Chamomile, Cardamom, Cassia, Coriander Seed, Elderflower, Lemon Myrtle, Orange Peel, Orris Root, Sloe Berry & Caster Sugar (aged in Pinot Noir Casks)

TASTING NOTES: Plum jam, cacao, and spearmint lead the nose, tart red cherry and sweet syrupy plums on the palate, dry blood plum, with a herbal character and a chewy tannin to finish.

SERVING SUGGESTION: Enjoy with Fever-Tree Lemon Tonic Water.

Turbo Gin 58.0%

BOTANICALS: Juniper, Coriander Seed, Angelica Root, Liquorice, Orange Peel, Cardamom, Chamomile, Native Pepperberry, Rose Petal, Hibiscus, Lemon Myrtle, Elderflower, Cassia, Orris Root, Lemon Peel, Lime Peel, Wattleseed, Almond, Black Peppercorn, Rosemary & Nutmeg

TASTING NOTES: Raw almond, pine and subtle lemon myrtle on the nose, bitter almond with cardamom and liquorice on palate, sweet liquorice and cardamom continue with mellowing lemon myrtle to finish.

SERVING SUGGESTION: Enjoy with Fever-Tree Aromatic Tonic Water.

Alfred Wiley Distillery
Tweed Heads, NSW

Based in northern NSW just south of the border with the Gold Coast, Alfred Wiley is a very small craft distillery owned and operated by Will Eather, who took the plunge to follow his passion for craft spirits and a pet-friendly lifestyle with his dog Alfie. They focus on using local botanicals which are garden-grown where possible, in their pursuit of original and unpretentious spirits.

River Standard 40.0%

BOTANICALS: Juniper, Coriander Seed, Orris Root, Native Tamarind, Lilly Pilly, River Mint, Rose Petal & Mandarin

TASTING NOTES: Fruity tones with lilly pilly and river mint on the nose, lilly pilly carries through with coriander seed and citrus on the palate, finishing with floral rose and lingering peppermint.

SERVING SUGGESTION: Enjoy with Fever-Tree Premium Indian Tonic Water.

Border Run 43.0%

BOTANICALS: Juniper, Coriander Seed, Angelica Root, Atherton Raspberry, Native Lemongrass, Lemon-Scented Gum, Finger Lime, Rosella & Cubeb Pepper

TASTING NOTES: Strong florals and citrus on the nose, initial finger lime and rosella rounded with juniper and coriander on the palate, drying pine to finish.

SERVING SUGGESTION: Enjoy with Fever-Tree Refreshingly Light Indian Tonic Water.

Jumper & Thongs 43.0%

BOTANICALS: Juniper, Coriander Seed, Orris Root, Cinnamon Myrtle, Wattleseed, Native Pepperberry, Sunrise Lime, Vanilla Bean, Orange Peel, All Spice & Clove

TASTING NOTES: Clove, cinnamon, and orange undertones lead the nose, dusty juniper with baking spice and orange on the palate, bright florals and lemon oil on the finish.

SERVING SUGGESTION: Enjoy with Fever-Tree Aromatic Tonic Water.

AmberChes Spirits Distillery
Perth, WA

Established in the stunning and fertile Swan Valley near Perth in Western Australia, AmberChes Spirits Distillery is family owned and operated with a love of fruity gins and seasonal flavours, and whose namesake is their dog, Chester, an Irish Setter. They specialise in London Dry style gins with a contemporary flair and use local botanicals and fruits where available.

Botanical Gin 42.0%

BOTANICALS: Juniper, Elderflower, Apple, Cardamom, Orange Peel, Orris Root & Angelica Root

TASTING NOTES: Broad juniper and floral tones on the nose, balanced fresh apple and elderflower with supporting citrus on the palate, a refreshing fruity-floral finish.

SERVING SUGGESTION: Enjoy with Fever-Tree Elderflower Tonic Water.

Orange Infusion Gin 42.0%

BOTANICALS: Juniper, Orange, Cinnamon, Lemon Peel, Coriander Seed, Liquorice, Orris Root & Angelica Root

TASTING NOTES: Strong orange leads the nose, bold orange continues on the palate with a touch of perfumed orris, coriander warmth and oily orange to finish.

SERVING SUGGESTION: Enjoy with Fever-Tree Mediterranean Tonic Water.

Raspberry Delight Gin 42.0%

BOTANICALS: Juniper, Raspberry, Apple, Cinnamon, Lemon Peel, Coriander Seed, Liquorice, Orris Root & Angelica Root

TASTING NOTES: Green banana with a hint of apple and tart raspberry on the nose, juniper forward with supporting dried fruit tea alongside lemon on the palate, dry raspberry and orris to finish.

SERVING SUGGESTION: Enjoy with Fever-Tree Refreshingly Light Indian Tonic Water.

Ambleside Distillers
Hahndorf, SA

Sitting in the picturesque Adelaide Hills, known for its wine and food, Ambleside Distillers keeps a respect for the traditional art form of distilling while challenging conventional mindsets as craftsmen that focus on attention to detail in every aspect. Built 'from the garden up', a large number of the ingredients they use are grown and picked in their own distillery garden.

Big Dry Gin 45.0%

BOTANICALS: Juniper, Jalapeño, Lime Leaf, Sage, Rosemary & Thyme

TASTING NOTES: Fresh herbs and green pepper on the nose, bright waxy lime leaf followed by rosemary and salty jalapeño on the palate, salty spice and lime leaf on the finish.

SERVING SUGGESTION: Enjoy with Fever-Tree Mediterranean Tonic Water.

No.8 Botanical Gin 40.0%

BOTANICALS: Juniper, Orange, Lime, Star Anise, Cassia & Others

TASTING NOTES: Star anise studded orange leads the nose, sharp juniper with bold peppery star anise on the palate, fresh orange peel with lingering spice to finish.

SERVING SUGGESTION: Enjoy with Fever-Tree Aromatic Tonic Water.

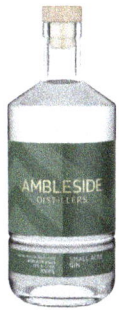

Small Acre Gin 42.0%

BOTANICALS: Juniper, Rhubarb, Apple, Pear, Native Pepperberry, Bay Leaf & Others

TASTING NOTES: Bright fresh juniper with supporting green herbs on the nose, juniper backbone supported by bay leaf and peppery heat on the palate, dry peppery spice to finish.

SERVING SUGGESTION: Enjoy with Fever-Tree Mediterranean Tonic Water.

Ambra Spirits
Adelaide, SA

Standing near the bustling heart of Adelaide in the hip, up-and-coming area of Thebarton, Ambra Spirits makes a range of traditionally inspired, locally produced spirits. They use traditional family recipes from Italy as the basis for their spirits, combined with fresh local Australian ingredients.

Citrus Gin 40.0%

BOTANICALS: Juniper, Coriander Seed, Angelica Root, Orris Root, Liquorice, Cardamom, White Peppercorn, Lemon Myrtle & Sage

TASTING NOTES: Eucalyptus, liquorice, and cardamom on the nose, sweet lemon and cardamom heat lead the palate, liquorice and slight floral musk on the finish.

SERVING SUGGESTION: Enjoy with Fever-Tree Refreshingly Light Indian Tonic Water.

Blood Orange Gin 30.0%

BOTANICALS: Juniper, Coriander Seed, Angelica Root, Orris Root, Orange, Lemon, Liquorice, Cardamom, Nutmeg & White Peppercorn

TASTING NOTES: Floral orange blossom leads the nose, sweet buttery orange peel with a touch of pepper on the palate, thick creamy orange to finish.

SERVING SUGGESTION: Enjoy with Fever-Tree Mediterranean Tonic Water.

Navel Gin 61.0%

BOTANICALS: Juniper, Coriander Seed, Angelica Root, Orange, Lemon, Liquorice, Cardamom, Nutmeg & White Peppercorn

TASTING NOTES: Zesty citrus, bold juniper, and baking spice lead the nose, white pepper, fresh pine and warming spice on the palate, pine needle and juniper linger to finish.

SERVING SUGGESTION: Enjoy with Fever-Tree Aromatic Tonic Water.

Watermelon + Mint Gin 40.0%

BOTANICALS: Juniper, Coriander Seed, Mint, Angelica Root, Cardamom, Cinnamon, Nutmeg, Ruby Red Grapefruit Peel, Lime Peel & Lemon Peel

TASTING NOTES: Mint, peppery spice, and watermelon on the nose, floral potpourri with peppery spice on the palate, lingering mint and watermelon to finish.

SERVING SUGGESTION: Enjoy with Fever-Tree Elderflower Tonic Water.

Ambrosia Distillery

Canberra, ACT

Sheltered next to the Jerrabomberra Wetlands in southeast Canberra, Ambrosia Distillery is named for the mythical food of the Greek gods with a different god paired with and depicted on each product. They combine years of bartending and distilling experience with medical science knowledge to create their range of spirits, focusing on purification and flavour infusion.

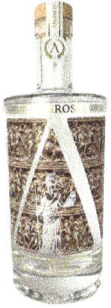

Athena 40.0%

BOTANICALS: Juniper, Lemon Myrtle, Strawberry Gum, Coriander Seed, Angelica Root, Davidson Plum, Riberry & Rosella

TASTING NOTES: Pronounced hibiscus and lavender on the nose, sweet citrus notes with growing florals on the palate, lingering lemon oil and lemon balm to finish.

SERVING SUGGESTION: Enjoy with Fever-Tree Elderflower Tonic Water.

Animus Distillery

Kyneton, VIC

Rooted in the former gold rush town of Kyneton in the idyllic Macedon Ranges, Animus Distillery was founded by four friends with a philosophy of capturing the soul of the freshest ingredients in their gin and footprint minimisation. They grow many of their own botanicals, which are exchanged frequently throughout production to improve flavour extraction and allows for tasting while making each batch, and are then reutilised to create fertiliser.

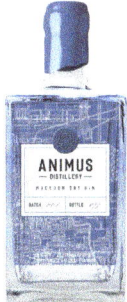

Macedon Dry Gin 50.0%

BOTANICALS: Juniper, Native Pepperberry, Cardamom, Angelica Root, Clove, Cinnamon, Coriander Seed, Lemon Myrtle, Sarsaparilla, Star Anise, Lemon, Lime, Turmeric & Rosemary

TASTING NOTES: Creamy nutty character with baking spice on the nose, initial burst of cinnamon with a supporting array of spices and warming lemon undertones on the palate, harmonising sweet spice lingers to finish.

SERVING SUGGESTION: Enjoy with Fever-Tree Premium Indian Tonic Water.

Ambrosian Gin 50.0%

BOTANICALS: Juniper, Cardamom, Angelica Root, Clove, Coriander Seed, Mandarin, Sesame Seed, Galangal, Ginger, Lemon, Makrut Lime, Lime, Turmeric, Lemon Myrtle & Star Anise

TASTING NOTES: Ginger, sesame, and savoury tones on the nose, lime leaf and sharp ginger spice alongside an array of classic botanicals on the palate, savoury spice to finish.

SERVING SUGGESTION: Enjoy with Fever-Tree Premium Indian Tonic Water.

Arboretum Gin 50.0%

BOTANICALS: Juniper, Capsicum, Cardamom, Angelica Root, Bay Leaf, Bush Tomato, Clove, Coriander Seed, Sarsaparilla, Lemon Thyme, Native Pepperberry, Star Anise, Lemon, Orange, Strawberry Gum Leaf, Rosemary, Turmeric & Lemon Myrtle

TASTING NOTES: Chilli, green cardamom, and tomato leaf on the nose, bright Thai spices with peppery heat emphasis on the palate, lingering spicy pepper on the finish.

SERVING SUGGESTION: Enjoy with Fever-Tree Mediterranean Tonic Water.

Barrel Aged Gin 55.9%

BOTANICALS: Juniper, Cardamom, Angelica Root, Clove, Coriander Seed, Mandarin, Sesame Seed, Galangal, Ginger, Lemon, Makrut Lime, Lime, Turmeric, Lemon Myrtle & Star Anise (aged in new French Oak Barrels)

TASTING NOTES: Ginger, sweet pineapple with caramel, and clove on the nose, oily texture of winter spice mix with galangal on the palate, clove and mandarin to finish.

SERVING SUGGESTION: Enjoy neat or with Fever-Tree Ginger Ale.

Davidsonia Gin 39.8%

BOTANICALS: Juniper, Davidson Plum & Others (used a variation of their over-proofed Macedon Dry recipe as a base for steeping the Davidson Plums)

TASTING NOTES: Distinctive plum on the nose, burst of plum with bold cinnamon spice and a slight fruity acidity on the palate, a bright finish with an elegant sweetness.

SERVING SUGGESTION: Enjoy with Fever-Tree Lemon Tonic Water.

Test Pressing 2 50.0%

BOTANICALS: Juniper, Ginger, Turmeric, Galangal, Makrut Lime, Pineapple, Sage, Lemon Verbena, Lemon Myrtle, Lemon Balm & Others (12 month vat maceration in Pineapple Flesh and Juice)

TASTING NOTES: Juicy pineapple with hints of clove and brown sugar on the nose, dried tarragon and sage with steeped fruit and toasted nuttiness on the palate, slight fruitiness with warming spice to finish.

SERVING SUGGESTION: Enjoy with Fever-Tree Ginger Ale.

Antagonist Spirits
Melbourne, VIC

Located in the laid-back multicultural suburb of Brunswick in Melbourne known for its live music and drinking scene, Antagonist Spirits strives to produce a full-bodied collection of gins inspired by the bright and floral essence of spring. They were founded with the goal of achieving complexity through simplicity and distil in small quantities to afford more distillate control followed by a method of post-distillation maceration to soften and balance their gins' finishes.

Hard Cut Gin 43.0%

BOTANICALS: Juniper, Orris Root, Angelica Root, Coriander Seed, Cassia, Dehydrated Orange Peel & Kikuyu Grass

TASTING NOTES: Fresh cut grass with earthy elements on the nose, musky hay bale with sweet orange and heated cassia spice on the palate, grassy linger to finish.

SERVING SUGGESTION: Enjoy with Fever-Tree Premium Indian Tonic Water.

Distillers Cut Gin 57.0%

BOTANICALS: Juniper, Orris Root, Angelica Root, Coriander Seed, Cassia, Dehydrated Orange Peel & Kikuyu Grass

TASTING NOTES: Cut grass and warm sea breeze notes on the nose, a burst of coriander spice with lingering bitter citrus on the palate, developing orris and drying grass tones to finish.

SERVING SUGGESTION: Enjoy with Fever-Tree Premium Indian Tonic Water.

Anther Spirits Distillery
Geelong, VIC

Settled at the innovation park in Geelong's historic Federal Woollen Mills building, Anther Spirits Distillery is named for the part of a plant that makes pollen. They extract and distil in a place of science, history, curiosity, collaboration, and female empowerment. Their co-founders combine their respective PhD in microbiology and experience in the liquor industry to produce spirits informed by science and born from history.

Australian Dry Gin 44.0%

BOTANICALS: Juniper (Macedonian), Juniper (Hungarian), Egyptian Brown Coriander Seed, Indian Green Coriander Seed, Cassia, Orris Root, Angelica Root, Tarragon, Lemon-Scented Gum, Eucalyptus Radiata, Wormwood, Clove, Nutmeg, Ginger, Finger Lime & Grains of Paradise

TASTING NOTES: Coriander, subtle cinnamon, and lemon myrtle on the nose, Moroccan-like spice mix infused with citrus oil and tarragon on the palate, mellow slightly-sweet herbs with a touch of violet to finish.

SERVING SUGGESTION: Enjoy with Fever-Tree Mediterranean Tonic Water.

Charismatica Gin 47.0%

BOTANICALS: Juniper, Egyptian Brown Coriander Seed, Indian Green Coriander Seed, Orris Root, Angelica Root, Cassia, Fennel Seed, Cinchona Bark, Blood Orange Peel, Wattleseed, Ginger, River Mint, Rosemary, Lavender, White Grapefruit Peel, Alpine Green Tea & Grains of Paradise

TASTING NOTES: Fennel, rosemary, and coriander on the nose, roasted wattleseed, geraldton wax and lemon myrtle on the palate, lingering saltbush to finish.

SERVING SUGGESTION: Enjoy with Fever-Tree Mediterranean Tonic Water.

Cherry Gin 27.5%

BOTANICALS: Juniper (Macedonian), Juniper (Hungarian), Black Cherry, Egyptian Brown Coriander Seed, Indian Green Coriander Seed, Cassia, Orris Root, Angelica Root, Tarragon, Lemon-Scented Gum, Eucalyptus Radiata, Wormwood, Clove, Nutmeg, Ginger, Finger Lime & Grains of Paradise

TASTING NOTES: Dark cherry fruit with tarragon on the nose, thick cherry with touches of warming spice and garden herbs on the palate, cherry lingers with warming spice on the finish.

SERVING SUGGESTION: Enjoy with Fever-Tree Lemon Tonic Water.

Geelong Dry Gin 40.0%

BOTANICALS: Juniper, Egyptian Brown Coriander Seed, Indian Coriander Seed, Cassia, Orris Root, Angelica Root, Eucalyptus Citriodora, Saltbush, Geraldton Wax, Clove, Nutmeg, Liquorice & Finger Lime

TASTING NOTES: Rounded nutmeg and geraldton wax on the nose, coriander, pine resin, and honey drive the palate, developing finger lime and eucalypt tones to finish.

SERVING SUGGESTION: Enjoy with Fever-Tree Premium Indian Tonic Water.

Goddess Strength Gin 54.0%

BOTANICALS: Juniper (Macedonian), Egyptian Brown Coriander Seed, Indian Green Coriander Seed, Cassia, Orris Root, Angelica Root, Lemon-Scented Gum, Eucalyptus Radiata, Artemisia, Clove, Nutmeg, Ginger, Finger Lime, Grains of Paradise, Damiana, Sarsaparilla, Saltbush, Cubeb Pepper, Honey & Maple Syrup

TASTING NOTES: Sweet florals and angelica lead the nose, dry spice with sharp eucalypt and citrus on the palate, mellow lemon myrtle to finish.

SERVING SUGGESTION: Enjoy with Fever-Tree Mediterranean Tonic Water.

Anther x Royal Botanic Gardens Florescence Gin 40.0%

BOTANICALS: Juniper, Alpine Pepper, Violet Kunzea, Lemon-Scented Ziera, Honey, Cymbopogon Obtectus, Baeckea Gunniana, Waratah Flower, Coriander Seed, Cassia, Orris Root, Angelica Root, Orange Peel, Eucalyptus Citriodora, Lemon Peel, Lemon Myrtle, Red Ginger, Nutmeg, Finger Lime, Liquorice & Waratah Water

TASTING NOTES: Soft florals with supporting honey on the nose, floral cucumber and violet lead with hints of delicate citrus and soft native botanicals on the palate, leading to a definitively savoury finish.

SERVING SUGGESTION: Enjoy with Fever-Tree Elderflower Tonic Water.

Apollo Bay Distillery

Apollo Bay, VIC

Looking out at the gorgeous Apollo Bay on the Great Ocean Road in Victoria, Apollo Bay Distillery is located in the town's old Post Office and aims to preserve the tales of the town and embody the spirit of Apollo Bay. They do this by making gins inspired by the ships that sailed off the treacherous coast many years ago with local botanicals wherever possible.

SS Casino Dry Gin 42.0%

BOTANICALS: Juniper, Cinnamon Myrtle, Saltbush & Fennel Seed

TASTING NOTES: Juniper and leafy myrtle notes on the nose, juniper and fennel lead with ocean saltiness on the palate, juniper and citrus linger on the finish.

SERVING SUGGESTION: Enjoy with Fever-Tree Premium Indian Tonic Water.

Amphitrite Gin Elixir 25.0%

BOTANICALS: Juniper, Elderflower, Aniseed & Native Lemongrass

TASTING NOTES: Caramelised quince with fruity-herbaceous tea on the nose, stewed fruit with a tea-like character and supporting spice on the palate, vanilla and honey linger to finish.

SERVING SUGGESTION: Enjoy with Fever-Tree Ginger Ale.

Australian Ocean Gin 42.0%

BOTANICALS: Juniper, Saltbush, Rosemary, Lemon, Ginger, Calamus & Coriander Seed

TASTING NOTES: Ginger and saltbush with strong umami tones on the nose, ocean spray alongside crystalized ginger and salty juniper on the palate, delicate salty herbs to finish.

SERVING SUGGESTION: Enjoy with Fever-Tree Mediterranean Tonic Water.

Captain Chapmans Navy Strength Gin 57.0%

BOTANICALS: Juniper, Sichuan Pepper, Ginger, Sesame Seed & Bay Leaf

TASTING NOTES: Juniper and waxy bay leaf on the nose, bold juniper with Sichuan pepper and ginger heat on the palate, savoury herbs and pine linger to finish.

SERVING SUGGESTION: Enjoy with Fever-Tree Premium Indian Tonic Water.

Speculant Grapefruit Gin 42.0%

BOTANICALS: Juniper, Grapefruit, Lemon Verbena & Fennel Seed

TASTING NOTES: Subtle lemon verbena and fresh-floral grapefruit on the nose, fresh fennel and dry spices on the palate, floral grapefruit peel to finish.

SERVING SUGGESTION: Enjoy with Fever-Tree Mediterranean Tonic Water.

Applewood Distillery
Gumeracha, SA

Nestled at the foot of the pristine Adelaide Hills, known for its wine and food, on the edge of Gumeracha, Applewood Distillery crafts gins inspired by the land around them in what was once a cold store built in the 1920s. They utilise the distinct flavours of endemic flora, sharing them with the rest of the world, and generate an avenue for two way agricultural practices and native reforestation to take place, supporting farmers who opt for more sustainable farming methods, crops, and orchards.

Applewood Gin 43.0%

BOTANICALS: Juniper, Desert Lime, Peppermint Gum, Wattleseed & Others

TASTING NOTES: Herbaceous lead with eucalyptus and a touch of creamy nuttiness on the nose, eucalyptus and garden herbs lead with pepper and tart lime on the palate, developing garden herbs, eucalyptus, and citrus to finish.

SERVING SUGGESTION: Enjoy with Fever-Tree Mediterranean Tonic Water.

Alpine Gin 43.0%

BOTANICALS: Juniper, Finger Lime, Native Pepperleaf, Tarragon & Others

TASTING NOTES: Pine forest, pepper, and tarragon notes on the nose, initial alpine breeze with pepperleaf and waxy juniper growing on the palate, cardamom and coriander linger to finish.

SERVING SUGGESTION: Enjoy with Fever-Tree Premium Indian Tonic Water.

Coral Gin 43.0%

BOTANICALS: Juniper, Riberry, Strawberry Gum, Karkalla & Others

TASTING NOTES: Bold strawberry gum and light fruity undertones on the nose, mentholic spice and striking strawberry sweetness with a slight salty undertone on the palate, a pleasant strawberry sherbet finish.

SERVING SUGGESTION: Enjoy with Fever-Tree Refreshingly Light Indian Tonic Water.

Archie Rose Distilling Co.
Sydney, NSW

Ensconced in the trendy inner Sydney suburb of Rosebery where old and new collide, Archie Rose Distilling Co. strive to redefine Australia's rich tradition in distilling through diversity, collaboration, and experiences. They are guided by a belief in transparency and an unwavering drive to universally expand people's knowledge and appreciation of spirits and hospitality, finding inspiration in the quality and diversity of crops and produce grown across Australia.

Signature Dry Gin 42.0%

BOTANICALS: Juniper, Sunrise Lime, Geraldton Waxflower, Blood Lime, Dorrigo Pepperleaf, Lemon Myrtle, Mint & Others

TASTING NOTES: Pithy lime, light peppery spice and minty tones on the nose, pepper spice and lime lead with river mint freshness on the palate, minty spice lingers to finish.

SERVING SUGGESTION: Enjoy with Fever-Tree Mediterranean Tonic Water.

Bone Dry Gin 44.0%

BOTANICALS: Juniper, Coriander Seed, Lemon-Scented Gum, Emerald Green Finger Lime, Tahitian Lime, River Mint, Dorrigo Pepperleaf & Orris Root

TASTING NOTES: Juniper and coriander lead with dried citrus and a touch of orris on the nose, initial citrus and fresh pine supported by orris root and pepperleaf on the palate, pepperleaf, pine, and mint to finish.

SERVING SUGGESTION: Enjoy with Fever-Tree Premium Indian Tonic Water.

Distiller's Strength Gin 52.4%

BOTANICALS: Juniper, Pear, Orange, Rose Petal, Elderflower, Honey & Others

TASTING NOTES: Rich rose and elderflower harmonise alongside tropical elements on the nose, rose and elderflower continue on the palate alongside juicy tropical fruits, floral undertones and complex fruits build to finish.

SERVING SUGGESTION: Enjoy with Fever-Tree Elderflower Tonic Water.

Artemis Winery & Distillery
Mittagong, NSW

Situated in the cool climate of the picturesque Southern Highlands wine region of NSW, Artemis Winery & Distillery is family run and takes its name from the Greek goddess of the hunt, the wilderness, and moon. They use age old methods and hands on techniques with traditional pot stills and fresh Australian citrus as they strive to produce the finest spirits.

Goddess Gin Original 43.0%

BOTANICALS: Juniper, Rose Petal, Lemon Myrtle & Star Anise

TASTING NOTES: Potpourri like florals with gentle spice on the nose, dried flowers and sweet candy with an earl grey tea note on the palate, florals with subtle savoury herbs to finish.

SERVING SUGGESTION: Enjoy with Fever-Tree Elderflower Tonic Water.

Eau De Vie Pinot Noir Navy Strength Gin 58.0%

BOTANICALS: Juniper, Artemisia, Kakadu Plum & Others

TASTING NOTES: Juniper leads with a touch of fruitiness on the nose, strong pine backbone with a slight bitter edge and hints of fruit on the palate, juniper and bitterness drive the finish.

SERVING SUGGESTION: Enjoy with Fever-Tree Premium Indian Tonic Water.

Goddess Pink Pinot Noir Gin 43.0%

BOTANICALS: Juniper, Damascus Rose, Strawberry & Others

TASTING NOTES: Rose petals with a slight green stem note on the nose, rose, pepper, and dried strawberries on the palate, fruits develop and florals linger to finish.

SERVING SUGGESTION: Enjoy with Fever-Tree Elderflower Tonic Water.

Goddess Sicilian Orange Gin 43.0%

BOTANICALS: Juniper, Orange, Blood Orange, Mandarin & Orange Blossom

TASTING NOTES: Blood orange and orange blossom lead the nose, zesty orange with a touch of juniper on the palate, thick zingy orange to finish.

SERVING SUGGESTION: Enjoy with Fever-Tree Mediterranean Tonic Water.

Kakadu, Manuka & Saffron Navy Strength Gin 58.0%

BOTANICALS: Juniper, Kakadu Plum, Manuka Honey, Saffron & Others

TASTING NOTES: Saffron and a touch of pine on the nose, juniper and saffron continue on the palate and open to a slight honey sweetness, honey drives the finish with hints of pine.

SERVING SUGGESTION: Enjoy with Fever-Tree Premium Indian Tonic Water.

Artillery Artisan Distillery
Melbourne, VIC

Set amongst the sprawl of the vibrant and diverse suburb of Preston in north-side Melbourne, Artillery Artisan Distillery aren't content with the usual distilling processes and recipes, referring to their crew as 'alchemists'. They aim to make their mark on the industry by designing their spirits around the idea of an assault on your tastebuds and sensibilities.

Juniper Bomb 37.0%

BOTANICALS: Juniper (Macedonian), Preserved Lemon, Rosemary, Coriander Seed, Angelica Root, Orris Root, Cassia, Cardamom & Pink Rose Petal

TASTING NOTES: Juniper, minty freshness and savoury honey on the nose, upfront juniper with eucalyptus tones on the palate, herbal heat develops to finish.

SERVING SUGGESTION: Enjoy with Fever-Tree Refreshingly Light Indian Tonic Water.

Big Island Gin 37.0%

BOTANICALS: Juniper (Macedonian), Coriander Seed, Orange Peel, Dried Lemon, Honey, Macadamia, Angelica Root, Aniseed Myrtle, Cassia, Cinnamon, Native Pepperleaf, Saltbush, Spearmint, Cardamom, Caraway Seed, Lavender, Fennel Seed, Tonka Bean & Nutmeg

TASTING NOTES: Sea breeze and grassy eucalyptus on the nose, dry woody-earthy angelica with eucalyptus developing on the palate, angelica and a touch of orange to finish.

SERVING SUGGESTION: Enjoy with Fever-Tree Premium Indian Tonic Water.

Australian Distilling Co.
Adelaide, SA

Stationed at the edge of Hackney, just a stone's throw from the rich Adelaide Parklands in the centre of the city, Australian Distilling Co. has traditional roots but takes inspiration from the here and now. They partner with local distilleries across the country and explore local ingredients to create flavours that embrace the spirit of the city or region.

Australian Distilling Co. Gin 40.0%
BOTANICALS: Juniper, Coriander Seed, Cardamom & Nutmeg & Others
TASTING NOTES: Coriander, green cardamom, and a touch of lemon myrtle on the nose, cardamom and dry pine on the palate, mentholic cardamom spice carries to finish.
SERVING SUGGESTION: Enjoy with Fever-Tree Premium Indian Tonic Water.

Navy Gin 57.0%
BOTANICALS: Juniper, Cardamom, Nutmeg & Others
TASTING NOTES: Juniper with lemon myrtle and cardamom on the nose, piny juniper, thyme, and a touch of nutty character on the palate, lengthy cardamom to finish.
SERVING SUGGESTION: Enjoy with Fever-Tree Mediterranean Tonic Water.

Rhapsody Ruby Gin 40.0%
BOTANICALS: Juniper, Coriander Seed, Cardamom & Nutmeg (infused with T BAR's Serendipi-T fruit tea blend)
TASTING NOTES: Fruity florals and berry tea notes on the nose, dry tropical fruits, black tea and an array of baking spice on the palate, tea-like tannins with a potpourri undertone to finish.
SERVING SUGGESTION: Enjoy with Fever-Tree Wild Raspberry Tonic Water.

Shiraz Gin 38.5%

BOTANICALS: Juniper, Coriander Seed, Cardamom & Nutmeg (steeped with Shiraz Grapes)

TASTING NOTES: Candied blackcurrant and honey water open on the nose, sweet blackcurrants with a hint of spice on the palate, drying spice and tannin character to finish.

SERVING SUGGESTION: Enjoy with Fever-Tree Lemon Tonic Water.

BABY Pink Gin
Melbourne, VIC

Located in the hip Melbourne suburb of Collingwood, known for its music scene and converted warehouses, BABY Pink Gin was created to be a pink gin that stays pink when mixed, using certified organic pink rose petals as the cornerstone. They are 100% female owned and aim to give female gin drinkers something both beautiful and premium to enjoy.

BABY Pink Gin 40.0%

BOTANICALS: Juniper, Coriander Seed, Pink Rose Petal, Chamomile, Raspberry Leaf & Lemon Verbena

TASTING NOTES: Lemon verbena and coriander lead the nose, rose petals and soft raspberry open on the palate with a hint of chamomile and dry coriander following, florals and peppery spice develop to finish.

SERVING SUGGESTION: Enjoy with Fever-Tree Elderflower Tonic Water.

Backwoods Distilling Co.
Yackandandah, VIC

Sequestered away in the small tourist town of Yackandandah near the Stanley State Forest and steeped in the legacy of gold, Backwoods Distilling Co. creates gins that are inspired by the Australian landscape using 100% Australian farmed and malted grains from growers with sustainable agricultural practices. They aim to bring friends and family together over a high-quality boutique drink that celebrates the unique flavour of the Victorian High Country.

High Country Gin 43.0%

BOTANICALS: Juniper, Coriander Seed, Cardamom, Angelica Root, Orris Root, Native Pepperberry, Strawberry Gum, Peppermint Gum, Wattleseed & Lemon Myrtle

TASTING NOTES: Wattleseed, angelica, and lemon myrtle on the nose, initial pepperberry and cardamom with strawberry and peppermint gum following on the palate, light green tea notes with lemon zest to finish.

SERVING SUGGESTION: Enjoy with Fever-Tree Refreshingly Light Indian Tonic Water.

Salted Lime Gin 43.0%

BOTANICALS: Juniper, Desert Lime, Finger Lime, Coriander Seed, Macadamia, Boab Nut, Orris Root, Pink Salt (Murray River), Old Man Saltbush, Native Pepperleaf & Eucalyptus Leaf

TASTING NOTES: Earthy nuttiness with saltbush and coriander on the nose, bitter eucalyptus, a soft salty note, and subtle peppery spice on the palate, peppery heat develops to finish.

SERVING SUGGESTION: Enjoy with Fever-Tree Premium Indian Tonic Water.

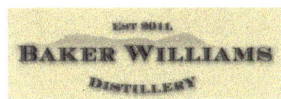

Baker Williams Distillery
Mudgee, NSW

Surrounded by the rolling hills and vineyards to the north of the wine town Mudgee, Baker Williams Distillery is a micro-distillery that focuses on capturing locally grown and Australian ingredients, flavours, and influences. Named for its co-founders, Helen Baker and Nathan Williams, they make a range of small batch spirits, including gin, liqueurs, whisky, rum, and hybrids.

Gin XLCR 40.0%

BOTANICALS: Juniper, Kumquat, Orange, Coriander Seed, Cassia, Angelica Root, Lemon Myrtle & Native Pepperberry

TASTING NOTES: Toasted coconut, orange blossom, and buttery pineapple on the nose, sweet orange and coconut flesh with resinous pine needles on the palate, sweet herbs to finish.

SERVING SUGGESTION: Enjoy with Fever-Tree Mediterranean Tonic Water.

Rum Barrel Gin 46.0%

BOTANICALS: Juniper, Coriander Seed, Cassia, Angelica Root, Native Pepperberry, Cardamom, Lemon Myrtle, Orange & Kumquat (aged for 18 months in ex-Baker Williams Rum American Oak Barrels)

TASTING NOTES: Rum-raisin-like spice and orange zest lead the nose, sharp oak and savoury spice followed by coriander and angelica on the palate, lingering ginger spice to finish.

SERVING SUGGESTION: Enjoy neat or with Fever-Tree Ginger Ale.

Shiraz Gin 40.0%

BOTANICALS: Juniper, Shiraz Grapes, Coriander Seed, Cinnamon Myrtle, Lemon Myrtle, Orange, Kumquat, Native Pepperberry & Cardamom

TASTING NOTES: Rich dark fruits with angelica and cassia on the nose, juicy sweet red grapes, subtle cardamom with dry spice and mint on the palate, pepperberry spice and dry tannins to finish.

SERVING SUGGESTION: Enjoy with Fever-Tree Lemon Tonic Water.

Banks & Solander Distillery

Sydney, NSW

Hidden in the back streets of the Sydney suburb of Botany with its village-style atmosphere, Banks & Solander Distillery is a small family owned and operated micro-distillery that takes its name from two botanists that catalogued and collected hundreds of samples of Australian flora and fauna around the Botany area. They like to experiment with new ingredients and different combinations of flavours and aromas as they create their next generation of drinks.

Signature Gin 48.0%

BOTANICALS: Juniper, Orris Root, Coriander Seed, Angelica Root, Green Cardamom, Navel Orange, Native Pepperberry, Lemon Myrtle, Wattleseed, Macadamia, Strawberry Gum, Star Anise & Cassia.

TASTING NOTES: Lemon myrtle, pepper spice and eucalyptus lead the nose, lemon leads with eucalypt tones and a hint of strawberry gum on the palate, lemon myrtle develops with hints of fruit on the finish.

SERVING SUGGESTION: Enjoy with Fever-Tree Mediterranean Tonic Water.

Endeavour (Aged) Gin 48.0%

BOTANICALS: Juniper, Orris Root, Coriander Seed, Angelica Root, Green Cardamom, Valencia Orange, Native Pepperberry, Lemon Myrtle, Wattleseed, Macadamia, Strawberry Gum, Star Anise & Cassia (aged in toasted American Oak)

TASTING NOTES: Dark roasted wattleseed with baking spice on the nose, dry green cardamom and coriander with an array of supporting citrus tones on the palate, zesty lime to finish.

SERVING SUGGESTION: Enjoy neat or with Fever-Tree Ginger Ale.

Barossa Distilling Co.
Nuriootpa, SA

Positioned just south of Nuriootpa at the heart of the renowned Barossa Valley wine region, Barossa Distilling Co. is housed in the Old Penfolds Distillery with one of only a handful of Coffey Stills in the world, which allows for continuous rather than batch distillation. They produce a range of gins driven by the desire for great flavour and inspired by discovery.

Australian Garden Gin 40.0%
BOTANICALS: Juniper, Lilly Pilly, Pink Peppercorn, Bee Pollen, Lemon Verbena, Juniper Needle, Saltbush, Buddha's Hand & Others

TASTING NOTES: Pine needle and zesty citrus with a slightly sweet rose and rhubarb note on the nose, bursting citrus with saltbush and pink peppercorn on the palate, citrus and pepperberry linger to finish.

SERVING SUGGESTION: Enjoy with Fever-Tree Mediterranean Tonic Water.

Barossa Shiraz 2021 38.0%
BOTANICALS: Juniper, Shiraz Grapes & Others

TASTING NOTES: Rich Shiraz and blackberry lead the nose, black tea notes and rich sweet Shiraz on the palate, fruity characters linger with chalky tannins on the finish.

SERVING SUGGESTION: Enjoy with Fever-Tree Lemon Tonic Water.

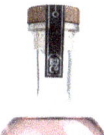

Budburst Gin 40.0%
BOTANICALS: Juniper, Orange, Macadamia, Vanilla, Ginger & Others (blended with an aromatic Barossa Wine)

TASTING NOTES: Vanilla and candied orange lead the nose, orange peel, toasted almond, and smoky rosemary with a touch of cassia on the palate, lingering potpourri-like florals to finish.

SERVING SUGGESTION: Enjoy with Fever-Tree Elderflower Tonic Water.

Generations Gin 40.0%

BOTANICALS: Juniper, Orange, Toasted French Oak, Almond, Chamomile & Others

TASTING NOTES: Hints of oakiness and sandalwood with orange oil on the nose, light baking spice with hints of juniper, orange, and almond on the palate, a touch of cedar with soft orange to finish.

SERVING SUGGESTION: Enjoy with Fever-Tree Premium Indian Tonic Water.

Bathurst Grange Distillery
Brewongle, NSW

Stationed on The Grange heritage estate and farm in the Central Tablelands to the west of Brewongle, Bathurst Grange Distillery is family-run and loves to collaborate with other local producers in their region. They use local and native Australian botanicals, some of which are grown on their own farm, and are passionate about sustainably produced paddock to bottle spirits, committing to zero waste sustainable practices.

Australian Dry Gin 40.0%

BOTANICALS: Juniper, Lemon Myrtle, Orange & Others

TASTING NOTES: Green cardamom with a slight herbaceous sweetness on the nose, cardamom and resin lead with slightly sweet citrus on the palate, menthol and candied orange to finish.

SERVING SUGGESTION: Enjoy with Fever-Tree Mediterranean Tonic Water.

Blue Mountain Gin 40.0%

BOTANICALS: Juniper, Orange, Native Pepperberry & Others

TASTING NOTES: Dried savoury herbs on the nose, intermingling fennel and rosemary with the support of pepper spice on the palate, sweet orange developing to finish.

SERVING SUGGESTION: Enjoy with Fever-Tree Mediterranean Tonic Water.

Rose Garden Gin 40.0%

BOTANICALS: Juniper, Rose Petal, Cassia, Wattleseed & Others

TASTING NOTES: Full-bodied spirit with earthy tones on the nose, rose florals with wattleseed and a touch of vanilla on the palate, grain notes to finish.

SERVING SUGGESTION: Enjoy with Fever-Tree Elderflower Tonic Water.

Battery Point Distillery
Hobart, TAS

Founded by the historic Lenna of Hobart Hotel, a colonial-era sandstone mansion on the doorstep of Hobart's vibrant waterfront, Battery Point Distillery was born from a passion for Tasmania and the traditions of master whisky distilling. They are committed to crafting small-batch, hand-crafted quality spirits that champion Tasmania with creative use of cask and barrel influence.

House of Lenna Dry Gin Blend No.1 44.0%

BOTANICALS: Juniper, Native Pepperberry, Vanilla Bean, Tonka Bean, Rosemary, Cucumber, Orange Peel, Chamomile, Basil, Lemon, Orris Root, Coriander Seed & Sea Salt (Tasmanian)

TASTING NOTES: Basil leaf and chamomile supported by a juniper backbone on the nose, complex green herbs with juniper, hints of citrus and tonka on the palate, green herbs and a nutty character to finish.

SERVING SUGGESTION: Enjoy with Fever-Tree Mediterranean Tonic Water.

House of Lenna Pink Gin Blend No.2 44.0%

BOTANICALS: Juniper, Coriander Seed, Strawberry, Vanilla Bean, Tonka Bean & Orange

TASTING NOTES: Stewed strawberry jam with fruity rhubarb and a touch of vanilla on the nose, candied orange with creamy strawberries on the palate, zesty orange to finish.

SERVING SUGGESTION: Enjoy with Fever-Tree Wild Raspberry Tonic Water.

Beachtree Distilling Co.
Caloundra, QLD

Based in the aquatic paradise of Caloundra on the southern cusp of the Sunshine Coast, Beachtree Distilling Co.'s mission is to follow their ancestors by using ethical and sustainable methods to source and produce high-quality products. They seek to tell their story and that of the Australian landscape with native botanicals by amplifying ancient generational knowledge with science and engineering.

Organic Koala Gin 42.0%

BOTANICALS: Juniper, Coriander Seed, Cardamom, Lemon Myrtle, Vanilla & Cinnamon

TASTING NOTES: Hints of citrus and powdered spice on the nose, lemon myrtle, vanilla and cardamom blend on the palate, lemon myrtle and a dusting of cinnamon to finish.

SERVING SUGGESTION: Enjoy with Fever-Tree Mediterranean Tonic Water.

Organic Quokka Gin 42.0%

BOTANICALS: Juniper, Coriander Seed, Cardamom, Elderberry, Finger Lime, Native Pepperberry, Lemon Myrtle & Hibiscus

TASTING NOTES: Summer breeze with hints of earthy florals and supporting spice on the nose, baking spice with lemon and baked fruit notse on the palate, tart lemon and a hint of spice to finish.

SERVING SUGGESTION: Enjoy with Fever-Tree Premium Indian Tonic Water.

Bellarine Distillery
Drysdale, VIC

Positioned just north of Drysdale on the breath-taking Bellarine Peninsula to the south of Melbourne, Bellarine Distillery believes in a less is more approach when it comes to the flavour and creation of their small-batch gins, letting just a few botanicals be the stars of the show. They grow a range of botanicals on their property, which sits at the foot of three valleys with rich black soil and plentiful water, which they combine with other botanicals from Australia and around the world.

Teddy & The Fox 42.0%

BOTANICALS: Juniper, Valencia Orange, Lemon Myrtle, Coriander Seed, Star Anise & Orris Root

TASTING NOTES: Juicy orange with candied lemon on the nose, sweet lemon and citrus coriander notes developing on the palate, sweet lemon myrtle lingers on the finish.

SERVING SUGGESTION: Enjoy with Fever-Tree Mediterranean Tonic Water.

Bear & The Koalas 42.0%

BOTANICALS: Juniper, Lemon-Scented Gum Leaf, Macadamia, Coriander Seed, Cinnamon & Orris Root

TASTING NOTES: Oily lime leaf with fresh cut finger lime on the nose, toasted coriander, waxy lime leaf, and pithy citrus on the palate, warming spice with thick lime leaf to finish.

SERVING SUGGESTION: Enjoy with Fever-Tree Mediterranean Tonic Water.

Rosey & The Rabbits - Barrel Aged 42.0%

BOTANICALS: Juniper, Apricot, Black Lime, Grains of Paradise & Angelica Root (aged in ex-Scotchman's Hill Pinot Noir Barrels)

TASTING NOTES: Perfumed spice with angelica on the nose, soft apricot sweetness with cardamom on the palate, light pepper and fruity tones to finish.

SERVING SUGGESTION: Enjoy with Fever-Tree Refreshingly Light Indian Tonic Water.

The Old Dodger - Navy Strength 57.0%

BOTANICALS: Juniper, Rosemary, Saltbush, Walnut, Tarragon, Lemon Zest & Angelica Root

TASTING NOTES: Ocean breeze with a supporting nutty character on the nose, upfront juniper and rosemary with light florals and a salty edge on the palate, savoury herbs and an array of florals drive the finish.

SERVING SUGGESTION: Enjoy with Fever-Tree Mediterranean Tonic Water.

Trooper & The Roo 42.0%

BOTANICALS: Juniper, Wattleseed, Cacao, Almond, Yellow Grapefruit, Pink Peppercorn & Orris Root

TASTING NOTES: Subtle smoke with baking spice and notes of mocha on the nose, delicate roasted coffee with supporting chocolate and tart citrus on the palate, dry cocoa to finish.

SERVING SUGGESTION: Enjoy with Fever-Tree Premium Indian Tonic Water.

Big River Distilling Co.
Canberra, ACT

Sheltered next to the Jerrabomberra Wetlands in southeast Canberra, Big River Distilling Co. is named for when European settlers were first exploring the region in search of 'The Big River' and came across the Murrumbidgee to the west of the city. They are guided, but not bound, by tradition as they seek to create spirits that reflect the unique Canberra environs and evoke a sense of time and space.

Dry Gin 42.0%

BOTANICALS: Juniper, Coriander Seed, Lemon Myrtle, Lime, Navel Orange, Cassia, Cardamom, Liquorice, Orris Root, Angelica Root, Native Pepperleaf, Hops, Ginger & Lebanese Cucumber

TASTING NOTES: Layered citrus of creamy lemon and tart peel with a touch of juniper on the nose, Meyer lemon, pepper spice and pine needle drive the palate, lingering pine oil and pepper to finish.

SERVING SUGGESTION: Enjoy with Fever-Tree Mediterranean Tonic Water.

Cinn Gin 44.0%

BOTANICALS: Juniper, Coriander Seed, Angelica Root, Pink Lady Apple, Cinnamon, Clove, Nutmeg & Star Anise

TASTING NOTES: Sweet orange with cinnamon and an array of baking spice on the nose, dry green spice, cinnamon, and pine needle on the palate, ginger spice and heat lingers to finish.

SERVING SUGGESTION: Enjoy with Fever-Tree Aromatic Tonic Water.

Pink Gin 40.0%

BOTANICALS: Juniper, Coriander Seed, Angelica Root, Rhubarb, Vanilla & Ginger

TASTING NOTES: Juniper leads with a touch of ginger on the nose, subtle ginger and juniper tingle with a touch of rhubarb fruitiness on the palate, ginger spice lingers to finish.

SERVING SUGGESTION: Enjoy with Fever-Tree Aromatic Tonic Water.

Big Tree Distillery
Newham, VIC

Tucked away in the middle of the idyllic Macedon Ranges overlooking the Cobaw area, Big Tree Distillery was born out of the love of flavour exploration with premium Australian ingredients and is distilled on Jack's Spring Farm. They use botanicals grown on their farm, foraged from local neighbours, or when harder to obtain, sourced by their gin-loving botanist.

Elegant Dry Gin 42.0%

BOTANICALS: Juniper, Coriander Seed, Cardamom, Star Anise, Kumquat, Orange, Cassia, Southern Sassafras & Bay Leaf

TASTING NOTES: Juniper with dry earthy spice and orange on the nose, coriander and cardamom with star anise on the palate, bay leaf and an almond-like character to finish.

SERVING SUGGESTION: Enjoy with Fever-Tree Mediterranean Tonic Water.

Claude Navy Strength 58.0%

BOTANICALS: Juniper, Coriander Seed, Cardamom, Star Anise, Cumquat, Orange, Cassia, Southern Sassafras & Bay Leaf

TASTING NOTES: Lemon myrtle and kumquat lead with undertones of green herbs on the nose, strong cardamom and cassia with bay leaf and orange on the palate, pepper spice driven finish.

SERVING SUGGESTION: Enjoy with Fever-Tree Mediterranean Tonic Water.

Cumquat Double Distilled 42.0%

BOTANICALS: Juniper, Coriander Seed, Cardamom, Star Anise, Cumquat, Orange, Cassia, Southern Sassafras & Bay Leaf

TASTING NOTES: Candied cumquat, salty bay leaf and green cardamom on the nose, coriander with dried thyme and citrus tones on the palate, sweet star anise and cumquat hints to finish.

SERVING SUGGESTION: Enjoy with Fever-Tree Mediterranean Tonic Water.

Billson's
Beechworth, VIC

Occupying a complex of restored Victorian-era buildings, centred on a 'tower brewery', in the historic gold-mining town of Beechworth, Billson's is a family-owned, small-batch craft distillery with a commitment to locality and a belief in restoration over reinvention. They use pristine alpine spring water from an on-site well in the crafting of their products while taking as much inspiration as possible from the past.

George's Dry Gin 40.0%

BOTANICALS: Juniper, Finger Lime & Others

TASTING NOTES: Coriander and delicate anise on the nose, sweet warming spice with coriander and pithy undertones on the palate, warming anise lingers to finish.

SERVING SUGGESTION: Enjoy with Fever-Tree Premium Indian Tonic Water.

Alfred's Peculiar Gin 40.0%

BOTANICALS: Juniper, Butterfly Pea Flower & Others

TASTING NOTES: Slightly sweet lemon myrtle with lemon verbena leads the nose, initial eucalypt tones with supporting lemon myrtle on the palate, zesty lemon develops and carries to finish.

SERVING SUGGESTION: Enjoy with Fever-Tree Mediterranean Tonic Water.

Durif Gin 40.0%

BOTANICALS: Juniper & Others (blended with Rutherglen Durif Wine)

TASTING NOTES: Plum jam and dry spice drive the nose, cardamom and white pepper to open with a dried black fruit on the palate, savoury coriander and anise to finish.

SERVING SUGGESTION: Enjoy with Fever-Tree Premium Indian Tonic Water.

Isabella's Barrel Aged Gin 40.0%

BOTANICALS: Juniper & Others (aged in ex-Fortified Wine Barrels)

TASTING NOTES: Honey water and citrus blossom on the nose, grassy coriander and dry cassia lead the palate, orange develops with cassia lingering to finish.

SERVING SUGGESTION: Enjoy with Fever-Tree Premium Indian Tonic Water.

Blackmans Bay Distillery

Blackmans Bay, TAS

Standing on the bluff overlooking Blackmans Bay south of Hobart, Blackmans Bay Distillery is a family-owned and operated micro-distillery named for the area, which in turn is named for James Blackman who occupied the land in the 1820s. They produce everything in-house, including their own base spirit made from Australian sugar cane, with seasonal botanicals from both Tasmania and afar.

Botanical Gin 43.0%

BOTANICALS: Juniper, Coriander Seed, Lavender, Orange Peel, Kumquat, Lemon Peel, Mandarin, Native Pepperberry, Almond, Vanilla & Cardamom

TASTING NOTES: Vanilla, roasted nuts and subtle orange on the nose, creamy almond with lavender and soft citrus notes following on the palate, creamy almond carries to the finish.

SERVING SUGGESTION: Enjoy with Fever-Tree Mediterranean Tonic Water.

Harvest Gin 43.0%

BOTANICALS: Juniper, Coriander Seed, Almond, Cherry, Five Spice, Lavender & Vanilla Bean

TASTING NOTES: Rich vanilla and almond meal on the nose, caramelised baking spice with juniper and developing savoury spice on the palate, pronounced spice to finish.

SERVING SUGGESTION: Enjoy with Fever-Tree Premium Indian Tonic Water.

Smoky Gin 43.0%

BOTANICALS: Juniper, Coriander Seed, Smoked Almond, Native Pepperberry, Sichuan Pepper, African Pepperberry, Cherry & Vanilla Bean

TASTING NOTES: Warm pepper and roasted almond with tart undertones on the nose, pepperberry with a slight creamy note and smoky sweetness on the palate, dry linger to finish.

SERVING SUGGESTION: Enjoy with Fever-Tree Premium Indian Tonic Water.

Blackwood Valley Distillery

Bridgetown, WA

Nestled in picturesque Bridgetown in the heart of Western Australia's apple growing region, Blackwood Valley Distillery is a small family-run operation within the local institution of The Cidery that focuses on gins and liqueurs. They began recipe testing during the early days of the COVID-19 pandemic when their distiller, a pilot by trade, was grounded from flying.

Grounded Gin 43.0%

BOTANICALS: Juniper, Coriander Seed, Orange Peel, Lemon Peel, Lemon Myrtle, Native Pepperleaf, Cassia, Green Cardamom, Liquorice, Chamomile, Angelica Root & Orris Root

TASTING NOTES: Lemon myrtle with earthy liquorice and chamomile on the nose, zesty lemon peel and pepperleaf lead the palate, peppermint and lemon tones linger to finish.

SERVING SUGGESTION: Enjoy with Fever-Tree Mediterranean Tonic Water.

Blend Etiquette Craft Distillery

Adelaide, SA

Sitting on the outskirts of Bedford Park near the bustling Flinders University in southern Adelaide, Blend Etiquette Craft Distillery is a second generation gin distillery with a female-led team. They use a 300-litre copper pot still named Frank, which was commissioned to match the one at KIS that was initially used for making their product.

Yours & Mine 42.0%

BOTANICALS: Juniper, Native Lemongrass, Long Pepper, False Cardamom, Sea Parsley, Lemon, Vanilla, Coriander Seed & Angelica Root

TASTING NOTES: Delicate fresh herbs with subtle lemon on the nose, soft vanilla with bold pepper, ginger spice, and fresh lemon on the palate, lingering pepper and zest to finish.

SERVING SUGGESTION: Enjoy with Fever-Tree Mediterranean Tonic Water.

Floral as Hell 42.0%

BOTANICALS: Juniper, Riberry, Raspberry, Lavender, Rosella, Orange, Apple Mint, Za'atar, Coriander Seed & Angelica Root

TASTING NOTES: Stewed green apple with earthy spice mix on the nose, lemon pepper leads with dried bay leaf and gingery juniper on the palate, settling into a bitter apple-mint finish.

SERVING SUGGESTION: Enjoy with Fever-Tree Mediterranean Tonic Water.

Little Bitter Plum Gin 2021 22.7%

BOTANICALS: Juniper, Satsuma Plum, Blood Orange, Gentian Root & Others

TASTING NOTES: Gentian and nutmeg lead the nose, juicy plum and dry gentian tones across the palate, dry grassy gentian to finish.

SERVING SUGGESTION: Enjoy with Fever-Tree Elderflower Tonic Water.

Strangely Savoury 42.0%

BOTANICALS: Juniper, Blood Lime, Sandalwood Nut, Native Pepperberry, Sea Lettuce, Native Lemongrass, Lemon Myrtle, Coriander Seed & Angelica Root

TASTING NOTES: Coriander and juniper supported by dried nut and pepperberry notes on the nose, lemon oil with soft herbs and peppery heat on the palate, dry slightly salty lime driven finish.

SERVING SUGGESTION: Enjoy with Fever-Tree Mediterranean Tonic Water.

Blue Mountains Gin Company
Katoomba, NSW

Huddled at the western edge of the Blue Mountains in the charmingly quirky tourist town of Katoomba, Blue Mountains Gin Company is dedicated to producing small batch craft spirits that highlight the most outstanding aspects of the Blue Mountains. Their Mountain Devil gin range is named for the attractive native shrub that has long been an emblem of the region.

Mountain Devil Classic 40.0%
BOTANICALS: Juniper, Coriander Seed, Liquorice, Lemon Myrtle, Dried Orange, Cassia, Angelica Root, Orris Root, Native Pepperberry & Ginger

TASTING NOTES: Sweet shortbread, hints of soft cinnamon, and candied citrus on the nose, initial ginger and citrus rounding out to dried herb on the palate, delicate liquorice and herbs to finish.

SERVING SUGGESTION: Enjoy with Fever-Tree Mediterranean Tonic Water.

Mountain Devil Black Label 40.0%
BOTANICALS: Juniper, Coriander Seed, Liquorice, Dried Lemon, Dried Orange, Cassia, Angelica Root, Native Pepperberry, Peppercorn & Chilli

TASTING NOTES: Sweet liquorice, cassia and juniper on the nose, zingy citrus, fresh pepperberry and savoury coriander on the palate, chilli heat to finish.

SERVING SUGGESTION: Enjoy with Fever-Tree Aromatic Tonic Water.

Mountain Devil Magic 40.0%
BOTANICALS: Juniper, Coriander Seed, Butterfly Pea Flower, Liquorice, Lemon Myrtle, Dried Orange, Cassia, Angelica Root, Orris Root, Native Pepperberry & Ginger

TASTING NOTES: Fresh citrus and cassia on the nose, ginger and angelica lead with liquorice in support on the palate, fennel and developing florals to finish.

SERVING SUGGESTION: Enjoy with Fever-Tree Mediterranean Tonic Water.

The Devil 57.0%

BOTANICALS: Juniper, Coriander Seed, Liquorice, Dried Lemon, Dried Orange, Cassia, Native Pepperberry, Black Peppercorn & Chilli

TASTING NOTES: Dry lemon and coriander with a hint of chilli on the nose, coriander and lemon lead with supporting chilli and pepperberry on the palate, cassia undertones and chilli heat to finish.

SERVING SUGGESTION: Enjoy with Fever-Tree Premium Indian Tonic Water.

Boatrocker Brewers and Distillers
Melbourne, VIC

Established in the southeastern Melbourne suburb of Braeside, known for its industry and large conservation park, Boatrocker Brewers and Distillers is family-owned and run with a mindset of challenging the status quo and changing the rules. They celebrate tradition while pushing boundaries, seeking to find new and exciting flavour profiles without straying from quality-driven values.

Original Gin 41.5%

BOTANICALS: Juniper, Coriander Seed, Orris Root, Angelica Root, Green Cardamom, Lavender, Almond, Pink Grapefruit, Lemon, Strawberry Gum & Native Pepperberry

TASTING NOTES: Dry rose, grapefruit peel, and strawberry gum on the nose, savoury green cardamom and a hint of turmeric with light florals on the palate, florals develop with lemon oil to finish.

SERVING SUGGESTION: Enjoy with Fever-Tree Elderflower Tonic Water.

Jungle Gin 42.0%

BOTANICALS: Juniper, Coriander Seed, Orris Root, Angelica Root, Makrut Lime Leaf, Ginger, Lemongrass & Kumquat

TASTING NOTES: Initial lime leaf with undertones of juniper on the nose, spicy ginger and coriander to open with oily lemongrass and lime leaf supporting on the palate, soft ginger, florals and citrus to finish.

SERVING SUGGESTION: Enjoy with Fever-Tree Mediterranean Tonic Water.

Raspberry Gin 40.0%

BOTANICALS: Juniper, Coriander Seed, Orris Root, Angelica Root, Almond, Strawberry Gum, Earl Grey Tea & Lemon

TASTING NOTES: Juicy raspberry and strawberry gum on the nose, dried raspberries and black tea on the palate, drying herbal tea-like finish.

SERVING SUGGESTION: Enjoy with Fever-Tree Wild Raspberry Tonic Water.

Bombak Distillery
Perth, WA

Rooted in the suburb of Osborne Park with its history of market gardens in Perth, Bombak Distillery is family-owned and run by the fourth-generation of an immigrant family that previously worked the land. They have a passion for creating small-batch contemporary style gins with a focus on native Western Australian botanicals and fresh ingredients.

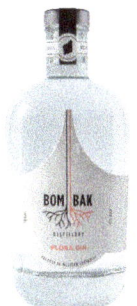

Flora Gin 41.0%

BOTANICALS: Juniper, Geraldton Wax, Bottlebrush, Peppermint Myrtle Leaf & Others

TASTING NOTES: Gentle waxflower with eucalyptus and minty freshness on the nose, fresh waxy citrus with oily peppermint with hints of honey and ginger on the palate, lemon, honey, and ginger spice develop to finish.

SERVING SUGGESTION: Enjoy with Fever-Tree Mediterranean Tonic Water.

Citrus Gin 41.0%

BOTANICALS: Juniper, Lemongrass, Peppermint Myrtle Leaf & Others

TASTING NOTES: Mint tea with supporting citrus on the nose, peppermint leads with liquorice, candied zest, and peppery warmth on the palate, zesty lemongrass and lime to finish.

SERVING SUGGESTION: Enjoy with Fever-Tree Mediterranean Tonic Water.

Navy Gin 57.0%

BOTANICALS: Juniper, Lemongrass, Peppermint Myrtle Leaf & Others

TASTING NOTES: Peppermint, sweet liquorice, and lemongrass on the nose, oily lemongrass leads with pine and pepper heat supporting, pepper and lemongrass develop to finish.

SERVING SUGGESTION: Enjoy with Fever-Tree Mediterranean Tonic Water.

Pickle Gin 41.0%

BOTANICALS: Juniper, Pickle, Dill, Cucumber, Coriander Seed, Habanero & Pickle Spices

TASTING NOTES: Pine needles and dill pickles on the nose, initial bold pickle flavour with jalapeño and coriander seed on the palate, anise and fennel character to finish.

SERVING SUGGESTION: Enjoy with Fever-Tree Mediterranean Tonic Water.

Bond Store Wallaroo
Wallaroo, SA

Huddled in the heart of the historic seaside town of Wallaroo on the east coast of Spencer Gulf, Bond Store Wallaroo is a microbrewery, distillery, and restaurant built around the vision of sharing an experience with friends and family, and bringing people together. They blend flavours from around the world with native Australian herbs and botanicals, including blood oranges and herbs from their home garden.

Lime and Pandan Gin 40.0%

BOTANICALS: Juniper, Makrut Lime, Lime, Pandan, Coconut & Others

TASTING NOTES: Toasted coconut with almond and lime leaf on the nose, oily lime leaf with supporting citrus and coriander seed on the palate, a long coconut driven finish.

SERVING SUGGESTION: Enjoy with Fever-Tree Mediterranean Tonic Water.

Quandong and Blood Orange Gin 42.0%

BOTANICALS: Juniper, Blood Orange, Quandong & Others

TASTING NOTES: Peaches and cream with bold orange peel and thyme on the nose, peppery notes with blood orange and fresh slightly-sweet quandong on the palate, dried fruity notes to finish.

SERVING SUGGESTION: Enjoy with Fever-Tree Refreshingly Light Indian Tonic Water.

True Blue Gin 40.0%

BOTANICALS: Juniper, Aniseed Myrtle, Butterfly Pea Flower, Lemon Myrtle, Desert Lime & Others

TASTING NOTES: Light floral lemon myrtle with a touch of hay and anise on the nose, bright zest with aniseed and warming lemon on the palate, Parma violet and lemon driven finish.

SERVING SUGGESTION: Enjoy with Fever-Tree Mediterranean Tonic Water.

Wattleseed Malt Gin 40.0%

BOTANICALS: Juniper, Wattleseed, Cinnamon, Malt, Star Anise, Native Pepperberry & Others

TASTING NOTES: Rich malt, warming juniper, orange, and baking spice on the nose, initial liquorice, juniper, and warming spice on the palate, malt undertones develop to finish.

SERVING SUGGESTION: Enjoy with Fever-Tree Aromatic Tonic Water.

Bondi Liquor Co.
Sydney, NSW

Sitting in the heart of Sydney's iconic and bustling Bondi Beach, Bondi Liquor Co. was born out of a love of the liquor industry by three mates with a vision of what Bondi means to them. They use organic and Australian grown botanicals where possible and get their base spirit from a sustainable supplier, putting flavour and quality above all else.

Original Dry Gin 40.0%
BOTANICALS: Juniper, Coriander Seed, Angelica Root, Lemon, Wattleseed & Cassia

TASTING NOTES: Coriander leads with juniper and a hint of fig on the nose, coriander continues on the palate with an earthy musk in support, perfumed angelica develops to finish.

SERVING SUGGESTION: Enjoy with Fever-Tree Premium Indian Tonic Water.

Bondi Liquor Co. x Morning Bondi Citrus Gin 40.0%
BOTANICALS: Juniper, Coriander Seed, Mandarin, Lemon Myrtle, Ginger & River Mint

TASTING NOTES: Juniper and citrus on the nose, zesty mandarin with ginger spice and a strong juniper backbone on the palate, lemon myrtle and cooling mint to finish.

SERVING SUGGESTION: Enjoy with Fever-Tree Mediterranean Tonic Water.

Saltwater Gin 40.0%
BOTANICALS: Juniper, Seaweed, Rock Salt, Citrus & Others

TASTING NOTES: Sea spray with herbaceous rosemary and dill on the nose, fresh sea breeze with almond, fennel, and a touch of lemon on the palate, light-crisp lemon builds to finish.

SERVING SUGGESTION: Enjoy with Fever-Tree Mediterranean Tonic Water.

Brogan's Way Distillery
Melbourne, VIC

Surrounded by the rich multi-culturalism of the Richmond suburb in Melbourne, Brogan's Way Distillery was started by a father-daughter duo with a passion for combining science and the art of distilling. They believe there is a gin drink for everyone as they combine creativity with science using native Australian ingredients and botanicals to connect and create lasting memories.

Everyday Salvation Gin 42.0%
BOTANICALS: Juniper, Coriander Seed, White Grapefruit Peel, Lavender, Rose, Orris Root, Angelica Root, Strawberry Gum, Native Pepperberry & Wattleseed

TASTING NOTES: Coriander with citrus, pepperberry, and warm juniper on the nose, initial pepperberry with wattleseed and sweet citrus on the palate, subtle juniper and developing wattleseed to finish.

SERVING SUGGESTION: Enjoy with Fever-Tree Mediterranean Tonic Water.

Evening Light Gin 42.0%
BOTANICALS: Juniper, Mango, Raspberry, White Grapefruit, Coriander Seed, Rose, Lavender, Cassia, Strawberry Gum, Lilly Pilly & River Mint

TASTING NOTES: Fresh tart raspberry and strawberry with strong juniper and lilly pilly on the nose, fresh citrus with funky river mint and coriander on the palate, fresh fruits and citrus linger to finish.

SERVING SUGGESTION: Enjoy with Fever-Tree Refreshingly Light Indian Tonic Water.

Hearts Afire Gin 42.0%
BOTANICALS: Juniper, Orange Peel, Strawberry Gum, Lilly Pilly, Aniseed Myrtle, Clove, Nutmeg, Cassia, Green Cardamom, Black Peppercorn & Wattleseed

TASTING NOTES: Slightly sweet rhubarb with bright juniper and pepper on the nose, baking spice of nutmeg and clove supported by warming orange on the palate, sharp citrus to finish.

SERVING SUGGESTION: Enjoy with Fever-Tree Premium Indian Tonic Water.

Royal Blood Gin 57.2%

BOTANICALS: Juniper, Rosemary, Bay Leaf, Olive Leaf, Black Peppercorn, Native Pepperleaf, Saltbush, Sea Parsley, Wattleseed & Green Cardamom

TASTING NOTES: Wattleseed with saltbush and olive on the nose, bay leaf and olive lead with peppery spice and resinous pine on the palate, savoury spice with peppery heat on the finish.

SERVING SUGGESTION: Enjoy with Fever-Tree Mediterranean Tonic Water.

Mother's Way Gin 38.5%

BOTANICALS: Juniper, Pine, Strawberry Gum, Native Pepperberry, Lime, Pink Grapefruit, Rose & Lavender

TASTING NOTES: Bright citrus with strawberry and floral perfume on the nose, strawberry with lemon and floral pepperberry spice on the palate, soft juniper and fruity strawberry to finish.

SERVING SUGGESTION: Enjoy with Fever-Tree Elderflower Tonic Water.

Strawberries and Cream Gin 38.0%

BOTANICALS: Juniper, Strawberry & Others

TASTING NOTES: Sweet strawberries with light juniper on the nose, strawberries and cream with a touch of spice and a hint of sweetness on the palate, juniper develops with dry strawberry on the finish.

SERVING SUGGESTION: Enjoy with Fever-Tree Refreshingly Light Indian Tonic Water.

Brunswick Aces
Melbourne, VIC

Located in the buzzing food and culture scene of the Brunswick East suburb of Melbourne, Brunswick Aces is a distillery started by a group of neighbours, with a collective skillset that included engineering and science, in need of a drink they could all share. They developed their own process of making non-alcoholic gin and have it as their mission to make everyone feel welcome in every social situation, making both non-alcoholic and alcoholic spirits.

Spades Gin 40.0%

BOTANICALS: Juniper, Green Cardamom, Lemon Myrtle, Parsley, Coriander Seed, Lime & Native Pepperberry

TASTING NOTES: Pronounced cardamom with hints of dried citrus peel and peppery notes on the nose, slight citrus sweetness opening to bold cardamom spice and pepperberry on the palate, lingering dried spice with tart citrus to finish.

SERVING SUGGESTION: Enjoy with Fever-Tree Aromatic Tonic Water.

Hearts Gin 40.0%

BOTANICALS: Juniper, Star Anise, Clove, Cassia, Wattleseed, Pink Grapefruit & Ginger

TASTING NOTES: Strong spice of cassia, clove, and star anise on the nose, upfront star anise with hints of ginger and a touch of juniper on the palate, lingering star anise and clove with peppery heat to finish.

SERVING SUGGESTION: Enjoy with Fever-Tree Aromatic Tonic Water.

Diamonds Gin 40.0%

BOTANICALS: Juniper, Mandarin, Desert Lime, Lemon, Sage & Angelica Root

TASTING NOTES: Dried lime peel with sage undertones on the nose, floral mandarin with light touches of angelica and peppery juniper on the palate, developing warmth with tart citrus to finish.

SERVING SUGGESTION: Enjoy with Fever-Tree Mediterranean Tonic Water.

Bruny Island House of Whisky
Bruny Island, TAS

Secluded on the north-western side of the wild and popular Bruny Island off the coast from Hobart, Bruny Island House of Whisky is a specialty tasting bar home to the largest collection of Tasmanian single malts. They collaborate with distilleries, such as McHenry Distillery, to create a range of limited release, and exclusive, whiskies and gins.

Seclusion Original Gin 42.1%
BOTANICALS: Juniper, Cassia, Orange Peel, Orange & Coriander Seed

TASTING NOTES: Orange oil leads with pine resin and bright anise on the nose, floral lemon myrtle, liquorice, fresh lime zest, and a slight mentholic heat on the palate, lingering heat and citrus to finish.

SERVING SUGGESTION: Enjoy with Fever-Tree Mediterranean Tonic Water.

Seclusion Saffron Gin 39.6%
BOTANICALS: Juniper, Saffron, Coriander Seed, Cardamom, Orange Peel & Star Anise

TASTING NOTES: Light hints of orange zest with dry cooking spice on the nose, cardamom with coriander seed and orange on the palate, subtle pepper spice lingers to finish.

SERVING SUGGESTION: Enjoy with Fever-Tree Premium Indian Tonic Water.

Seclusion Satellite Gin 42.1%
BOTANICALS: Juniper, Butterfly Pea Flower, Cassia, Orange Peel, Orange & Coriander Seed

TASTING NOTES: Anise and fennel with oily orange peel on the nose, burst of lemon and orange supported by star anise and myrtle-like notes on the palate, hints of florals with lingering citrus oil to finish.

SERVING SUGGESTION: Enjoy with Fever-Tree Mediterranean Tonic Water.

Buffalo Vale Distillery

Sydney, NSW

Founded on the banks of Buffalo Creek, a tributary of Sydney Harbour, now in the suburb of Rhodes, Buffalo Vale Distillery produces small batch craft spirits with the values of simplicity, ingenuity, purity, and quality at their core. They use their own base spirit with a combination of home-grown and locally sourced botanicals, blended to reflect the character of their gentle locale and aiming to allow a moment of pause.

Clair De Lune Gin 40.0%

BOTANICALS: Juniper, Stinging Nettle, Cassia, Lemon Myrtle, Cardamom, Angelica Root, Nigella, Lemon Zest, Coriander Seed, Wattleseed, Chamomile, Native Pepperberry & Bergamot

TASTING NOTES: Hints of banana with a slight oak note on the nose, chamomile and nettle lead the palate with wattleseed in support, a spiced citrus finish.

SERVING SUGGESTION: Enjoy with Fever-Tree Mediterranean Tonic Water.

Clair De Lune Gin Extreme 55.0%

BOTANICALS: Juniper, Stinging Nettle, Cassia, Lemon Myrtle, Cardamom, Angelica Root, Nigella, Lemon Zest, Coriander Seed, Wattleseed, Chamomile, Native Pepperberry & Bergamot

TASTING NOTES: Grassy grain notes with earthy characters on the nose, musky lavender with pepperberry on the palate, herbaceous pepperberry develops to finish.

SERVING SUGGESTION: Enjoy with Fever-Tree Mediterranean Tonic Water.

Camden Valley Distilling Company
Camden, NSW

Secreted away in the Camden Valley between the historic town of Camden and Sydney, Camden Valley Distilling Company use a combination of traditional and local ingredients in their gins, including some from their neighbours' properties. They steep, boil, and basket infuse their botanicals in varying combinations using a 50L copper pot still and use water from a spring in the Southern Highlands near Mittagong.

Post Modern Dry Gin 44.0%

BOTANICALS: Juniper, Meyer Lemon, Thyme, Walnut, Coriander Seed, Angelica Root & Liquorice

TASTING NOTES: Juniper and lemon lead the nose, initial burst of juniper and thyme with a touch of coriander on the palate, lingering lemon and coriander with a slight earthy musk to finish.

SERVING SUGGESTION: Enjoy with Fever-Tree Mediterranean Tonic Water.

Sloe Gin 28.0%

BOTANICALS: Juniper, Meyer Lemon, Thyme, Walnut, Coriander Seed, Angelica Root, Liquorice & Sloe Berry

TASTING NOTES: Tart raspberry, almond blossom, and plum jam on the nose, hints of peppery spice, marzipan, and thick tart plum the palate, firm acid and an elegant sweetness to finish.

SERVING SUGGESTION: Enjoy with Fever-Tree Lemon Tonic Water.

Cape Byron Distillery
McLeods Shoot, NSW

Sheltered on a 95-acre macadamia farm and 30-year-old regenerated subtropical rainforest in the hills and hinterland behind the beachside town of Byron Bay, Cape Byron Distillery are passionate about sustainability and are B Corp Certified. They keep to the time honoured traditions and art of distillation whilst trying to capture and showcase the terroir of the Northern Rivers region.

Brookie's Byron Dry Gin 46.0%

BOTANICALS: Juniper, Finger Lime, Aniseed Myrtle, Cinnamon Myrtle, Macadamia, Native Ginger, Native Raspberry & Others

TASTING NOTES: Dry citrus with spiced myrtle and subtle juniper on the nose, bright peppery fruit with cinnamon and a macadamia texture on the palate, peppery spice on the finish.

SERVING SUGGESTION: Enjoy with Fever-Tree Mediterranean Tonic Water.

Brookie's Shirl the Pearl Cumquat Gin 37.7%

BOTANICALS: Juniper, Finger Lime, Aniseed Myrtle, Cinnamon Myrtle, Macadamia, Ginger, Raspberry, Cumquat & Others

TASTING NOTES: Candied cumquat with gentle ginger spice and raspberry leaf on the nose, initial aniseed progressing into sweeter cinnamon and kumquat on the palate, kumquat and ginger spice to finish.

SERVING SUGGESTION: Enjoy with Fever-Tree Refreshingly Light Indian Tonic Water.

Brookie's Byron Slow Gin 26.0%

BOTANICALS: Juniper, Davidson Plum, Rose & Watermelon

TASTING NOTES: Creamy apricot and plum flesh with a touch of thyme on the nose, apricot, red currant, and tart red plum skin on the palate, bright acidity and restrained sweetness with plum and ripe red cherry finish.

SERVING SUGGESTION: Enjoy with Fever-Tree Lemon Tonic Water.

Capricorn Distilling Co.
Gold Coast, QLD

Stationed in the picturesque Burleigh Heads on the southern end of the Gold Coast, Capricorn Distilling Co. started life as The Salesyard Distillery in Rockhampton before moving south and changing their name to reflect their origin in the Tropic of Capricorn. They value sustainability at all stages of their distillation and production process, using local ingredients, free from added sugars, colours, and artificial flavours.

Summer Gin 42.0%

BOTANICALS: Juniper, Orris Root, Finger Lime, Ruby Red Grapefruit, Lemon Myrtle, Lavender, Rose, Cinnamon, Coriander Seed & Others

TASTING NOTES: Pine notes with sweet pink grapefruit and lemon myrtle on the nose, bright finger lime, floral grapefruit, and dry spice of cardamom and coriander on the palate, dried grapefruit peel on the finish.

SERVING SUGGESTION: Enjoy with Fever-Tree Mediterranean Tonic Water.

Oak Aged Gin 42.0%

BOTANICALS: Juniper, Orris Root, Finger Lime, Ruby Red Grapefruit, Lemon Myrtle, Lavender, Rose, Cinnamon, Coriander Seed & Others (aged in ex-Barossa Valley French and American Oak Barrels)

TASTING NOTES: Toasted coconut with tropical pineapple and lime on the nose, soft nutty character with pine oil and spice developing on the palate, cedar and spice with coconut to finish.

SERVING SUGGESTION: Enjoy neat or with Fever-Tree Ginger Ale.

Old Tom Gin 42.0%

BOTANICALS: Juniper, Coriander Seed, Orange, Orris Root, Angelica Root, Star Anise, Frankincense, Myrrh & Others

TASTING NOTES: Woody pine with sappy forest notes on the nose, dry and woody notes to open with rich honey and oily juniper on the palate, drying pine driven finish.

SERVING SUGGESTION: Enjoy with Fever-Tree Aromatic Tonic Water.

Castle Glen Distillery
The Summit, QLD

Set amongst the farmland, vineyards, and cooler climate of The Summit in southern Queensland, Castle Glen Distillery is environmentally conscious, developing organic practices and using a combination of solar and wind power. Initially a winery, they began producing a wide variety of different spirits, which are all 100% natural, alongside their wines in the late 2000s.

Castle Glen Gin 40.0%
BOTANICALS: Juniper & Others
TASTING NOTES: Bold base notes with steeped fruits on the nose, peppery heat with strong dark fruit on the palate, prune and preserved fruits to finish.
SERVING SUGGESTION: Enjoy with Fever-Tree Premium Indian Tonic Water.

Castle Glen Elderflower Gin 40.0%
BOTANICALS: Juniper, Elderflower & Others
TASTING NOTES: Elderflower and stewed fruits with a touch of grain on the nose, dried apricot with a touch of nutty character on the palate, dried fruity character with grain notes to finish.
SERVING SUGGESTION: Enjoy with Fever-Tree Elderflower Tonic Water.

Cedar Fox Distilling Co.
Melbourne, VIC

Positioned in the northern Melbourne suburb of Coburg North, Cedar Fox Distilling Co. was founded by a brewer/distiller/musician and a journalist/lawyer who immerse themselves in the Australian independent art and music scene as well as craft brewing and distilling. They strive to create products that reflect their ideas on achieving complexity and quality through simple and minimal means alongside unconventionality and DIY approaches.

Cedar Fox Gin 42.0%

BOTANICALS: Juniper, Coriander Seed, Meyer Lemon, Lebanese Cucumber, Sichuan Peppercorn, Rosemary, Lemon Verbena & Others

TASTING NOTES: Lemon verbena and cucumber peel with a hint of pepper on the nose, floral lemon with smoky rosemary and sweet pepper on the palate, long lingering citrus to finish.

SERVING SUGGESTION: Enjoy with Fever-Tree Mediterranean Tonic Water.

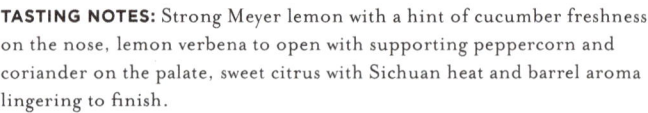

Oak Gin 45.0%

BOTANICALS: Juniper, Coriander Seed, Meyer Lemon, Lebanese Cucumber, Sichuan Peppercorn, Rosemary, Lemon Verbena & Others (aged in ex-Whisky Barrels)

TASTING NOTES: Strong Meyer lemon with a hint of cucumber freshness on the nose, lemon verbena to open with supporting peppercorn and coriander on the palate, sweet citrus with Sichuan heat and barrel aroma lingering to finish.

SERVING SUGGESTION: Enjoy with Fever-Tree Mediterranean Tonic Water.

Clarence Distillery
Yamba, NSW

Looking out on the mouth of the Clarence River in the vibrant marine town of Yamba, Clarence Distillery looks to inspire more free spirits with their slow living style. They draw on the produce made in the local area, which is home to a broad range of agriculture from small farm producers to large sugar cane plantations.

Duke 42.0%
BOTANICALS: Juniper, Makrut Lime, Lemon Myrtle, Orange, Dorrigo Pepper, Cardamom, Coriander Seed, Vetiver & Native Ginger

TASTING NOTES: Waxy lime leaf with supporting lemon citrus on the nose, lime leaf continues on the palate with sharp lemon and developing green herbs, herbaceous driven finish with bright spots of citrus.

SERVING SUGGESTION: Enjoy with Fever-Tree Mediterranean Tonic Water.

Ruby 42.0%
BOTANICALS: Juniper, Lemon Myrtle, Rosella Flower, Makrut Lime, Orange, Geranium, Coriander Seed, Strawberry Gum, Rosebud & Cassia

TASTING NOTES: Ginger spice with hints of dried fruits on the nose, an array of spice leads with earthy angelica and tart plum juice on the palate, musky perfumed angelica to finish.

SERVING SUGGESTION: Enjoy with Fever-Tree Lemon Tonic Water.

Sailor King Navy Gin 58.0%
BOTANICALS: Juniper, Makrut Lime, Orange, Dorrigo Pepper, Macadamia, Coriander Seed, River Mint, Aniseed Myrtle

TASTING NOTES: Thyme and aniseed with a hint of nuttiness on the nose, aniseed and thyme lead with peppery heat on the palate, pepperberry and spice linger to finish.

SERVING SUGGESTION: Enjoy with Fever-Tree Premium Indian Tonic Water.

Clark & Kealey Distilling
Wamboin, NSW

Occupying a spot in the middle of the Wamboin area of the Southern Tablelands northeast of Canberra, Clark & Kealey Distilling is a small-batch artisan distillery named for its co-founders. They produce spirits inspired by the flavours and simplicity of the Australian bush using traditional methods, with particular times or occasions in mind for their enjoyment.

Tymephora Gin featuring Strawberry Gum 44.0%

BOTANICALS: Juniper, Strawberry Gum, Orris Root, Angelica Root & Almond

TASTING NOTES: Strawberry gum leads with a hint of pine on the nose, initial burst of strawberry gum with orris earthiness and a touch of pine on the plate, lingering strawberry gum to finish.

SERVING SUGGESTION: Enjoy with Fever-Tree Mediterranean Tonic Water.

Christmas Gin featuring Cinnamon Myrtle 44.0%

BOTANICALS: Juniper, Cinnamon Myrtle, Orris Root, Angelica Root, Currant, Raisin, Prune, Cranberry, Clove, Allspice, Nutmeg & Mandarin Peel

TASTING NOTES: Hints of spiced fruit with allspice and cinnamon on the nose, Christmas spice mix leads with a hint of mandarin and an almond texture on the palate, spiced fruit mix lingers to finish.

SERVING SUGGESTION: Enjoy with Fever-Tree Aromatic Tonic Water.

Tymephora Gin featuring Anise Myrtle 44.0%

BOTANICALS: Juniper, Aniseed Myrtle, Orris Root, Angelica Root & Almond

TASTING NOTES: Black liquorice leads with a hint of sea breeze on the nose, salty character features alongside developing liquorice on the palate, settling anise to finish.

SERVING SUGGESTION: Enjoy with Fever-Tree Aromatic Tonic Water.

Critters Distillery
Woolgoolga, NSW

Established in the seaside town of Woolgoolga and surrounded by the rugged beauty of the mid-north coast, Critters Distillery produces small batch spirits inspired by the Australian marine environment with full traceability from 'paddock to glass'. They strive to support sustainable practices throughout their business and take the angler fish as their logo for the resonance between it and the authentic craftsmanship of brewing, fermenting, and distilling, in their reliance on their senses for survival.

Critters Distillery Gin 42.0%

BOTANICALS: Juniper, Davidson Plum, Finger Lime, Lemon Myrtle, Aniseed Myrtle, Rosella Flower & Others

TASTING NOTES: White pepper, fermented peach, and white florals on the nose, anise with supporting lemon and stone fruit flavour on the palate, anise led finish with subtle supporting spice.

SERVING SUGGESTION: Enjoy with Fever-Tree Refreshingly Light Indian Tonic Water.

Cuprum Distillery
Bunbury, WA

Based in the cosmopolitan coastal city of Bunbury, which acts as the northern gateway to Australia's South West, Cuprum Distillery began with an idea to create quality spirits in handmade copper pot stills using indigenous botanicals that capture the spirit of the South West. They take their name from the Latin word for copper, given its importance as the material of choice for stills, and use its atomic symbol and number in their logo.

West Coast Signature Gin 40.0%

BOTANICALS: Juniper, Orange Peel, Cinnamon, Cassia & Others

TASTING NOTES: Dry tea leaves with cinnamon and juniper on the nose, dry woody tea-like characters leads the palate with heated spice in support, cassia driven finish.

SERVING SUGGESTION: Enjoy with Fever-Tree Aromatic Tonic Water.

Raspberry Gin 40.0%

BOTANICALS: Juniper, Orris Root, Raspberry & Others

TASTING NOTES: Raspberry and florals lead the nose, initial fruity notes with orris root and developing florals on the palate, dried berry notes with balancing orris root to finish.

SERVING SUGGESTION: Enjoy with Fever-Tree Wild Raspberry Tonic Water.

Darling Distillery
Melbourne, VIC

Located within the walls of the iconic 130-year-old Royal Hotel in the bohemian inner-city Clifton Hill suburb of Melbourne, Darling Distillery was started by three mates with time, space, and a passion for process. They have a desire to create exceptional small batch products with sustainability and community in mind, using locally sourced premium botanicals.

Darling Distillery Gin 42.0%

BOTANICALS: Juniper, Orange, Mandarin, Native Pepperberry, Coriander Seed, Lemongrass, Rosemary, Green Tea, Honey & Others

TASTING NOTES: Classic nose led by juniper, coriander and citrus, juniper and coriander continue with pepper heat on the palate, lasting juniper and pepper to finish.

SERVING SUGGESTION: Enjoy with Fever-Tree Premium Indian Tonic Water.

Darwin Distilling Co.
Darwin, NT

Planted right in the heart of balmy Darwin's colourful city centre, Darwin Distilling Co. was started within a restaurant by a passionate entrepreneur and botanical lover with a long history in the hospitality industry. They regularly forage for Territorian botanicals as well as working with various communities to bring local but exotic flavours to their spirits.

Darwin Gin 40%
BOTANICALS: Juniper, Kakadu Plum, Native Lemongrass, Water Lily & Others

TASTING NOTES: Strong earthy tones lead the nose, rich fruitiness with developing florals on the palate, pepper spice and lingering florals continue to finish.

SERVING SUGGESTION: Enjoy with Fever-Tree Premium Indian Tonic Water.

Salty Plum Gin 40%
BOTANICALS: Juniper, Plums, Ginger, Lime & Others

TASTING NOTES: Bold hits of tamarind and fermented fruit on the nose, a sweet-sour fruit driven palate, long and dry with notes of sichuan and eastern spice to finish.

SERVING SUGGESTION: Enjoy with Fever-Tree Premium Indian Tonic Water.

Distil on the Hill
Kuranda, QLD

Secluded amongst the lush hills of Jumrum Springs near picturesque Kuranda in the tropical rainforest to the north of Cairns, Distil on the Hill is a small batch micro-distillery whose founders have a strong family heritage of distilling. They use a base spirit made with 100% Australian grown Barossa Valley grapes along with a range of botanicals, including fresh local citrus, which they combine in their copper pot still in a one-shot vapour distillation.

Jindilli Gin 41.0%

BOTANICALS: Juniper, Coriander Seed, Angelica Root, Atherton Raspberry, Orange, Elderflower, Pink Peppercorn, Vanilla, Lemongrass, Orange Blossom, Mint, Macadamia & Lime

TASTING NOTES: Strong florals, resinous peppercorn and lemongrass on the nose, coriander spice with mint and lime on the palate, hints of mint carry with honeydew to finish.

SERVING SUGGESTION: Enjoy with Fever-Tree Mediterranean Tonic Water.

Mandarin Gin 42.0%

BOTANICALS: Juniper, Coriander Seed, Cardamom, Angelica Root, Mandarin, Lemon Myrtle, Long Pepper, Cubeb Pepper & Vanilla

TASTING NOTES: Pepper spice with bitter mandarin on the nose, subtle cardamom with cubeb pepper and tart mandarin on the palate, vanilla rounds out the finish.

SERVING SUGGESTION: Enjoy with Fever-Tree Aromatic Tonic Water.

Distillery Botanica
Erina, NSW

Tucked away on the beautiful Central Coast of New South Wales between Sydney and Newcastle in the suburb of Erina, Distillery Botanica is set amongst three acres of gardens, owned and distilled by an astute herbalist with a long history in horticulture, They grow many botanicals in their gardens which serve as the inspiration and ingredients for their products.

Moore's Dry Gin 40.0%

BOTANICALS: Juniper, Coriander Seed, Liquorice, Angelica Root, Pink Peppercorn, Macadamia, Illawarra Plum & Desert Lime

TASTING NOTES: Coriander and liquorice lead with a hint of angelica on the nose, fruity notes with angelica and pepper spice on the palate, coriander lingers with growing fruity notes to finish.

SERVING SUGGESTION: Enjoy with Fever-Tree Refreshingly Light Indian Tonic Water.

Moore's Dry Gin Distillers Cut Juniper 45.0%

BOTANICALS: Juniper, Grapefruit, Orange, Liquorice, Angelica Root & Cardamom

TASTING NOTES: Coriander, angelica and bold juniper on the nose, juniper and angelica lead the palate with liquorice sweetness in support, resinous juniper and earthy roots to finish.

SERVING SUGGESTION: Enjoy with Fever-Tree Premium Indian Tonic Water.

Moore's Dry Gin Roots & Leaves 40.0%

BOTANICALS: Juniper, Angelica Root, Galangal, Ginger, Turmeric, Makrut Lime Leaf, Lemon Verbena, Mandarin Leaf & Curry Leaf

TASTING NOTES: Strong herbaceous characters with curry leaf and woody ginger on the nose, pronounced citrus with eucalypt honey and orange sweetness on the palate, citrus oils linger to finish.

SERVING SUGGESTION: Enjoy with Fever-Tree Mediterranean Tonic Water.

DIVINERS
DISTILLERY

Diviners Distillery
Ballandean, QLD

Situated in the midst of the hills and vineyards to the west of Ballandean in the Granite Belt, Diviners Distillery revels in the wonder of the invisible and believes in creating divine experiences that are beyond physical by crafting in a place between science and art. They use Australian botanicals with a cold vacuum distillation process to achieve flavours that traditional methods cannot.

Apparition Gin 40.0%

BOTANICALS: Juniper, Wattleseed, Macadamia, Cassia, Angelica Root, Coriander Seed & Others

TASTING NOTES: Citrus, angelica and a touch of cassia on the nose, dry spice, coriander and wattleseed provide a strong nutty flavour on the palate, deep warming spice to finish.

SERVING SUGGESTION: Enjoy with Fever-Tree Aromatic Tonic Water.

Outlier Gin 46.0%

BOTANICALS: Juniper, Strawberry Gum, Cassia, Finger Lime, Allspice & Coriander Seed

TASTING NOTES: Pronounced finger lime with strawberry gum on the nose, peppery spice, juniper, and cassia drive the palate, sweet touch of rhubarb to finish.

SERVING SUGGESTION: Enjoy with Fever-Tree Refreshingly Light Indian Tonic Water.

Dunalley Bay Distillery
Dunalley, TAS

Nestled directly on the southern end of the sweeping, ruggedly tranquil Dunalley Bay shoreline north of Port Arthur, Dunalley Bay Distillery was founded in the spirit of rebirth and renewal following the local area's bushfires in 2013. They craft gins blended with locally sourced Tasmanian fruits, flowers, and native botanicals to reflect their natural environment.

JJJ Gin 43.0%

BOTANICALS: Juniper, Kakadu Plum, Lemon Myrtle, Strawberry Gum, Native Pepperleaf, Wattleseed, Cinnamon Myrtle, Celerytop Pine, Quandong & Oyster Shell

TASTING NOTES: Striking lemon and cinnamon myrtle with pine on the nose, burst of fresh citrus and fennel seed with developing juniper on the palate, lingering lemon myrtle and fruity tones to finish.

SERVING SUGGESTION: Enjoy with Fever-Tree Mediterranean Tonic Water.

Blue Blue Gin 42.0%

BOTANICALS: Juniper, Kakadu Plum, Lemon Myrtle, Strawberry Gum, Native Pepperleaf, Wattleseed, Cinnamon Myrtle, Celerytop Pine, Quandong, Oyster Shell & Others

TASTING NOTES: Burnt orange rind with cinnamon quill on the nose, drying ground spices with coriander seed and citrus on the palate, lingering spice and citrus to finish.

SERVING SUGGESTION: Enjoy with Fever-Tree Aromatic Tonic Water.

Chartreuse Gin 42.0%

BOTANICALS: Juniper, Kakadu Plum, Lemon Myrtle, Strawberry Gum, Native Pepperleaf, Wattleseed, Cinnamon Myrtle, Celerytop Pine, Quandong, Oyster Shell & Others

TASTING NOTES: Strong lemon with a touch of salt and earthiness on the nose, initial dried fennel leaf leading to oily lemon and pepperberry on the palate, citrus lingers to finish.

SERVING SUGGESTION: Enjoy with Fever-Tree Mediterranean Tonic Water.

Princess Sloe Gin 40.0%

BOTANICALS: Juniper, Kakadu Plum, Lemon Myrtle, Strawberry Gum, Native Pepperleaf, Wattleseed, Cinnamon Myrtle, Celerytop Pine, Quandong, Oyster Shell, Sloe Berry, Star Anise, Coriander Seed & Cardamom

TASTING NOTES: Light marzipan with raisins and dried apricot on the nose, baking spice with sweet sultanas, honey, and cinnamon on the palate, honey, spice, and sweetness linger to finish.

SERVING SUGGESTION: Enjoy with Fever-Tree Lemon Tonic Water.

Rosie & Hip Gin 42.0%

BOTANICALS: Juniper, Kakadu Plum, Lemon Myrtle, Strawberry Gum, Native Pepperleaf, Wattleseed, Cinnamon Myrtle, Celerytop Pine, Quandong, Oyster Shell & Others

TASTING NOTES: Fennel seed with bitter almond and hints of pine on the nose, tones of dried fruits with eucalypt notes and supporting fresh citrus on the palate, lingering fresh lemon zest to finish.

SERVING SUGGESTION: Enjoy with Fever-Tree Refreshingly Light Indian Tonic Water.

Spiced Sloe Gin 40.0%

BOTANICALS: Juniper, Kakadu Plum, Lemon Myrtle, Strawberry Gum, Native Pepperleaf, Wattleseed, Cinnamon Myrtle, Celerytop Pine, Quandong, Oyster Shell, Sloe Berry, Orange Peel & Clove

TASTING NOTES: Cinnamon with quandong sweetness on the nose, strong pepper with clove, orange, and a touch of raisin on the palate, pepper continues to develop and leads the finish.

SERVING SUGGESTION: Enjoy with Fever-Tree Lemon Tonic Water.

Dune Distilling Co.
Wilyabrup, WA

Situated in Wilyabrup, in the Margaret River wine region of Western Australia's beautiful South West region, Dune Distilling Co. is inspired by its home along the stunning coastline, taking the rugged terrain and beautiful native flora as their muse. They source as much local produce and native botanicals as possible to produce flavours that reflect a sense of place.

Signature Gin 41.0%
BOTANICALS: Juniper, Navel Orange, Coriander Seed & Lemon Rind

TASTING NOTES: Striking orange and lemon oil on the nose, classic juniper at first with supporting bitter lemon peel on the palate, mellowing into a sweeter citrus that lingers to finish.

SERVING SUGGESTION: Enjoy with Fever-Tree Mediterranean Tonic Water.

Lime and Green Tea Gin 43.0%
BOTANICALS: Juniper, Davidson Plum, Lemon Myrtle, Coriander Seed, Saltbush, Green Tea & Lime

TASTING NOTES: Classic juniper and coriander with supporting saltbush on the nose, juniper punch with saltbush and lemon myrtle on the palate, dry coriander and curry spice to finish.

SERVING SUGGESTION: Enjoy with Fever-Tree Mediterranean Tonic Water.

Pink Grapefruit Gin 42.0%
BOTANICALS: Juniper, Davidson Plum, Lemon Myrtle, Coriander Seed, Salt Bush, Pink Grapefruit, Navel Orange & Lemon Peel

TASTING NOTES: Candied grapefruit zest with fresh squeezed grapefruit juice on the nose, citrus driven with lemon myrtle, navel orange, and grapefruit juice on the palate, saltbush develops late with a fresh zesty finish.

SERVING SUGGESTION: Enjoy with Fever-Tree Mediterranean Tonic Water.

Earp Distilling Co.
Newcastle, NSW

Cloistered on either side by Throsby Creek and Hunter River in the suburb of Carrington next to the Port of Newcastle, Earp Distilling Co. was established by two brothers, from whom it takes its name, with a passion for the creative and experiential. They embrace modern distilling technology in the pursuit of speed, accuracy, control, and consistency in producing their spirits.

Just Juniper 42.0%

BOTANICALS: Juniper

TASTING NOTES: Herbaceous lead with juniper and lifted heat on the nose, peppery spice with strong juniper on the palate, classic finish led by juniper with supporting spice.

SERVING SUGGESTION: Enjoy with Fever-Tree Refreshingly Light Indian Tonic Water.

No. 8 Dry Gin 42.0%

BOTANICALS: Juniper, Coriander Seed, Angelica Root, Cardamom, Dried Apple, Raspberry, Chamomile & Cinnamon

TASTING NOTES: Cinnamon and cardamom lead the nose, peppery heat with angelica and cardamom on the palate, perfumed angelica continues with cardamom heat lingering to finish.

SERVING SUGGESTION: Enjoy with Fever-Tree Premium Indian Tonic Water.

Portside Gin 57.0%

BOTANICALS: Juniper, Coriander Seed, Angelica Root, Wattleseed, Orris Root, Chamomile & Lemon Myrtle

TASTING NOTES: Wattleseed and orris root on the nose, initial sweetness with dark roasted wattleseed, lemon myrtle, and dry chamomile on the palate, tea florals and lemon myrtle to finish.

SERVING SUGGESTION: Enjoy with Fever-Tree Mediterranean Tonic Water.

Echuca Distillery
Echuca Moama, VIC

Seated in the charming and historic river port town of Echuca Moama between the Murray and Campaspe Rivers, Echuca Distillery is committed to creating 100% natural products with the purest water they can source. They craft their spirits using Australian base spirit made from grain or grapes and plant-based natural botanicals from around the world in their still called Lavender.

High Street Gin 40.0%

BOTANICALS: Juniper, Angelica Root, Aniseed Myrtle, Coriander Seed, Orange, Lemon Myrtle, Liquorice, Native Pepperberry & Wild Thyme

TASTING NOTES: Wild thyme, rosemary, and liquorice root lead the nose, coriander seed with light hints of citrus alongside earthy herbaceous tones carry the palate, drying pepper with citrus oil on the finish.

SERVING SUGGESTION: Enjoy with Fever-Tree Mediterranean Tonic Water.

Cadell's Navy Strength Gin 57.0%

BOTANICALS: Juniper, Angelica Root, Cassia, Coriander Seed, Ginger, Lemon Myrtle, Liquorice, Mace & West Indian Lime

TASTING NOTES: Ginger root spice with lemon myrtle and juniper on the nose, bold juniper leads with pronounced coriander and liquorice root on the palate, juniper and lemon myrtle linger to finish.

SERVING SUGGESTION: Enjoy with Fever-Tree Premium Indian Tonic Water.

Hopwood's Yuzu & Ginger Gin 40.0%

BOTANICALS: Juniper, Allspice, Angelica Root, Caraway Seed, Coriander Seed, Cubeb Peppercorn, Yuzu, Ginger & Lemongrass

TASTING NOTES: Coriander, ginger and sweet yuzu lead the nose, green garden herbs to open with bright lemongrass and earthy ginger on the palate, green herbaceous finish with hints of citrus.

SERVING SUGGESTION: Enjoy with Fever-Tree Refreshingly Light Indian Tonic Water.

Emerald Island Distillery
Emerald Beach, NSW

Looking out from Emerald Beach, New South Wales, at the broad expanse of the Pacific Ocean with the Great Dividing Range at its back, Emerald Island Distillery takes its name from a local phantom island first sighted in 1821 but never confirmed to exist since. They draw inspiration from the pristine coastline and sea-kissed hinterland around them.

Premium Dry Gin 42.0%

BOTANICALS: Juniper, Kumquat, Raspberry, Makrut Lime, Lemon Myrtle & Others

TASTING NOTES: Lime leaf with fruit tones and soft honey on the nose, bright citrus and waxy lime leaf with a juniper backbone on the palate, lingering lime leaf with zesty lemon to finish.

SERVING SUGGESTION: Enjoy with Fever-Tree Mediterranean Tonic Water.

Berry Slow Gin 40.0%

BOTANICALS: Juniper, Kumquat, Raspberry, Makrut Lime, Lemon Myrtle & Others (steeped with Seasonal Local Berries)

TASTING NOTES: Bright tart raspberry with touches of jam sweetness on the nose, moderate berry sweetness and light acidity with supporting pepperberry on the palate, drying fruit notes to finish.

SERVING SUGGESTION: Enjoy with Fever-Tree Lemon Tonic Water.

Ginger Bee Gin 40.0%

BOTANICALS: Juniper, Honey, Ginger & Others (aged in ex-Shiraz Barrels)

TASTING NOTES: Resounding honey and ginger on the nose, hints of lemon oil with rich honey and notes of fresh baked bread on the palate, thick honey and lemon linger to finish.

SERVING SUGGESTION: Enjoy with Fever-Tree Mediterranean Tonic Water.

Mirage Gin 42.0%

BOTANICALS: Juniper, Kumquat, Raspberry, Makrut Lime, Lemon Myrtle & Butterfly Pea Flower

TASTING NOTES: Earthy tones with dry lemon myrtle on the nose, pine oil with lemon myrtle continuing on the palate, grapefruit, light rosemary and subtle anise to finish.

SERVING SUGGESTION: Enjoy with Fever-Tree Mediterranean Tonic Water.

Spice Chest Gin 40.0%

BOTANICALS: Juniper, Cocoa Husk & Others

TASTING NOTES: Heavy spice blend with clove, cardamom, cinnamon, and orange zest on the nose, sweet spices with supporting orange continue on the palate, sweet spice driven finish.

SERVING SUGGESTION: Enjoy with Fever-Tree Aromatic Tonic Water.

Envy Distilling
Melbourne, VIC

Hidden away in the urban sprawl of dynamic Melbourne, Envy Distilling is a small craft distillery that takes its name from the first letter of each of its owners and runners' first names, N and V. They are inspired by a love for traditional alembic methods and the produce from their local community which they use to highlight the love, diversity, and uniqueness of their relationships, friends, family, and neighbours in their spirits.

Sea & Stars Gin 40.0%

BOTANICALS: Juniper, Coriander Seed, Cardamom, Cassia, Lime Peel, Orange Peel, Orris Root, Makrut Lime Leaf, Long Pepper & Angelica Root

TASTING NOTES: Oily lime leaf with baking spice on the nose, bright fresh citrus with cardamom, coriander, and lime leaf on the palate, peppery led finish with hints of citrus.

SERVING SUGGESTION: Enjoy with Fever-Tree Mediterranean Tonic Water.

Picnic Gin 40.0%

BOTANICALS: Juniper, Coriander Seed, Cardamom, Cassia, Orange Peel, Lime Peel, Elderberry, Aniseed Myrtle, Wormwood & Dill

TASTING NOTES: Bright fruit notes of pear and apple with elderflower and honey on the nose, subtle juniper with elderflower followed by anise notes and menthol spice on the palate, cassia and subtle juniper to finish.

SERVING SUGGESTION: Enjoy with Fever-Tree Elderflower Tonic Water.

Esperance Distillery Co
Esperance, WA

Standing on Wudjari Nyungar Boodjar land in the paradise-like town of Esperance, with its pristine white sands and turquoise waters, Esperance Distillery Co is run by a father and son duo and launched as one of the smallest distilleries in Australia, with just a 30L pot still at the time. They work with botanists, traditional owners, and locals to create spirits that showcase the diversity of the Esperance biosphere while focusing on sustainability.

Cut & Run Gin 42.0%

BOTANICALS: Juniper, Vanilla Acacia, Coriander Seed, Lemon Myrtle & Others

TASTING NOTES: Pine with slight wood sap and dry angelica on the nose, lemon oil with juniper, angelica, and woody earth notes on the palate, citrus and earthy notes linger to finish.

SERVING SUGGESTION: Enjoy with Fever-Tree Mediterranean Tonic Water.

Middle Island Pink Gin 40.0%

BOTANICALS: Juniper, Esperance Wax, Rosella, Bush Lemon & Blood Orange

TASTING NOTES: Delicate florals, soft rosella and a touch of rose jam on the nose, gentle rhubarb and gardenia with bright bird's eye chilli kick on the palate, chilli and florals develop and linger to finish.

SERVING SUGGESTION: Enjoy with Fever-Tree Elderflower Tonic Water.

Ester Spirits

ESTER SPIRITS **Sydney, NSW**

Located in the fun and friendly inner-city Marrickville suburb of Sydney, Ester Spirits was founded by a husband-and-wife team with a long history in hospitality and a passion for creating flavour and fun. They combine their different approaches by exploring the conflicting ideas and flavours with an 'all in' method of distillation and using Australian botanicals wherever possible.

Dry Gin 43.0%

BOTANICALS: Juniper, Coriander Seed, Liquorice, Cardamom, Orris Root, Angelica Root, Cassia, Macadamia, Clove, Native Pepperberry, Mandarin Peel, Finger Lime & Lemon Myrtle

TASTING NOTES: Juniper, cardamom and coriander lead the nose, coriander, cardamom and lemon myrtle on the palate, continuing coriander and citrus level off to finish.

SERVING SUGGESTION: Enjoy with Fever-Tree Premium Indian Tonic Water.

Strong Gin 57.0%

BOTANICALS: Juniper, Finger Lime, Coriander Seed, Cardamom, Orris Root, Liquorice, Angelica Root, Cassia, Macadamia, Clove, Native Pepperberry & Lemon Myrtle

TASTING NOTES: Musty juniper with black cardamom and oily citrus on the nose, finger lime and cardamom menthol with coriander and orange on the palate, cardamom and orange oil carry and linger to finish.

SERVING SUGGESTION: Enjoy with Fever-Tree Aromatic Tonic Water.

Eventide Hills Distillery
Kalunga, QLD

Founded near Kalunga in the diverse and idyllic Atherton Tablelands of Queensland, Eventide Hills Distillery was founded by two locals to creates spirits that pay homage to, and showcase, their local region. They combine quality ingredients, sourced from local farmers and businesses where possible, with the pure water and clean air of their mountainous environment to produce flavour profiles distinctive to the region.

Reflection Gin 40.0%

BOTANICALS: Juniper, Strawberry Gum, Lemon Myrtle & Native Pepperberry

TASTING NOTES: Strawberry gum leads with a hint of menthol character on the nose, steamed herbs with strawberry gum, juniper, and supporting heat on the palate, heat builds and lingers with a touch of lemon myrtle to finish.

SERVING SUGGESTION: Enjoy with Fever-Tree Mediterranean Tonic Water.

The Farmer's Wife Distillery
Allworth, NSW

Conceived on a farm in the small village of Allworth, The Farmer's Wife Distillery all started with a farmer's wife and her love of gin, and were inspired to share their love of country life and passion for creating something unique as 3rd generation farmers. They make small batch one-shot distilled gin in homage to the traditions of gin making and native flavours of Australia using neutral Australian sugarcane base spirit and purified rainwater harvested from their farm.

Autumn Dry Gin 48.0%

BOTANICALS: Juniper, Ruby Red Grapefruit Peel, Native Sage, Sugarbag Honey, Native Pepperberry, Aniseed Myrtle, Lemon Myrtle, Coriander Seed, Angelica Root, Orris Root, Liquorice, Cardamom & Makrut Lime

TASTING NOTES: Eucalyptus with fresh green herbs and native sage drive the nose, strong citrus with earthy angelica, pepperleaf, and myrtle on the palate, lingering myrtle character and bitter honey to finish.

SERVING SUGGESTION: Enjoy with Fever-Tree Mediterranean Tonic Water.

Finders Distillery
Sydney, NSW

Seated in the business-oriented St Leonards suburb of Sydney's north shore, Finders Distillery was born from a multi-year trip around the world where visiting distilleries and trying local produce became a common occurrence. They aim to create stories about Australian produce through their spirits, including a location series made using botanicals sourced from specific Australian regions to highlight both local ingredients and the towns they come from.

Australian Dry Gin 41.5%

BOTANICALS: Juniper, Coriander Seed, Angelica Root, Orris Root, Cassia, Orange Peel, Chamomile Flower, Wattleseed & Others

TASTING NOTES: Strong cardamom with lemon myrtle and hints of fruit on the nose, cardamom leads with crushed pepper, coriander, and lemon oil on the palate, strawberry and eucalyptus to finish.

SERVING SUGGESTION: Enjoy with Fever-Tree Mediterranean Tonic Water.

Native Red Lime Gin 43.0%

BOTANICALS: Juniper, Coriander Seed, Angelica Root, Orris Root, Cassia, Chamomile Flower, Blood Lime, Red Finger Lime, Tahitian Lime & Makrut Lime Leaf

TASTING NOTES: Lime flesh with hints of peppery oil and angelica on the nose, peppermint and river mint with finger lime oil on the palate, lime lingers with a touch of angelica to finish.

SERVING SUGGESTION: Enjoy with Fever-Tree Mediterranean Tonic Water.

Flowstate Brewers and Distillers
Torquay, VIC

Surrounded by the vibrant surfing culture and beauty of the seaside town of Torquay, Flowstate Brewers and Distillers was started by two brothers and is a result of their eclectic backgrounds in the building, brewing, and horticulture industries. They are influenced by their surroundings and community, combining their practical creativity and botanical sensibility in their production processes and drink styles.

Craft Gin 40.0%

BOTANICALS: Juniper, Coriander Seed, Angelica Root, Orris Root, Cinnamon, Coastal Daisy-Bush, Native Pepperberry, Hops, Grapefruit & Lemon

TASTING NOTES: Dried citrus peel with Mediterranean herbs on the nose, fruity hops and sweet lime leaf with salty notes on the palate, peppery heat and hops lingering to finish.

SERVING SUGGESTION: Enjoy with Fever-Tree Mediterranean Tonic Water.

Fonzie Abbott
Brisbane, QLD

Positioned in the inner-city suburb of Albion just northeast of Brisbane's CBD, Fonzie Abbott was founded on making good coffee and is now home to a roaster, brewery, and distillery all under one roof. They are passionate about curating quality products through hard work while constantly evolving and innovating, and use all Australian ingredients with organic botanicals in their spirits.

Wishbone Gin 40.0%

BOTANICALS: Juniper, Orange, Grapefruit, Makrut Lime Juice, Coriander Seed, Cardamom & Cassia

TASTING NOTES: Lime leaf with anise and sweet citrus on the nose, fresh lime peel with dry coriander seed spice on the palate, spice notes with sharp citrus developing and lingering to finish.

SERVING SUGGESTION: Enjoy with Fever-Tree Mediterranean Tonic Water.

Fossey's Distillery
Mildura, VIC

Housed in the historic The Setts pub in the vibrant regional city of Mildura along the Murray River near the outback, Fossey's Distillery is family-owned and operated, and embraces family history, local produce, and storytelling through distilling. They embrace the culture of Australian distilled spirits using Australian botanicals and locally-sourced products to showcase the best that Mildura and Australia have to offer.

Original Gin 40.0%

BOTANICALS: Juniper, Coriander Seed, Aniseed Myrtle, Native Pepperleaf, Lemon Myrtle Leaf, Lavender, Cardamom, Angelica Root, Cassia, Lemon, Tangelo, Valencia Orange & Bergamot

TASTING NOTES: Cardamom, coriander, and pepperberry lead the nose, cardamom and lemon myrtle with an array of bright herbaceous characters on the palate, lemon myrtle leads the finish.

SERVING SUGGESTION: Enjoy with Fever-Tree Mediterranean Tonic Water.

Desert Lime Gin 40.0%

BOTANICALS: Juniper, Desert Lime, Coriander Seed, Aniseed Myrtle, Native Pepperleaf, Lemon Myrtle Leaf, Lavender, Cardamom, Angelica Root, Cassia, Lemon, Tangelo, Valencia Orange & Bergamot

TASTING NOTES: Dried lime peel with tea characters and supporting florals on the nose, lime and lavender lead with an oily array of herbs on the palate, lemon myrtle develops with a touch of florals to finish.

SERVING SUGGESTION: Enjoy with Fever-Tree Mediterranean Tonic Water.

Navel Strength Gin 57.0%

BOTANICALS: Juniper, Coriander Seed, Aniseed Myrtle, Native Pepperleaf, Lemon Myrtle Leaf, Lavender, Cardamom, Angelica Root, Cassia, Ginger, Lemon & Navel Orange

TASTING NOTES: Lavender, honey, and pepperberry on the nose, citrus leads with pepperberry and cardamom on the palate, sweet citrus oil and pepperberry linger to finish.

SERVING SUGGESTION: Enjoy with Fever-Tree Mediterranean Tonic Water.

Shiraz Gin 40.0%

BOTANICALS: Juniper, Shiraz Grapes, Coriander Seed, Aniseed Myrtle, Native Pepperleaf, Lemon Myrtle Leaf, Lavender, Cardamom, Angelica Root, Cassia, Lemon, Tangelo, Valencia Orange & Bergamot

TASTING NOTES: Dry earl grey tea with eucalyptus and spice heat on the nose, baking spice with juicy grapes, bright lavender florals and pepperberry heat on the palate, dry juniper with a hint of honey to finish.

SERVING SUGGESTION: Enjoy with Fever-Tree Lemon Tonic Water.

Four Pillars
Healesville, VIC

Standing in the regional wine and food hub of Healesville in the stunning Yarra Valley near Melbourne, Four Pillars is named loosely on the idea that the three founders' favourite cocktails are usually a blend of four ingredients. All of their stills are named for important women in their lives. They believe that Australia is the most delicious, diverse, and creative place to make gin, using whole fresh citrus in every gin as their signature.

Rare Dry Gin 41.8%

BOTANICALS: Juniper, Orange, Coriander Seed, Lemon Myrtle, Green Cardamom, Cassia, Star Anise, Lavender, Angelica Root & Native Pepperleaf

TASTING NOTES: Juniper, green cardamom, lemon, and musky lavender on the nose, upfront juniper, pronounced star anise and cardamom accented by angelica on the palate, long warming spice finish.

SERVING SUGGESTION: Enjoy with Fever-Tree Aromatic Tonic Water.

Bloody Shiraz Gin 37.8%

BOTANICALS: Juniper, Shiraz Grapes, Orange, Coriander Seed, Lemon Myrtle, Green Cardamom, Cassia, Star Anise, Lavender, Angelica Root & Native Pepperleaf

TASTING NOTES: Dry coriander and angelica with plum marmalade and warm orange oil on the nose, fresh ripe red cherry and ripe plum skin with notes of hibiscus and light supporting spice on the palate, sweet but light fruity finish.

SERVING SUGGESTION: Enjoy with Fever-Tree Lemon Tonic Water.

Fresh Yuzu Gin 41.8%

BOTANICALS: Juniper, Yuzu, Ginger, Sencha Genmaicha, Turmeric, Coriander Seed, Angelica Root, Lavender, Lemon Myrtle, Finger Lime & Dried Apple

TASTING NOTES: Vibrant citrus with garden herbs and light florals on the nose, pine with juicy yuzu flesh and creamy warming spice on the palate, dry citrus peel alongside pepper heat to finish.

SERVING SUGGESTION: Enjoy with Fever-Tree Refreshingly Light Indian Tonic Water.

Modern Australian Gin 41.8%

BOTANICALS: Juniper, Quandong, Macadamia, Red Sichuan Peppercorn, Rosie Glow Apple, Coriander Seed, Green Cardamom, Cassia, Star Anise, Lavender, Angelica Root, Native Pepperleaf, Orange, Green Sichuan & Grapefruit Peel

TASTING NOTES: Floral geranium, hints of fresh fruit and orange blossom on the nose, anise and orange blossom with peppery heat on the palate, fruity stewed apple character with pepper and lemon myrtle to finish.

SERVING SUGGESTION: Enjoy with Fever-Tree Premium Indian Tonic Water.

Navy Strength Gin 58.8%

BOTANICALS: Juniper, Coriander Seed, Green Cardamom, Cassia, Star Anise, Lavender, Angelica Root, Native Pepperleaf, Lemon Myrtle, Orange, Finger Lime, Turmeric & Ginger

TASTING NOTES: Cracked pepper with lavender and warming spice on the nose, cardamom, liquorice, lime, and juniper lead the palate, slightly sweet liquorice with strong pepper heat to finish.

SERVING SUGGESTION: Enjoy with Fever-Tree Aromatic Tonic Water.

Olive Leaf Gin 43.8%

BOTANICALS: Juniper, Olive Leaf Tea, Lemon, Bay Leaf, Olive Oil, Macadamia, Rosemary, Grapefruit Peel, Coriander Seed, Lavender & Orris Root

TASTING NOTES: Savoury rosemary and thyme with lemon peel on the nose, harmony of green herbs, juniper, citrus peel, and dried tea on the palate, dry juniper and rosemary with touches of warming pepper and liquorice to finish.

SERVING SUGGESTION: Enjoy with Fever-Tree Mediterranean Tonic Water.

Spiced Negroni Gin 43.8%

BOTANICALS: Juniper, Coriander Seed, Green Cardamom, Cassia, Star Anise, Lavender, Angelica Root, Native Pepperleaf, Lemon Myrtle, Orange, Ginger, Grains of Paradise & Cubeb Pepper

TASTING NOTES: Star anise, cardamom with oily orange and a hint of florals on the nose, upfront juniper with strong cardamom and star anise on the palate, long lingering liquorice, star anise and orange sweetness to finish.

SERVING SUGGESTION: Enjoy with Fever-Tree Blood Orange Soda.

Gindu
Newham, VIC

Settled in the small town of Newham in the idyllic Macedon Ranges, Gindu is a distillery that was born out of a desire to create something that could be shared, engage the senses, and evoke the joy that discovery brings. They focus on discovery and nurturing a sense of pride in the land by blending the botanicals that grow in different destinations in Australia.

An Australian Dry 42.0%

BOTANICALS: Juniper, Blood Lime, Aniseed Myrtle, Old Man Saltbush, Wattleseed & Native Pepperberry

TASTING NOTES: Saltbush, wattleseed, and earthy juniper with hints of blood lime on the nose, juniper and aniseed followed by pepperberry and hints of dried herbs on the palate, wattleseed and aniseed linger to finish.

SERVING SUGGESTION: Enjoy with Fever-Tree Aromatic Tonic Water.

A Coastal Gin 48.0%

BOTANICALS: Juniper, Sunrise Lime, Rainforest Lychee, Muntrie, Native Pepperleaf, Coastal Rosemary, Coast Saltbush & Sallow Wattleseed

TASTING NOTES: Balanced native botanicals with sweet fruits and classic dry spice on the nose, coriander with saltbush, subtle wattleseed and pepperleaf on the palate, leading to a fresh and dry green herb finish.

SERVING SUGGESTION: Enjoy with Fever-Tree Mediterranean Tonic Water.

Rainforest Cherry Gin 42.5%

BOTANICALS: Juniper, Native Pepperleaf, Lemon Myrtle, Wild Basil, Boab Tuber, Native Pepperberry, Native Currant, Geraldton Wax, Desert Lime & Rainforest Cherry

TASTING NOTES: Basil, geraldton wax and lime lead the nose, dry pepperleaf, steeped basil and eucalyptus tones on the palate, basil tones linger with dry cherry to finish.

SERVING SUGGESTION: Enjoy with Fever-Tree Mediterranean Tonic Water

An Australian Gin 42.0%

BOTANICALS: Juniper, Native Pepperleaf, Lemon Myrtle, Wild Basil, Boab Tuber, Native Pepperberry, Native Currant, Geraldton Wax & Desert Lime

TASTING NOTES: Bright fruit aromatics with lime leaf and fresh herbs on the nose, anise and geraldton wax drying to woody juniper notes on the palate, lingering lemon and juniper to finish.

SERVING SUGGESTION: Enjoy with Fever-Tree Mediterranean Tonic Water.

GinFinity
Melbourne, VIC

Inaugurated in bustling Belgrave on the outskirts of Melbourne with the lush Sherbrooke Forest at its back, GinFinity is an open source gin project focused on innovation and experimentation that values the creation of unique experiences. This is typified in their BubbleGum Gin range that is inspired by Jamaican rum, with a high ester content.

BubbleGum Gin 45.0%

BOTANICALS: Juniper, Pineapple & Mandarin

TASTING NOTES: Candied pineapple with citrus peel and fruity banana on the nose, citrus freshness with funky tropical fruit notes drive the palate, slight mandarin sweetness with lengthy banana and bubblegum to finish.

SERVING SUGGESTION: Enjoy with Fever-Tree Premium Indian Tonic Water.

Mango Bubblegum Gin 45.0%

BOTANICALS: Juniper, Mango & Apricot

TASTING NOTES: Bold bubblegum, coconut cream and mango on the nose, sweet and juicy tropical fruits with apricot flesh on the palate, sweet tropical fruits linger to finish.

SERVING SUGGESTION: Enjoy with Fever-Tree Premium Indian Tonic Water.

Open Source #03 45.0%

BOTANICALS: Juniper, Orange Zest, Ginger, Coriander Seed, Nutmeg & Chamomile

TASTING NOTES: Warming nutmeg with orange oil, ginger and coriander seed on the nose, dried orange zest with fresh ginger and coriander drive the palate, oily orange and ginger spice linger to finish.

SERVING SUGGESTION: Enjoy with Fever-Tree Aromatic Tonic Water.

Ginny Pig Distillery
McLaren Vale, SA

Settled in McLaren Vale at the epicentre of South Australia's wine industry on the Fleurieu Peninsula, Ginny Pig Distillery is run by a husband and wife team that started out with the goal of recreating the flavour of hot cross buns in gin form. They use traditional distilling techniques, native botanicals, and home-grown ingredients in their gins which are inspired by the seasons and happy memories of family and friends.

Classic Dry Gin 42.0%

BOTANICALS: Juniper, Coriander Seed, Angelica Root, Orris Root, Elderflower, Mandarin & Grapefruit

TASTING NOTES: Juniper, orris and hints of the forest floor on the nose, classic juniper and coriander lead with mandarin peel and rosemary on the palate, lengthy slightly earthy warming finish.

SERVING SUGGESTION: Enjoy with Fever-Tree Mediterranean Tonic Water.

Blueberry Gin 42.0%

BOTANICALS: Juniper, Coriander Seed, Blueberry & Vanilla

TASTING NOTES: Light berry fruits with a touch of sweetness on the nose, sweet cherry and raspberry with hints of pine needle and coriander on the palate, sweet berry to finish.

SERVING SUGGESTION: Enjoy with Fever-Tree Wild Raspberry Tonic Water.

Botanic Gin 44.0%

BOTANICALS: Juniper, Lemon Myrtle, Rosemary, Native Pepperberry, Elderflower & Others

TASTING NOTES: Fresh elderflower, dried rosemary and a touch of lemon myrtle on the nose, gentle elderflower and developing spice with a juniper backbone on the palate, lemon myrtle and angelica to finish.

SERVING SUGGESTION: Enjoy with Fever-Tree Elderflower Tonic Water.

Spiced Fig Gin 42.0%

BOTANICALS: Juniper, Coriander Seed, Fig, Cinnamon, Ginger & Clove

TASTING NOTES: Pronounced cinnamon with clove and hints of dried fig on the nose, sweet poached fig with baking spice and supporting clove on the palate, fig lingers to finish.

SERVING SUGGESTION: Enjoy with Fever-Tree Premium Indian Tonic Water.

Pink Gin 42.0%

BOTANICALS: Juniper, Coriander Seed, Angelica Root, Orris Root, Elderflower, Mandarin, Grapefruit & Raspberry

TASTING NOTES: Juniper, earthy roots and light pithy citrus on the nose, anise and orris lead with hints of elderflower on the palate, orris and angelica musk linger to finish.

SERVING SUGGESTION: Enjoy with Fever-Tree Elderflower Tonic Water.

Ginworth

Hobart, TAS

Conceived in Tasmania, Ginworth was started by a mother and son duo with an ethos centred on the important moments that ignite the human spirit. They develop their gin in collaboration with White Label Distillery in Hobart, drawing inspiration from their Italian and English heritage with the aim of creating premium gins to be shared in the company of family and friends.

Future Vintage 40.0%

BOTANICALS: Juniper, Coriander Seed, Angelica Root, Lemon, Orange, Lime & Orris Root

TASTING NOTES: Lime zest, juniper and orris root lead the nose, woody orris and angelica with fresh coriander and anise on the palate, warming woody spice continues to finish.

SERVING SUGGESTION: Enjoy with Fever-Tree Aromatic Tonic Water.

Gold Emotion Australia

Melbourne, VIC

Tucked away in the urban sprawl of dynamic Melbourne, Gold Emotion Australia is an opulent and exclusive concept product range made with 24K gold. They use edible 24K gold in their gins to make their bottles gleam and catch the eye, along with a combination of premium botanicals to create what they believe are timeless fresh infusions.

Pure Gold Gin 44.0%

BOTANICALS: Juniper, Coriander Seed, Orris Root, Lemon Myrtle, Cassia, Blood Orange, Native Pepperberry, Lavender, Finger Lime, Ginger, Quandong & Lime Peel

TASTING NOTES: Layered citrus of lemon myrtle, lime peel, finger lime, and subtle ginger on the nose, pronounced lemon myrtle with quandong and ginger root on the palate, zesty fresh finish.

SERVING SUGGESTION: Enjoy with Fever-Tree Mediterranean Tonic Water.

Rose Gold Gin 40.0%

BOTANICALS: Juniper, Blood Orange Pulp, Coriander Seed, Angelica Root, Burdock Root, Ruby Red Grapefruit, Macadamia, Lemon Aspen, Pink Rose, Orris Root, Lemon Myrtle, Cassia, Nutmeg & Spearmint

TASTING NOTES: Sweet roasted nuts with woody orris and an array of florals on the nose, angelica with notes of gardenia and camellia leaf on the palate, classic botanicals subtly developing to finish.

SERVING SUGGESTION: Enjoy with Fever-Tree Elderflower Tonic Water.

Goodradigbee Distillers
Sydney, NSW

Located in the relaxed Balgowlah suburb of northern Sydney with its stunning scenery and tree-lined streets, Goodradigbee Distillers is named after the river in the Snowy Mountains that its founder learnt to fly-fish on and was born from the idea of creating a spirit that is unique on the shelf. They use accelerated maturation technology and Australian hardwood cubes, rather than oak barrels, to age their spirits made with native Australian botanicals.

Freshwater Gin 43.0%

BOTANICALS: Juniper, Coriander Seed, Quandong, Kakadu Plum, Angelica Root, Native Pepperberry, Native Currant, Lemon Myrtle, Cinnamon Myrtle, Aniseed Myrtle, Finger Lime & Orange

TASTING NOTES: Native citrus, warming spice, quandong and aniseed myrtle on the nose, fruity spice with supporting citrus, liquorice root and aniseed on the palate, lingering zest to finish.

SERVING SUGGESTION: Enjoy with Fever-Tree Elderflower Tonic Water.

Freshwater Blush Gin 43.0%

BOTANICALS: Juniper, Coriander Seed, Kakadu Plum, Angelica Root, Desert Lime, Finger Lime, Muntrie, Native Raspberry, Native Pepperberry, Davidson Plum, Lemon Myrtle & Strawberry Gum

TASTING NOTES: Dried lime and lemon myrtle with hints of lavender on the nose, sweet berries with dried coriander seed and pepperberry on the palate, settling citrus with lingering pepperberry to finish.

SERVING SUGGESTION: Enjoy with Fever-Tree Mediterranean Tonic Water.

Sweetwater Gin 43.0%

BOTANICALS: Juniper, Apple, Angelica Root, Orange, Finger Lime, Lemon Myrtle, Cinnamon Myrtle, Aniseed Myrtle & Native Pepperleaf

TASTING NOTES: Pepper, cinnamon myrtle and citrus oil on the nose, dried orange with supporting cinnamon and pepperleaf on the palate, undertones of orange to finish.

SERVING SUGGESTION: Enjoy with Fever-Tree Premium Indian Tonic Water.

Grower's Own Distillery
Glaziers Bay, TAS

Set amongst the beauty and charm of the Huon Valley in Tasmania near Glaziers Bay, Growers Own Distillery is based on a farm that pioneered the saffron industry in Australia. They use saffron handpicked and processed from their own farm and pure filtered rainwater with a still designed to eliminate the need for filtration and carry through the full flavour of the saffron.

Saffron Gin 42.0%

BOTANICALS: Juniper, Saffron, Angelica Root, Cardamom, Cassia, Coriander Seed, Lemon & Orange Peel

TASTING NOTES: Light herbal notes with crushed almond on the nose, dried thyme with a touch of pine on the palate, lingering dried garden herbs and an earthy musk to finish.

SERVING SUGGESTION: Enjoy with Fever-Tree Mediterranean Tonic Water.

Hang 10 Distillery
Sydney, NSW

Located in the Warriewood suburb of Sydney's Northern Beaches, Hang 10 Distillery is a sustainable micro-distillery with a focus on creating a circular economy and a passion for making a difference. They use surplus bread from local bakeries to ferment their own base spirit as part of their mission to protect the environment and oceans by reducing food waste and the methane it would otherwise create.

The Classic Gin 43.0%

BOTANICALS: Juniper, Cinnamon, Grapefruit, Lemon-Scented Gum, Cassia, Almond & Cardamom

TASTING NOTES: Grapefruit and cassia lead the nose, sharp tart citrus with hints of cardamom and cassia on the palate, cardamom and cassia spice lead the finish.

SERVING SUGGESTION: Enjoy with Fever-Tree Premium Indian Tonic Water.

Baker's Dozen Gin 43.0%

BOTANICALS: Juniper, Coriander Seed, Sourdough Bread, Angelica Root, Allspice, Clove, Apple, Raspberry, Rose Hip, Almond, Lavender, Cardamom & Fennel Seed

TASTING NOTES: Herbaceous pepper with clove and spiced apple on the nose, clove and spiced apple continue with fresh herbs and spices on the palate, clove and pepper linger to finish.

SERVING SUGGESTION: Enjoy with Fever-Tree Mediterranean Tonic Water.

Happenstance Distillery
Adelaide, SA

Based near the bustling heart of Adelaide in the hip, up-and-coming area of Thebarton, Happenstance Distillery was born from a serendipitous conversation between two friends about alcohol production, from whence they take their name. They use alembic copper pot stills to craft their products with the aim of creating a gin that keeps you coming back at the heart of every bottle.

Happenstance Gin 42.0%

BOTANICALS: Juniper, Coriander Seed, Angelica Root, Lemon Peel, Mandarin Peel, Lemon Myrtle, Fennel Seed, Nutmeg, Strawberry Gum & Vanilla

TASTING NOTES: Citrus peel and nutmeg lead the nose, tart layered citrus peel develops on the palate, balanced yet bright citrus lingers to a drying finish.

SERVING SUGGESTION: Enjoy with Fever-Tree Mediterranean Tonic Water.

Fiesta Gin 42.0%

BOTANICALS: Juniper, Coriander Seed, Angelica Root, Makrut Lime, Star Anise, Chilli, Lime Peel & Chamomile

TASTING NOTES: Lime leaf and angelica lead the nose, slightly sweet star anise with punchy chilli and lime drives the palate, angelica musk leads the finish with tea-like florals developing.

SERVING SUGGESTION: Enjoy with Fever-Tree Mediterranean Tonic Water.

Fireside Gin 45.0%

BOTANICALS: Juniper, Coriander Seed, Angelica Root, Cardamom, Cinnamon, Ginger, Clove, Hazelnut & Orange Peel

TASTING NOTES: Cinnamon and orange lead the nose, ginger heat and clove on the palate with cardamom and coriander developing late, clove lingers across the finish with hints of angelica.

SERVING SUGGESTION: Enjoy with Fever-Tree Premium Indian Tonic Water.

Hartshorn Distillery
Birchs Bay, TAS

Ensconced amongst the charm and beauty of the Huon Valley in Tasmania near Birchs Bay, Hartshorn Distillery is family-owned with the goal of reducing waste from their sheep cheesery by turning it into quality products. They use leftover whey from the cheese-making process to make their base spirit and process it in a way that carries its character through into their finished spirits.

Sheep Whey Gin 40.0%

BOTANICALS: Juniper, Lemon Myrtle, Aniseed Myrtle, Wattleseed, Native Pepperberry & Others

TASTING NOTES: Sweet lemon with supporting floral notes and green pine on the nose, rose, cut grass and pepperberry on the palate, elegant florals to finish with subtle pepperberry.

SERVING SUGGESTION: Enjoy with Fever-Tree Mediterranean Tonic Water.

Headlands Distilling Company
Wollongong, NSW

Seated just to the north of vibrant Wollongong's city centre, Headlands Distilling Company was started by four friends with a can-do attitude and a grain to glass philosophy at its core. They do everything from scratch, from milling barley from local farms on-site to bottling and labelling, and focus on highlighting native Australian botanicals in their spirits.

Boobialla Australian Native Gin 40.0%

BOTANICALS: Boobialla, Lemon Aspen, Geraldton Wax, Atherton Almond, Cinnamon Myrtle, White Kunzea, Quandong, Muntrie & Native Tamarind

TASTING NOTES: Woody honey notes with creamy almond and tamarind on the nose, rich cinnamon and nutmeg with lemon oil and dry pepper on the palate, oily lemon and spice linger to finish.

SERVING SUGGESTION: Enjoy with Fever-Tree Aromatic Tonic Water.

Mt. & Sea Classic Australian Gin 43.0%

BOTANICALS: Juniper, Rainforest Lime, Coastal Wattleseed & Cinnamon

TASTING NOTES: Honey and coconut lead with hints of sweet cinnamon on the nose, spice leads with lime pith followed by dark chocolate and roasted coffee notes on the palate, warming spice with a slight burst of zest to finish.

SERVING SUGGESTION: Enjoy with Fever-Tree Aromatic Tonic Water.

Tidal Lines Illawara Plum Infused Gin 32.0%

BOTANICALS: Juniper, Rainforest Lime, Coastal Wattleseed, Cinnamon & Illawara Plum

TASTING NOTES: Baked cinnamon and lime with sweet-floral stone fruit on the nose, spiced almond and gingerbread with stone fruit developing on the palate, slightly sweet plum lingers to finish.

SERVING SUGGESTION: Enjoy with Fever-Tree Premium Indian Tonic Water.

Heathcote Gin
Heathcote, VIC

Situated in the tranquil town of Heathcote in the heart of regional Victoria, Heathcote Gin was founded in the area to take advantage of its rich Cambrian soils and the botanical growing possibilities. They make their range of gins using the landscape of Heathcote as the palate while maintaining a passion for ethical and sustainable agriculture.

Founders Gin 40%

BOTANICALS: Juniper, Lemon Myrtle, Orange Peel, Cassia, Coriander Seed, Angelica Root & Orris Root

TASTING NOTES: Classic juniper, coriander and angelica on the nose, continuing juniper grounded by angelica and coriander seed on the palate, a savoury warmth and a lightly sweet citrus finish.

SERVING SUGGESTION: Enjoy with Fever-Tree Premium Indian Tonic Water.

Chocolate Gin 40%

BOTANICALS: : Juniper, Orange, Lemon Myrtle, Almond, Hazelnut, Vanilla, Cassia, Coriander Seed, Angelica & Orris Root

TASTING NOTES: Rich milk chocolate carries the nose, continuing milk chocolate on the palate, sweet creamy white chocolate to finish.

SERVING SUGGESTION: Enjoy with Fever-Tree Ginger Ale.

Distillers' Navy Cut Gin 58%

BOTANICALS: Juniper, Lemon Myrtle, Orange Peel, Cassia, Coriander Seed, Orris Root & Angelica Root

TASTING NOTES: Sharp juniper notes lead the nose, fresh pine with supporting citrus and light spots of sharpness on the palate, mellowing juniper to finish.

SERVING SUGGESTION: Enjoy with Fever-Tree Mediterranean Tonic Water.

Fusion Gin 43%

BOTANICALS: Juniper, Lemongrass, Lime, Makrut Lime, Red Galangal, Grapefruit, Lemon Myrtle, Orange Peel, Star Anise, Coriander Seed, Cassia, Angelica Root & Orris Root

TASTING NOTES: Fragrant bouquette of native botaniacls leads the nose, wild lime and native leafy notes lead the palate, very dry with a dusty earthy tone to finish.

SERVING SUGGESTION: Enjoy with Fever-Tree Mediterranean Tonic Water.

Shiraz Reserve Gin 37%

BOTANICALS: : Juniper, Lemon Myrtle, Orange Peel, Coriander Seed, Cassia, Angelica Root, Orris Root & 2018 Barrel Aged Heathcote Shiraz Wine

TASTING NOTES: Coconut and raspberry jam lead the nose, rich and sweet red fruit on the palate, sweet cherry ripe with a powdery tannin to finish.

SERVING SUGGESTION: Enjoy with Fever-Tree Refreshingly Light Indian Tonic Water

Smokin' Chilli Gin 40%

BOTANICALS: Juniper, Lemon Myrtle, Orange Peel, Smoked Chilli, Cassia, Orris Root, Coriander Seed & Angelica Root

TASTING NOTES: Bold paprika and chipotle spice on the nose, smoky warmth with a light heat on the palate, lingering warm spice leads the finish.

SERVING SUGGESTION: Enjoy with Fever-Tree Aromatic Tonic Water.

Hellfire Bluff Distillery
Boomer Bay, TAS

Sheltered just outside of the peaceful Boomers Bay in south-eastern Tasmania, Hellfire Bluff Distillery is family-owned, taking its name from the rocky outcrop that their potato farm overlooks, with a passion for innovation in the pursuit of producing quality products. They use local rainwater and botanicals, including those that are quintessentially Tasmanian, in their spirits.

London Dry Gin 45.0%

BOTANICALS: Juniper, Coriander Seed, Cardamom, Cinnamon, Citrus Peel, Orris Root & Others

TASTING NOTES: Coriander and cinnamon lead the nose, coriander and cinnamon continue with cardamom developing on the palate, lingering spice drives the finish.

SERVING SUGGESTION: Enjoy with Fever-Tree Aromatic Tonic Water.

Summer Floral Gin 40.0%

BOTANICALS: Juniper, Brown Boronia Flower, Leatherwood Honey, Native Pepperberry, Sarsaparilla & Others

TASTING NOTES: Firm earthy notes of orris, sarsaparilla, liquorice and angelica on the nose, growing pepperberry with thick honey and hints of anise on the palate, pepperberry and anise carry and linger to finish.

SERVING SUGGESTION: Enjoy with Fever-Tree Premium Indian Tonic Water.

Piquant Herbal Gin 45.0%

BOTANICALS: Juniper, Native Pepperleaf, Olive Leaf, Lemon Myrtle, Lemongrass & Others

TASTING NOTES: Lemon myrtle with raspberry leaf and fruity juniper on the nose, leafy botanicals with strong pepper, lemongrass and olive leaf on the palate, lingering pepperberry and lemon to finish.

SERVING SUGGESTION: Enjoy with Fever-Tree Mediterranean Tonic Water.

Hepburn Distillery
Daylesford, VIC

Based in the spa and wellbeing town of Daylesford to the northwest of Melbourne, Hepburn Distillery began with the idea of being local and drawing from the mineral-rich soil, and abundant rainfall of Hepburn Shire. They source as many raw materials as they can locally, organically, and seasonally, including growing some of their own botanicals, as part of their commitment to sustainability along with stills that run on renewable energy, recycled packaging and composting all organic waste.

Lyonville Classic Dry Gin 40.0%

BOTANICALS: Juniper, Coriander Seed, Orris Root, Angelica Root & Others

TASTING NOTES: Resinous pine, rosemary, river mint and hints of fruit on the nose, sweet raisin with pine resin and supporting earthy florals on the palate, hints of lingering fruits to finish.

SERVING SUGGESTION: Enjoy with Fever-Tree Mediterranean Tonic Water.

Trentham Harvest Gin 40.0%

BOTANICALS: Juniper, Aniseed, Liquorice, Fennel Seed, Blackberry & Others

TASTING NOTES: Blackcurrant, orange oil and liquorice on the nose, sweet liquorice with thick orange oil and a touch of spice on the palate, slightly sweet baking spice lingers to finish.

SERVING SUGGESTION: Enjoy with Fever-Tree Mediterranean Tonic Water.

HG Hemp Gin
Sydney, NSW

Surrounded by the Parramatta River in the Sydney suburb of Rhodes, HG Hemp Gin was born from a university assignment, a career of innovation and development in the food industry, and a passion for high quality gin. They had their 'eureka' moment when hemp won legal approval for use in food and drink in 2017, becoming the first to use it in an Australian gin.

HG Hemp Gin 40.0%

BOTANICALS: Juniper, Hemp, Cardamom, Coriander Seed, Lemon, Liquorice & Vanilla

TASTING NOTES: Sweet hemp with hints of thyme and liquorice on the nose, cardamom, coriander and hemp with supporting lemon and liquorice on the palate, continuing liquorice and hemp to finish.

SERVING SUGGESTION: Enjoy with Fever-Tree Mediterranean Tonic Water.

HHH Distill
Perth, WA

Swaddled by the charm and bushland of the Bickley Valley to the west of Perth, HHH Distill is both a distillery and still manufacturer run by a father-daughter duo with a passion for creating beautiful experiences and a mission to prioritise people. They make gins designed to reflect the creative and down to earth nature of their creators.

Wax Lyrical 45.0%

BOTANICALS: Juniper, Coriander Seed, Angelica Root, Cassia, Liquorice, Calamus Root, Almond, Lemon Peel & Geraldton Wax Leaf

TASTING NOTES: Lemon and orange citrus with gingerbread spice on the nose, waxy citrus with strong almond and bitter root spice on the palate, lingering spice and nuttiness to finish.

SERVING SUGGESTION: Enjoy with Fever-Tree Mediterranean Tonic Water.

KLC 45.0%

BOTANICALS: Juniper, Coriander Seed, Angelica Root, Cassia, Liquorice, Almond, Makrut Lime Leaf & Kumquat

TASTING NOTES: Dusty cassia with supporting liquorice and citrus undertones on the nose, cassia continues throughout with lime leaf and kumquat oil on the palate, rounding out with slightly sweet baking spice to finish.

SERVING SUGGESTION: Enjoy with Fever-Tree Mediterranean Tonic Water.

Miss Myrtle 40.0%

BOTANICALS: Juniper, Coriander Seed, Cassia, Angelica Root, Liquorice, Orris Root, Lemon, Almond Meal & Honey Myrtle

TASTING NOTES: Aromatic lavender with jasmine and honeysuckle on the nose, sweet eucalypt with supporting almond creaminess and enrichening honey on the palate, creamy nuttiness lingers to finish.

SERVING SUGGESTION: Enjoy with Fever-Tree Refreshingly Light Indian Tonic Water.

Wax Lyrical Blue 40.0%

BOTANICALS: Juniper, Coriander Seed, Angelica Root, Cassia, Liquorice, Calamus Root, Almond, Lemon Peel, Butterfly Pea Flower & Geraldton Wax Leaf

TASTING NOTES: Geraldton wax and lemon rind with hints of cassia and angelica on the nose, soft cinnamon and anise with geraldton wax, almond and angelica on the palate, lingering spice to finish.

SERVING SUGGESTION: Enjoy with Fever-Tree Premium Indian Tonic Water.

Hickson House Distilling Co
Sydney, NSW

Housed in a heritage warehouse, almost directly under the Sydney Harbour Bridge, in The Rocks, Hickson House Distilling Co maintains a deep respect for their history, the environment, and future, by distilling what the land has to offer. They use ingredients sourced from all over New South Wales and Australia, some of which are grown exclusively for them.

Hickson Rd. London Dry Gin 40.0%

BOTANICALS: Juniper, Coriander Seed, Angelica Root, Orris Root & Old Man Saltbush

TASTING NOTES: Clean coriander, juniper, and orris root lead the nose, balanced juniper, coriander, and orris work in harmony on the palate, bold juniper lingers to finish.

SERVING SUGGESTION: Enjoy with Fever-Tree Premium Indian Tonic Water.

Hickson Rd. Australian Dry Gin 42.0%

BOTANICALS: Juniper, Coriander Seed, Angelica Root, Orris Root, Liquorice, Orange Peel, Oolong Tea, Native Thyme, Finger Lime & Aniseed Myrtle

TASTING NOTES: Juniper, sherbet-like lemon and savoury herbs on the nose, juniper and coriander continue with thyme and lemon on the palate, aniseed develops with bright citrus to finish.

SERVING SUGGESTION: Enjoy with Fever-Tree Mediterranean Tonic Water.

Hickson Rd. Harbour Strength Gin 57.0%

BOTANICALS: Juniper, Coriander Seed, Angelica Root, Orris Root & Old Man Saltbush

TASTING NOTES: Bold saltbush with supporting coriander on the nose, upfront citrus oil, soft orris with strong menthol, and saltbush on the palate, lengthy lingering heat to finish.

SERVING SUGGESTION: Enjoy with Fever-Tree Mediterranean Tonic Water.

HillsCrest Distillery
Mount Helena, WA

Sitting at the top of the Darling Scarp in the delightful town of Mount Helena just east of Perth, HillsCrest Distillery is family-run by two brothers who founded it together after more than a decade of discussion and dreaming became reality. They use traditional techniques with pure filtered rainwater and locally sourced ingredients when possible.

Australian Dry Gin 45.0%

BOTANICALS: Juniper, Coriander Seed, Rangpur Lime, Lemon, Mandarin, Cardamom, Cinnamon, Pink Peppercorn & Macadamia

TASTING NOTES: Subtle cinnamon with layered citrus peel and macadamia on the nose, bursting citrus oil with peppercorn and resinous juniper on the palate, light pepper and citrus oil to finish.

SERVING SUGGESTION: Enjoy with Fever-Tree Mediterranean Tonic Water.

Hurdle Creek Still
Milawa, VIC

Sheltered in a farm shed on a family property among the bustling hills of the King Valley in northeast Victoria, Hurdle Creek Still was born from an aversion to getting up and driving to work in the morning, and is named for the creek running through the property. They use a base spirit made from locally sourced grain and try to grow or locally source as many botanicals as they can for their spirits.

Yardarm Distilled Gin 42.0%

BOTANICALS: Juniper, Coriander Seed, Angelica Root, Clove, Cardamom, Orange Peel, Lime Leaf, Cassia, Ginger, Pink Peppercorn, Hops, Ginger & Lemon Myrtle Leaf

TASTING NOTES: Warming spice, ginger root and hints of lemon myrtle on the nose, initial peppercorn and juniper with developing orange and ginger on the palate, orange oil, cassia, and coriander to finish.

SERVING SUGGESTION: Enjoy with Fever-Tree Mediterranean Tonic Water.

Grain Jenever 38.0%

BOTANICALS: Juniper, Cinnamon Myrtle Leaf, Lemon Myrtle Leaf, Aniseed Myrtle Leaf, Pink Peppercorn & Eucalyptus Leaf

TASTING NOTES: Aromatic base notes with touches of honey and supporting spice on the nose, slightly sweet baking spice with grassy undertones and eucalyptus on the palate, grassy hay-like finish.

SERVING SUGGESTION: Enjoy with Fever-Tree Premium Indian Tonic Water.

Powder Monkey Navy Strength Gin 58.0%

BOTANICALS: Juniper, Cinnamon Myrtle Leaf, Lemon Myrtle Leaf, Aniseed Myrtle Leaf, Pink Peppercorn & Eucalyptus Leaf

TASTING NOTES: Anise, sweet rosemary and lemon myrtle on the nose, eucalypt resin with leafy greens, sweet juniper and pepper on the palate, peppery heat continues to finish.

SERVING SUGGESTION: Enjoy with Fever-Tree Mediterranean Tonic Water.

The Aniseed Gin 42.0%

BOTANICALS: Juniper, Coriander Seed, Angelica Root, Clove, Aniseed, Cardamom, Orange Peel, Lime Leaf, Cassia, Pink Peppercorn, Ginger, Cinnamon Myrtle Leaf, Lemon Myrtle Leaf, Aniseed, Star Anise, Fennel Seed, Liquorice & Aniseed Myrtle

TASTING NOTES: Orange, fennel seed and clove sweetness on the nose, ginger and juniper with striking liquorice on the palate, finishing with lingering orange blossom and star anise.

SERVING SUGGESTION: Enjoy with Fever-Tree Mediterranean Tonic Water.

Husk Distillers
North Tumbulgum, NSW

Tucked away in the calming ambience of North Tumbulgum along the Tweed River in New South Wales, Husk Distillers was started by a family with a dream of creating a plantation distillery on their cattle and cane farm. They began with a vision of making a farm to bottle agricole rum with an Australian expression and later expanded to making gin as well while recycling all of their organic distillery waste as cattle feed on their farm.

Ink Dry Gin 43.0%

BOTANICALS: Juniper, Butterfly Pea Flower, Elderflower, Cinnamon, Cardamom, Angelica Root, Orris Root, Liquorice, Lemon Peel, Lemon Myrtle Leaf, Coriander Seed, Native Pepperberry & Sundried Orange Peel

TASTING NOTES: Liquorice, cinnamon, and lemon peel lead the nose, lemon myrtle and liquorice lead with pepperberry spice growing on the palate, lemon lingers with a slight floral sweetness developing to finish.

SERVING SUGGESTION: Enjoy with Fever-Tree Mediterranean Tonic Water.

Ink Sloe & Berry Gin Liqueur 26.0%

BOTANICALS: Juniper, Coriander Seed, Angelica Root, Liquorice, Rosella Flower, Sloe Berry & Seasonal Berries

TASTING NOTES: Hibiscus with rosella and dried cranberry on the nose, sweet cranberry juice, fruity red currant, and rose undertones on palate, lively fruit acidity to finish.

SERVING SUGGESTION: Enjoy with Fever-Tree Lemon Tonic Water.

imbue distillery
Melbourne, VIC

Inaugurated in the leafy Melbourne suburb of Research on the edge of the city sprawl, Imbue distillery loves the power that taste has to unlock memories, and try to make spirits rich in flavour and imbued with their story. They use a combination of locally abundant botanicals as well as obscure and exotic ones to push boundaries and create both new and nostalgic experiences.

Sub-urban Gin 40.0%

BOTANICALS: Juniper, Coriander Seed, Cardamom, Cinnamon, Orris Root, Angelica Root, Dandelion, Lemon, Fennel Seed, Prickly Pear, Blackberry & Sunflower Seed

TASTING NOTES: Light juniper with supporting angelica and distinct dandelion root on the nose, grassy green cardamom with pine, fennel and caraway seed on the palate, lingering cardamom and coriander to finish.

SERVING SUGGESTION: Enjoy with Fever-Tree Refreshingly Light Indian Tonic Water.

Sub-urban Gin Barrel Aged Gin 40.0%

BOTANICALS: Juniper, Coriander Seed, Cardamom, Cinnamon, Orris Root, Angelica Root, Dandelion, Lemon, Fennel Seed, Prickly Pear, Blackberry & Sunflower Seed (aged in Oak ex-Spanish Sherry and Australian Apera Barrels)

TASTING NOTES: Cardamom, angelica, fennel and lemon oil drive the nose, fennel and cinnamon spice with dry citrus on the palate, undertones of spice with bright citrus lingers to finish.

SERVING SUGGESTION: Enjoy with Fever-Tree Mediterranean Tonic Water.

The Journey Gin 40.0%

BOTANICALS: Juniper, Coriander Seed, Angelica Root, Lemon, Sunflower Seed, Apple & Muntrie

TASTING NOTES: Bright lemon zest with floral apple and earthy coriander on the nose, dry fruity apple with sunflower seed and coriander on the palate, drying finish with developing coriander.

SERVING SUGGESTION: Enjoy with Fever-Tree Refreshingly Light Indian Tonic Water.

Imperial Measures Distilling
Adelaide, SA

Established near the bustling heart of Adelaide in the hip, up-and-coming area of Thebarton, Imperial Measures Distilling develop all of their products with their use in a bar at the forefront and never cutting corners as one of their goals. They use methods designed to balance in classic formats whilst bringing unique character to their drinks.

Ounce Gin Signature 42.0%

BOTANICALS: Juniper, Orange, Vanilla, Cardamom, Coriander Seed, Angelica Root & Others

TASTING NOTES: Orange, juniper, and coriander lead the nose, initial orange and juniper with coriander and cardamom supporting on the palate, lingering coriander and orange peel to finish.

SERVING SUGGESTION: Enjoy with Fever-Tree Mediterranean Tonic Water.

Ounce Gin Bold 47.0%

BOTANICALS: Juniper, Sage, Thyme, Black Cardamom, Peppercorn & Others

TASTING NOTES: Sage, thyme and pepper lead the nose, cardamom leads with a burst of juniper, thyme and pepper on the palate, minty-citrus notes from thyme linger with a heated pepper finish.

SERVING SUGGESTION: Enjoy with Fever-Tree Mediterranean Tonic Water.

Ounce Gin Bright 44.5%

BOTANICALS: Juniper, Lime, Mint, Dill, Rose Petal, Pink Peppercorn, Cardamom Seed, Nutmeg, Ginger, Liquorice, Coriander Seed & Angelica Root

TASTING NOTES: Dill and crushed mint lead with hints of pepper on the nose, initial juniper with dill, minty freshness and lifted pepper heat on the palate, fresh crushed mint with a touch of pepper linger to finish.

SERVING SUGGESTION: Enjoy with Fever-Tree Mediterranean Tonic Water.

Impression Spirits

Eden Valley, SA

Secluded in the small town of Eden Valley amongst the vineyards of the Barossa Valley, Impression Spirits was born from a desire to create non-traditional gin that could be enjoyed with soda as opposed to tonic water. They draw on one of their co-founder's background in health and fitness, and use ingredients rich with antioxidants.

Dry Gin 40.0%

BOTANICALS: Juniper, Mangosteen, Riberry, Lemon Myrtle, Calendula, Kakadu Plum, Finger Lime, Aloe Vera & Coriander Seed

TASTING NOTES: Lime zest and coriander with hints of fruity notes on the nose, dry florals and fruity characters with a touch of hay on the palate, lingering coriander to finish.

SERVING SUGGESTION: Enjoy with Fever-Tree Mediterranean Tonic Water.

Ironhouse Distillery

Four Mile Creek, TAS

Standing right on the beach on Tasmania's gorgeous east coast just south of Four Mile Creek, IronHouse Distillery is a family-owned brewery, vineyard, and distillery that takes inspiration from the enigmas and wonders of life. They use a combination of local ingredients, pristine water, and the clean ocean air of the east coast to balance and mature their spirits.

Strange Omen Small Batch Gin 45.0%

BOTANICALS: Juniper, Native Pepperberry, Liquorice, Cassia, Whole Orange, Lemon Myrtle, Coriander Seed, Rose Petal, Caraway Seed & Angelica Root

TASTING NOTES: Coriander and caraway lead with citrus undertones on the nose, woody cinnamon with citrus, caraway and fruity tones on the palate, cinnamon spice to finish.

SERVING SUGGESTION: Enjoy with Fever-Tree Premium Indian Tonic Water.

Strange Omen Navy Strength Gin 59.0%

BOTANICALS: Juniper, Native Pepperberry, Liquorice, Cassia, Whole Orange, Lemon Myrtle, Coriander Seed, Rose Petal, Caraway Seed & Angelica Root

TASTING NOTES: Striking pine resin with orange blossom and soft slightly sweet florals on the nose, orris and angelica lead with pepperberry and liquorice on the palate, juniper and invigorating heat to finish.

SERVING SUGGESTION: Enjoy with Fever-Tree Premium Indian Tonic Water.

Strange Omen Hopped Gin 48.0%

BOTANICALS: Juniper, Native Pepperberry, Liquorice, Cassia, Whole Orange, Lemon Myrtle, Coriander Seed, Rose Petal, Caraway Seed & Angelica Root (steeped in Hops and Hop Oils)

TASTING NOTES: Caraway seed with oily orange on the nose, fruity rose with caraway and liquorice on the palate, liquorice carries and lingers to finish.

SERVING SUGGESTION: Enjoy with Fever-Tree Premium Indian Tonic Water.

Joadja Distillery
Joadja, NSW

Withdrawn in the abandoned kerosene mining village of Joadja in the Southern Highlands of New South Wales, Joadja Distillery was started after the family that purchased the historically significant property discovered that the shed was licensed to be a distillery. They grow their own barley, use on-site natural spring water, and solar power in the pursuit of creating sustainable, quality spirits that reflect the character, nature, and heritage of the Joadja Valley.

Dry Gin 43.0%

BOTANICALS: Juniper, Aniseed, Angelica Root, Cardamom, Coriander Seed & Lemon Myrtle

TASTING NOTES: Hints of aniseed and cardamom with orange undertones on the nose, aniseed and cardamom continue with coriander on the palate, strong spice driven finish.

SERVING SUGGESTION: Enjoy with Fever-Tree Aromatic Tonic Water.

Highland Gin 43.0%

BOTANICALS: Juniper, Aniseed, Angelica Root, Cardamom, Coriander Seed, Lemon Myrtle, Strawberry Gum, Native Pepperberry, Cinnamon Myrtle & Aniseed Myrtle

TASTING NOTES: Pronounced spice with lemon myrtle and pine needle on the nose, dry juniper with citrus and peppery heat lead the palate, sweet spice to finish.

SERVING SUGGESTION: Enjoy with Fever-Tree Aromatic Tonic Water.

Kalki Moon
Bundaberg, QLD

Situated in the Svensson Heights suburb of the bountiful Bundaberg Region, Kalki Moon is family-owned and run, taking its name from the nearby Kalkie suburb where its founders built their home and were inspired by the view of expansive cane fields lit by the full moon. They aspire to embody the beauty of the region in their products, using locally sourced ingredients and Australian made equipment.

Classic Gin 37.0%

BOTANICALS: Juniper, Coriander Seed, Cardamom, Lemon Myrtle & Angelica Root

TASTING NOTES: Classic juniper and coriander lead the nose, zesty lemon with persistent juniper and coriander on the palate, juniper continues throughout with a touch of cardamom and lemon myrtle to finish.

SERVING SUGGESTION: Enjoy with Fever-Tree Premium Indian Tonic Water.

Australian Premium Gin 42.0%

BOTANICALS: Juniper, Coriander Seed, Cardamom, Lemon Myrtle, Angelica Root, Liquorice, Orange Peel, Finger Lime, Ginger & Cinnamon Myrtle

TASTING NOTES: Bright citrus, coriander, cardamom, and fresh ginger on the nose, earthy liquorice and cinnamon with bright spots of citrus on the palate, cardamom and zesty lemon linger to finish.

SERVING SUGGESTION: Enjoy with Fever-Tree Premium Indian Tonic Water.

Kylie's Summer Gin 45.0%

BOTANICALS: Juniper, Coriander Seed, Angelica Root, Orris Root, Orange Peel, Apple Peel, Liquorice, Ginger, Lemon Peel & Cinnamon

TASTING NOTES: Pronounced juniper, coriander and orris on the nose, heated ginger with warming cinnamon and angelica on the palate, oily lemon, lingering ginger and earthy undertones to finish.

SERVING SUGGESTION: Enjoy with Fever-Tree Premium Indian Tonic Water.

Navy Strength Gin 57.0%

BOTANICALS: Juniper, Coriander Seed, Angelica Root, Orris Root, Liquorice, Ginger & Lemon Peel

TASTING NOTES: Pronounced juniper with ginger, liquorice, and lemon on the nose, initial coriander seed with supporting liquorice on the palate, angelica root, ginger spice, and lemon linger to finish.

SERVING SUGGESTION: Enjoy with Fever-Tree Aromatic Tonic Water.

Pink Gin Liqueur 20.0%

BOTANICALS: Juniper, Coriander Seed, Cardamom, Lemon Myrtle & Angelica Root (blended with Elderflower & Rose Water)

TASTING NOTES: Rose water, sweet elderflower, and a touch of warmth on the nose, sweet rose with pronounced lemon myrtle on the palate, rose and lemon lingering to finish.

SERVING SUGGESTION: Enjoy with Fever-Tree Elderflower Tonic Water.

Kangaroo Island Spirits
Cygnet River, SA

Set amongst the bountiful farms of Kangaroo Island just down the coast from Adelaide, Kangaroo Island Spirits was Australia's first dedicated gin distillery, where they value creativity, resourcefulness, and the pioneering spirit. They make traditionally crafted spirits using botanicals from the island to set the stage for and capture the character that the land offers.

O Gin 43.5%

BOTANICALS: Juniper, Coastal Daisy-Bush & Others

TASTING NOTES: Crushed mint with fruit tea notes on the nose, pine resin and woody rosemary with notes of coastal herbs on the palate, peppery heat and woody herbs linger to finish.

SERVING SUGGESTION: Enjoy with Fever-Tree Mediterranean Tonic Water.

Mulberry Gin 28.0%

BOTANICALS: Juniper, Coastal Daisy-Bush & Others (steeped in Mulberry)

TASTING NOTES: Tart mulberry with slightly acidic jam notes on the nose, hibiscus and rosemary with distinct mulberry on the palate, slightly acidic tannins with herbal undertones to finish.

SERVING SUGGESTION: Enjoy with Fever-Tree Lemon Tonic Water.

Wild Gin 43.0%

BOTANICALS: Boobialla, Eau Du Cologne Mint, Lime Zest & Pink Peppercorn

TASTING NOTES: Crushed mint with crisp citrus and a slight woody edge on the nose, vibrant green pine needle with bright citrus and peppery heat on the palate, green herbs and subtle balanced pepper to finish.

SERVING SUGGESTION: Enjoy with Fever-Tree Mediterranean Tonic Water.

Karu Distillery
Grose Vale, NSW

Huddled at the base of the Blue Mountains National park in Grose Vale on the very edge of Sydney, Karu Distillery was established by a husband-and-wife team, their name comes from the Estonian word for bear, reflecting their distillers' family heritage and symbolises the qualities that drive them. They believe that quality, sustainability, and passion are essential ingredients, predominantly using home-grown and local ingredients in their spirits.

Affinity Gin 44.0%

BOTANICALS: Juniper, Orange Peel, Coriander Seed, Cardamom, Lemon Myrtle, Vanilla & Almond

TASTING NOTES: Striking coriander and warming spice on the nose, juniper leads with coriander and warming cardamom developing on the palate, lingering spice with hints of tart citrus to finish.

SERVING SUGGESTION: Enjoy with Fever-Tree Aromatic Tonic Water.

Lightning Gin 57.5%

BOTANICALS: Juniper, Rose Geranium, Lemon Myrtle, Ruby Red Grapefruit & Mandarin

TASTING NOTES: Floral lemon myrtle with sweet mandarin peel and juniper on the nose, initial sharp citrus with supporting geranium florals and juniper undertones on the palate, soft anise and juniper to finish.

SERVING SUGGESTION: Enjoy with Fever-Tree Mediterranean Tonic Water.

Kilderkin Distillery
Ballarat, VIC

Established in Mount Pleasant, the oldest residential suburb of the historic goldmining city of Ballarat, Kilderkin Distillery is family-owned and run, taking its name from an old English barrel measure. They strive to produce quality spirits that can be enjoyed neat as well as with selected mixers and in cocktails, using stills that are designed for lightness of spirit.

Larrikin Scoundrel London Dry 42.0%

BOTANICALS: Juniper, Coriander Seed, Lemon Peel, Green Cardamom, Brown Cardamom, Grains of Paradise, Aniseed, Cinnamon, Angelica Root, Orris Root, Orange & Lemon

TASTING NOTES: Layered citrus with anise and cinnamon undertones on the nose, lemon, cinnamon and cardamom on the palate, oily citrus peel with lingering baking spice to finish.

SERVING SUGGESTION: Enjoy with Fever-Tree Premium Indian Tonic Water.

Larrikin Buccaneer Navy Strength 57.0%

BOTANICALS: Juniper, Coriander Seed, Lemon Peel, Green Cardamom, Brown Cardamom, Grains of Paradise, Aniseed, Cinnamon, Angelica Root, Orris Root, Orange, Lemon & Lime

TASTING NOTES: Juniper balanced by cardamom and anise on the nose, dried lemon peel with coriander seed and subtle cinnamon on the palate, lingering pepper heat to finish.

SERVING SUGGESTION: Enjoy with Fever-Tree Mediterranean Tonic Water.

Larrikin Original Australian 42.0%

BOTANICALS: Juniper, Coriander Seed, Lemon Myrtle, Cinnamon Myrtle, Aniseed Myrtle, Native Pepperleaf, Wattleseed, River Mint & Lilly Pilly Berry

TASTING NOTES: Light cinnamon spice and subtle wattle seed on the nose, upfront cinnamon and aniseed with peppery heat and coriander undertones on the palate, coriander, aniseed and juniper to finish.

SERVING SUGGESTION: Enjoy with Fever-Tree Aromatic Tonic Water.

Larrikin Sunburnt Country Bush Tucker Gin 50.7%

BOTANICALS: Juniper, Coriander Seed, Wattleseed, Lemon Myrtle, Lemon Aspen, Kakadu Plum, Blood Lime, Desert Lime, Bush Tomato, Strawberry Gum, Davidson Plum & Finger Lime

TASTING NOTES: Mixed spices and dried fruit lead the nose, initial burst of fruitiness with pronounced supporting spice character and earthy orris on the palate, lingering earthiness and mixed spice to finish.

SERVING SUGGESTION: Enjoy with Fever-Tree Refreshingly Light Indian Tonic Water.

Kings Cross Distillery
Sydney, NSW

Settled in the centre of the late-night heart of Sydney at the intersection of Darlinghurst Road and Macleay Street, Kings Cross Distillery takes its name and inspiration from the area and its richly risqué history, housed in what was at different times an illegal casino, club, and private bookshop. They create small-batch vapour infused gins and other spirits using their pot still known affectionately as Miss Pottsy.

Australian Classic Dry Gin 42.0%

BOTANICALS: Juniper, Australian Myrtles, Lemon Peel, Cassia, Angelica Root & Others

TASTING NOTES: Cassia leads with dried tea leaf notes on the nose, steeped tea with woody forest element and sweet cassia on the palate, damp earthy driven finish.

SERVING SUGGESTION: Enjoy with Fever-Tree Aromatic Tonic Water.

Navy Strength Garden Island Gin 58.5%

BOTANICALS: Juniper, Gunpowder Tea, Australian Myrtles & Others

TASTING NOTES: Pronounced lemon myrtle with soft honey and brewed tea on the nose, hot tea notes with lemon myrtle and peppery heat on the palate, herbaceous undertones with a touch of lemon to finish.

SERVING SUGGESTION: Enjoy with Fever-Tree Mediterranean Tonic Water.

KNOCKLOFTY   Knocklofty Spirits
Hobart, TAS

Overlooking the Derwent River from the foothills of the beautiful Knocklofty Reserve in West Hobart, Knocklofty Spirits is a home-based micro-distillery run by three couples that bring together passion and knowledge from their diverse backgrounds. They use equipment made from recycled and second-hand materials to make their own grain-free base spirit and distil each botanical separately before blending to create their spirits.

All Juniper Gin 40.0%

BOTANICALS: Juniper

TASTING NOTES: Bold juniper forward with hints of green undertones on the nose, clean and warming juniper continues on the palate, mellowing hints of juniper to finish.

SERVING SUGGESTION: Enjoy with Fever-Tree Premium Indian Tonic Water.

Penn Gin 40.0%

BOTANICALS: Juniper, Orange, Basil, Thai Basil, Coriander Seed, Pepperberry, Wattleseed, Angelica Root, Lemongrass & Cardamom

TASTING NOTES: Juniper with citrus and herbaceous undertones on the nose, subtle juniper with pepperberry and cardamom lead the palate, lingering lemongrass and Thai basil heat mellow to finish.

SERVING SUGGESTION: Enjoy with Fever-Tree Mediterranean Tonic Water.

Quince Garden Gin 32.5%

BOTANICALS: Juniper (steeped in Quince)

TASTING NOTES: Rich steeped fruit character leads the nose, steeped fruit character continues with a touch of juniper on the palate, mellowing quince to finish.

SERVING SUGGESTION: Enjoy with Fever-Tree Premium Indian Tonic Water.

Ladbroken Distilling Co.
Tumbarumba, NSW

Bundled away in the charming town of Tumbarumba in New South Wales' spectacular Snowy Valley, Ladbroken Distilling Co. is a family business with a mission to make great tasting Australian single malt whisky, distinctive Australian botanical spirits, and liqueurs. They work to capture the beauty and richness of the High Country region in their spirits using locally and seasonally grown produce.

Eliksir Signature Dry Gin 40.0%

BOTANICALS: Juniper, Coriander Seed, Native Pepperberry, Liquorice, Almond, Cassia, Lavender, Lemon Myrtle & Hibiscus

TASTING NOTES: Fruitcake spice with supporting citrus on the nose, Christmas spice with pepperberry heat and supporting citrus on the palate, lingering sweet liquorice to finish.

SERVING SUGGESTION: Enjoy with Fever-Tree Aromatic Tonic Water.

Eliksir Blood Orange Gin 40.0%

BOTANICALS: Juniper, Blood Orange, Feijoa, Cardamom, Native Pepperberry & Cinnamon

TASTING NOTES: Striking cinnamon with orange peel undertones on the nose, upfront cinnamon with supporting cardamom and rounded orange peel on the palate, cardamom and cinnamon spice to finish.

SERVING SUGGESTION: Enjoy with Fever-Tree Premium Indian Tonic Water.

Lark Distillery
Hobart, TAS

Stationed in Tasmania's dynamic capital city of Hobart, Lark Distillery is a compilation of creativity, Tasmania's pure environment, and over 30 years of experience, started after the question of why no one was making malt whisky in Tasmania stuck with its founders. They create a range of spirits designed to give different ways to make your own drink in their certified carbon-neutral facility.

Forty Spotted Classic Tassie Gin 40.0%

BOTANICALS: Juniper, Native Pepperberry, Makrut Lime Leaf & Lemon Peel

TASTING NOTES: Sharp lemon with supporting spice and juniper undertones on the nose, distinct lemon with pronounced juniper and soft pepperberry spice on the palate, resin and lemon lingering to finish.

SERVING SUGGESTION: Enjoy with Fever-Tree Mediterranean Tonic Water.

Forty Spotted Citrus & Pepperberry 40.0%

BOTANICALS: Juniper, Native Pepperberry, Orange & Oyster Bay Pine

TASTING NOTES: Oily orange with undertones of fresh cut pine on the nose, zesty orange with a marmalade jamminess and pine resin in support on the palate, soft orange with lingering pine to finish.

SERVING SUGGESTION: Enjoy with Fever-Tree Mediterranean Tonic Water.

Forty Spotted Pinot Noir Gin 40.0%

BOTANICALS: Juniper, Pinot Noir Grapes, Coriander Seed, Angelica Root, Rose & Plum

TASTING NOTES: Passionfruit and natural wine-like character on the nose, fermented grapes with peppery spice and supporting rose on the palate, touches of passionfruit with pinot character and warming spice to finish.

SERVING SUGGESTION: Enjoy with Fever-Tree Lemon Tonic Water.

Forty Spotted Raspberry & Rose 20.0%

BOTANICALS: Juniper, Raspberry, Rose, Bergamot, Lime & Grapefruit

TASTING NOTES: Peaches and cream sweetness with background florals on the nose, rose water and sweet fruity florals on the palate, rounding creamy peach and rose to finish.

SERVING SUGGESTION: Enjoy with Fever-Tree Elderflower Tonic Water.

Forty Spotted Tassie Bush Honey 40.0%

BOTANICALS: Juniper, Star Anise, Rooibos, Honey & Others

TASTING NOTES: Honey with dry tea leaves and a hint of anise spice on the nose, steeped tea with dried fruit and hints of honey on the palate, drying herbaceous finish.

SERVING SUGGESTION: Enjoy with Fever-Tree Premium Indian Tonic Water.

Forty Spotted Wild Rose Gin 40.0%

BOTANICALS: Juniper, Rooibos, Black Lime, Frankincense & Rose

TASTING NOTES: Elegant rose water with rooibos tea-like tones on the nose, light dry rose with dark herbal characters on the palate, subtle lingering spice to finish.

SERVING SUGGESTION: Enjoy with Fever-Tree Elderflower Tonic Water.

Lawrenny Estate Distillery
Ouse, TAS

Seated on a 400 acre property in the picturesque Derwent Valley of Tasmania's Central Highlands, Lawrenny Estate Distillery was established as a paddock to bottle single malt whisky estate and now makes a range of spirits. They use water from Lake St Clair, the deepest freshwater lake in Australia, and botanicals found across their estate in their products.

Van Diemen's Gin 42.5%

BOTANICALS: Juniper, Coriander Seed, Fresh Citrus, Dried Citrus, Strawberry, Fennel Seed, Almond & Lime Flower

TASTING NOTES: Juniper with fennel seed and lime blossom on the nose, sweet candied citrus with subtle strawberry and hints of fennel on the palate, fennel lingers to finish.

SERVING SUGGESTION: Enjoy with Fever-Tree Mediterranean Tonic Water.

1818 Settlers Gin 52.5%

BOTANICALS: Juniper, Coriander Seed, Apple, Black Cardamom, Fresh Citrus, Dried Citrus, Rosemary & Elderberry

TASTING NOTES: Rosemary and baking spice with sea breeze undertones on nose, herbal tones with baking spice reinforced by a backbone of juniper and lemon on the palate, lingering spice with tart lemon and pine resin to finish.

SERVING SUGGESTION: Enjoy with Fever-Tree Mediterranean Tonic Water.

Highlands Gin 40.0%

BOTANICALS: Juniper, Coriander Seed, Blue Cypress, Mint, Grapefruit & Grains of Paradise

TASTING NOTES: Crushed mint and coriander seed with pine cones on the nose, upfront pine resin with savoury pepper and balanced grapefruit on the palate, cooling mint and grapefruit pith linger to finish.

SERVING SUGGESTION: Enjoy with Fever-Tree Mediterranean Tonic Water.

Meadowbank Pink Gin 38.5%

BOTANICALS: Juniper, Coriander Seed, Blood Orange, Coriander, Raspberry, Strawberry & Hibiscus

TASTING NOTES: Dried strawberry with blood orange and tea leaf undertones on the nose, dry hibiscus, blood orange with subtle angelica and coriander on the palate, dry fruity yet warming finish.

SERVING SUGGESTION: Enjoy with Fever-Tree Elderflower Tonic Water.

Legacy Spirit Distilling Co.
Melbourne, VIC

Hidden away in the urban sprawl of dynamic Melbourne, Legacy Spirit Distilling Co. was started by two good friends bonded over a shared loss and desire to create the taste of legacy to celebrate their mums that now extends to their families in general. They bring together their loves of science and creativity in their quest to make great gin with ingredients that reflect a story.

Marie Classic Dry Gin 43.0%

BOTANICALS: Juniper, Orange, Ginger, Coriander Seed, Cinnamon, Turmeric & Others

TASTING NOTES: Savoury garden herbs of thyme and oregano with juniper undertones on the nose, pine resin and mild lemon myrtle with hints of honey on the palate, heated spice to finish.

SERVING SUGGESTION: Enjoy with Fever-Tree Mediterranean Tonic Water.

Pride Classic Dry Gin 43.0%

BOTANICALS: Juniper, Rose, Lavender, Orange, Cinnamon, Grapefruit & Others

TASTING NOTES: Juniper leads with a hint of rose and lemon on the nose, initial juniper with garden herbs, sweet orange and peppery heat on the palate, spiced heat drives the finish.

SERVING SUGGESTION: Enjoy with Fever-Tree Mediterranean Tonic Water.

Libation Liquor
Sydney, NSW

Produced under contract in the spectacular Mount Glorious northwest of Brisbane, Libation Liquor was established on the foundation of service, passion, and the belief that exceptional experiences stem from the culmination of quality beverages, food, and atmosphere. They use triple distilled sugarcane and pure filtered water from Mount Glorious in their small batch spirits.

Honcho Gin 40.0%

BOTANICALS: Juniper, Sugarcane, Lemon, Coriander Seed & Angelica Root

TASTING NOTES: Coriander seed and sweet lemon lead the nose, bright lemon with supporting juniper and angelica earthiness on the palate, building pine resin and citrus to finish.

SERVING SUGGESTION: Enjoy with Fever-Tree Premium Indian Tonic Water.

Little Juniper Distilling Co.
Ashton, SA

Surrounded by fruit orchards in the small town of Ashton in the picturesque Adelaide Hills, Little Juniper Distilling Co. believe in quality and sustainability with a drive for invention that is anchored in tradition, with the 'Little' in their name referencing their focus on having the smallest footprint possible. They incorporate certified organic ingredients grown locally and from around the world with sustainable distilling and packaging practices.

Signature Gin 42.0%

BOTANICALS: Juniper, Coriander Seed, Orris Root, Liquorice, Star Anise, Cinnamon, Cardamom, Nutmeg, Pink Peppercorn, Ginger, Rosemary, Lavender, Bay Leaf, Thyme, Ruby Red Grapefruit, Makrut Lime, Fennel & Others

TASTING NOTES: Subtle juniper with hints of cardamom, lime leaf and layered citrus on the nose, juniper and coriander lead with earthy florals and lime leaf on the palate, mellowing anise with a touch of pepper to finish.

SERVING SUGGESTION: Enjoy with Fever-Tree Mediterranean Tonic Water.

Little Lon Distilling Co.
Melbourne, VIC

Housed in the last single story cottage in Melbourne's vibrant city centre, that once served as a grog shop and brothel, Little Lon Distilling Co. is named for the history of the area in which it stands, a former red-light district. They commemorate those that once trod the area's laneways with their range of gins using their own base spirit made from Australian malted barley and Melbourne water.

Constable Proudfoot 42.0%

BOTANICALS: Juniper, Coriander Seed, Angelica Root, Rosemary, Cardamom, Star Anise, Fennel Seed, Lemon, Lime & Lemon Myrtle

TASTING NOTES: Musky candy and tropical fruits with lemon myrtle on the nose, rosemary, cardamom and anise spice with hints of citrus on the palate, earthy musk with hints of mint to finish.

SERVING SUGGESTION: Enjoy with Fever-Tree Mediterranean Tonic Water.

Dutchy Thomas 42.0%

BOTANICALS: Juniper, Coriander Seed, Angelica Root, Ruby Red Grapefruit, Orange, Lemon, Lime, Cinnamon, Native Pepperberry & Ginger

TASTING NOTES: Rich and malty base notes on the nose, bold tones of caramel, liquorice and continued rich malt on the palate, lasting malty tones with a hint of butteriness to finish.

SERVING SUGGESTION: Enjoy with Fever-Tree Ginger Ale.

Ginger Mick 42.0%

BOTANICALS: Juniper, Coriander Seed, Angelica Root, Ruby Red Grapefruit, Orange, Lemon, Lime, Cinnamon, Native Pepperberry, Ginger, Blood Orange & Tangelo

TASTING NOTES: Baking spice and candied ginger with undertones of citrus on the nose, sweet spice and ginger heat lead with hints of pepper and tart citrus on the palate, drying spice to finish.

SERVING SUGGESTION: Enjoy with Fever-Tree Ginger Ale.

Little Miss Yoko 42.0%

BOTANICALS: Juniper, Coriander Seed, Angelica Root, Lychee, Vanilla, Cinnamon, Lemon, Lime & Lemongrass

TASTING NOTES: Hints of banana with candied lychee and vanilla undertones on the nose, lemongrass and coriander with supporting ginger and sweet fruitiness on the palate, drying coriander seed to finish.

SERVING SUGGESTION: Enjoy with Fever-Tree Mediterranean Tonic Water.

Loaded Barrel Distillery
Melbourne, VIC

Located in the rapidly growing and largely residential Rowville suburb of southeast Melbourne, Loaded Barrel Distillery is family-owned and run with the goal of creating a family legacy and spirits that you dream of drinking as you watch the clock tick down to 5pm on a weekday. They pride themselves on creating spirits that reinvent tradition using Australian and tropical botanicals.

Missfire Gin 42.0%

BOTANICALS: Juniper, Coriander Seed, Mango, Pineapple, Rose Petal, Lemon Myrtle & Orris Root

TASTING NOTES: Notes of green mango, papaya and lemongrass on the nose, fresh lime zest with juicy pineapple and hints of coriander seed on the palate, oily lemon and lasting coriander to finish.

SERVING SUGGESTION: Enjoy with Fever-Tree Refreshingly Light Indian Tonic Water.

LOBO Spirits
Lenswood, SA

Rooted in the fruit orchards that surround Lenswood on the eastern side of the picturesque Adelaide Hills, LOBO Spirits is run by a team of two, one that grows things and one that makes things, that started out making cider and then expanded into spirits. They use fruits from their orchard in all of their products.

Djinn Gin 41.6%

BOTANICALS: Juniper, Quince Peel, Coriander Seed, Cinnamon, Star Anise, Angelica Root, Orris Root & Others

TASTING NOTES: Spiced fruit of quince and pear on the nose, orris root and angelica drive with dry fruity undertones on the palate, drying earthy finish.

SERVING SUGGESTION: Enjoy with Fever-Tree Refreshingly Light Indian Tonic Water.

Quince Liqueur Gin 30.0%

BOTANICALS: Juniper, Quince Peel, Coriander Seed, Cinnamon, Star Anise, Angelica Root, Orris Root & Others

TASTING NOTES: Spiced quince with supporting clove on the nose, pronounced spice of anise, clove and cinnamon on the palate, drying yet tart notes to finish.

SERVING SUGGESTION: Enjoy with Fever-Tree Aromatic Tonic Water.

Loch Brewery & Distillery

Loch, VIC

Based in the quaint historic town of Loch among the rolling hills of Gippsland, Loch Brewery & Distillery was established by a creative duo as a grass-roots operation in a 100-year-old red brick bank and adjoining derelict butchery. They combine traditional methods with modern ingenuity to make their spirits in hand-beaten alembic copper pot stills.

Loch Gin 41.0%

BOTANICALS: Juniper, Cinnamon, Cardamom, Angelica Root, Liquorice, Mace, Cassia, Coriander Seed, Nutmeg, Orris Root, Orange & Ginger

TASTING NOTES: Liquorice and coriander with nutmeg and cinnamon on the nose, warming juniper with fresh ginger and eucalyptus tones on the palate, lengthy ginger with lime zest to finish.

SERVING SUGGESTION: Enjoy with Fever-Tree Aromatic Tonic Water.

The Weaver Australian Gin 50.0%

BOTANICALS: Juniper, Lemon Myrtle, Aniseed Myrtle, Cinnamon Myrtle, Wattleseed, Strawberry Gum, Mace, Cassia, Nutmeg & Coriander Seed

TASTING NOTES: Warming nutmeg and cinnamon with supporting strawberry gum on the nose, oily juniper with cinnamon and cassia following on the palate, lingering strawberry gum and dark wattleseed notes to finish.

SERVING SUGGESTION: Enjoy with Fever-Tree Premium Indian Tonic Water.

Lord Howe Island Distilling Co.
Lord Howe Island, NSW

Removed from the mainland, out on the spectacularly beautiful Lord Howe Island off of New South Wales, Lord Howe Island Distilling Co. was started by two mates who wanted to celebrate the island's natural flora through world-class spirits. They minimise their footprint on the island by distilling in Sydney under their own license and with other independent distillers, using wild and endemic botanicals to create their spirits.

Wild Lemon and Hibiscus Gin 40.0%

BOTANICALS: Juniper, Bush Lemon, Hibiscus & Others

TASTING NOTES: Musky earth with lemon peel and juniper on the nose, upfront pine with lemon balm and layered citrus oil on the palate, thick oils and pine resin to finish.

SERVING SUGGESTION: Enjoy with Fever-Tree Mediterranean Tonic Water.

Luxe Brew
Melbourne, VIC

Positioned in Melbourne's quiet eastern suburb of Knoxfield, Luxe Brew is driven by the mantra that 'A product is only as good as its base ingredients', to which end they source more than 90% of their ingredients from Australian growers and makers. They regularly hand select and test every ingredient that goes into their spirits, liqueurs, and cocktails.

Style 3 Gin 38.0%

BOTANICALS: Juniper, Grapefruit, Clove & Others

TASTING NOTES: Pronounced lavender and orris root with lemon myrtle on the nose, floral pine with orris and tart lemon on the palate, lingering lemon myrtle with touches of pine to finish.

SERVING SUGGESTION: Enjoy with Fever-Tree Mediterranean Tonic Water.

Manly Spirits Co. Distillery
Sydney, NSW

Situated in the Sydney suburb of Brookvale just to the north of the tranquil and iconic Manly Beach, Manly Spirits Co. was born from a passion to create distinctive Australian spirits capturing the carefree beach life and coastal influence of Manly's famed marine sanctuary. They use sustainably foraged and grown marine and native Australian botanicals in their range of spirits.

Australian Dry Gin 43.0%

BOTANICALS: Juniper, Angelica Root, Coriander Seed, Orris Root, Cardamom, Sea Lettuce, Finger Lime, Aniseed Myrtle, Native Pepperleaf & Orange Peel

TASTING NOTES: Salty sea breeze with sea lettuce and aniseed myrtle on the nose, coriander, orange zest and angelica supported by light anise on the palate, soft-mellowing anise and coriander to finish.

SERVING SUGGESTION: Enjoy with Fever-Tree Premium Indian Tonic Water.

Coastal Citrus Gin 43.0%

BOTANICALS: Juniper, Lemon Aspen, Sea Parsley, Lemon Myrtle, Coriander Leaf & Meyer Lemon

TASTING NOTES: Bright citrus with hints of fresh green grass and light sea spray on the nose, juniper with crisp lemon zest and sweet floral notes on the palate, lingering lemon and florals to finish.

SERVING SUGGESTION: Enjoy with Fever-Tree Mediterranean Tonic Water.

Lilly Pilly Pink Gin 40.0%

BOTANICALS: Juniper, Lilly Pilly, Riberry, Native Lime, Raspberry, Blood Orange, Coriander Seed, Angelica Root, Orris Root, Rosella, Sea Fig & Nasturtium

TASTING NOTES: Elegant lilly pilly with hints of raspberry and leafy herbs on the nose, dry cooking spice with hints of green herbs and dried florals on the palate, finishing with bright summer fruits.

SERVING SUGGESTION: Enjoy with Fever-Tree Mediterranean Tonic Water.

Maria River Distillery
Crescent Head, NSW

Tucked away on a family farm along the Maria River between easy-going Crescent Head and vibrant Port Macquarie, Maria River Distillery is based around old school spirit making with onsite small batch production. They grow many of their own botanicals on the farm, including juniper, and source the rest either locally or responsibly from overseas.

Dry Gin 40.0%

BOTANICALS: Juniper, Citrus, Liquorice, Angelica Root, Cinnamon, Coriander Seed & Others

TASTING NOTES: Aniseed, hazelnut and eucalyptus tones lead the nose, grassy anise with sweet thyme and hints of juniper on the palate, green herbs and juniper linger to finish.

SERVING SUGGESTION: Enjoy with Fever-Tree Mediterranean Tonic Water.

MRD Gin 40.0%

BOTANICALS: Juniper, Citrus & Others

TASTING NOTES: Dried fruits with mixed herbs and spices lead the nose, musky citrus with cooked spice and green herbs on the palate, tingly green herbs lasting to finish.

SERVING SUGGESTION: Enjoy with Fever-Tree Mediterranean Tonic Water.

Ginello 40.0%

BOTANICALS: Juniper & Others (blended with Maria River Distillery Limoncello)

TASTING NOTES: Candied creamy lemon on the nose, oily lemon zest with a slight sweetness on the palate, pithy lemon with an oily finish.

SERVING SUGGESTION: Enjoy with Fever-Tree Mediterranean Tonic Water.

Mountain Distilling Company
Gisborne, VIC

Established in the peaceful and attractive town of Gisborne at the gateway to the idyllic Macedon Ranges, Mountain Distilling Company puts innovation at their core, incorporating exploration into every product and every process. They take a blank canvas approach with their range of spirits, using locally foraged and native ingredients, and seeing where the journey takes them.

Mountain Gin 43.0%

BOTANICALS: Juniper, New Growth Pine Needle, Native Pepperberry, Orange Zest, Lemon Myrtle & Coriander Seed

TASTING NOTES: Pine with coriander and light lemon zest on the nose, juniper with pronounced pepper, orange and coriander on the palate, pepper heat lingers with a touch lemon myrtle to finish.

SERVING SUGGESTION: Enjoy with Fever-Tree Premium Indian Tonic Water.

Mt. Uncle Distillery
Walkamin, QLD

Nestled near the small town of Walkamin on the western side of the Great Dividing Range across from Cairns, Mt. Uncle Distillery sits on a family property of over 800 acres, taking inspiration from nature and approaching every botanical with curiosity and experimentation. They put a significant emphasis on using as many local and Australian ingredients as possible, including many botanicals grown on their farm, in their spirits.

Botanic Australis Gin 40.0%

BOTANICALS: Juniper, Aniseed Myrtle, Cinnamon Myrtle, Lemon Myrtle, Lemon-Scented Gum, Finger Lime, River Mint, Peppermint Gum, Wattleseed, Native Pepperberry, Lilly Pilly, Eucalyptus Olinda, Native Ginger & Bunya Nut

TASTING NOTES: Strawberry jam with tropical fruit notes and a touch of green herbs on the nose, dry strawberry gum with tart lemon and resinous heated herbal tones on the palate, lemon myrtle lingers to finish.

SERVING SUGGESTION: Enjoy with Fever-Tree Mediterranean Tonic Water.

Bushfire Smoked Botanic Australis Gin 48.4%

BOTANICALS: Juniper, Aniseed Myrtle, Cinnamon Myrtle, Lemon Myrtle, Lemon-Scented Gum, Finger Lime, River Mint, Peppermint Gum, Wattleseed, Native Pepperberry, Lilly Pilly, Eucalyptus Olinda, Native Ginger & Bunya Nut (all botanicals smoked with Ironbark)

TASTING NOTES: Smoked pine with hickory on the nose, herbaceous rosemary and river mint with striking smoked spice and hints of juniper on the palate, developing lengthy smokiness to finish.

SERVING SUGGESTION: Enjoy with Fever-Tree Aromatic Tonic Water.

Navy Strength Botanic Australis Gin 57.0%

BOTANICALS: Juniper, Aniseed Myrtle, Cinnamon Myrtle, Lemon Myrtle, Lemon-Scented Gum, Finger Lime, River Mint, Peppermint Gum, Wattleseed, Native Pepperberry, Lilly Pilly, Eucalyptus Olinda, Native Ginger & Bunya Nut

TASTING NOTES: Prominent native botanicals with eucalyptus and citrus oils on the nose, fresh finger lime with lemon zest and minty tones developing on the palate, tingling eucalyptus and mint to finish.

SERVING SUGGESTION: Enjoy with Fever-Tree Mediterranean Tonic Water.

Northern Gem Botanic Australis Gin 43.0%

BOTANICALS: Juniper, Mango Leaf, Vanilla Bean, Nerada Tea, Aniseed Myrtle, Cinnamon Myrtle, Lemon Myrtle, Lemon-Scented Gum, Finger Lime, River Mint, Peppermint Gum, Wattleseed, Native Pepperberry, Lilly Pilly, Eucalyptus Olinda, Native Ginger & Bunya Nut

TASTING NOTES: Lemon balm with eucalyptus tones and hints of vanilla on the nose, lemon verbena leads with rosemary and cardamom in support on the palate, lingering lemon and spiced undertone to finish.

SERVING SUGGESTION: Enjoy with Fever-Tree Mediterranean Tonic Water.

Ooray Botanic Australis Gin 31.0%

BOTANICALS: Juniper, Davidson Plum, Strawberry Eucalyptus, Aniseed Myrtle, Cinnamon Myrtle, Lemon Myrtle, Lemon-Scented Gum, Finger Lime, River Mint, Peppermint Gum, Wattleseed, Native Pepperberry, Lilly Pilly, Eucalyptus, Native Ginger & Bunya Nut

TASTING NOTES: Red currant, anise and eucalyptus lead the nose, tart plum with garden herbs, tannins and red currant on the palate, fruity notes with garden herbs developing to finish.

SERVING SUGGESTION: Enjoy with Fever-Tree Lemon Tonic Water.

Murray's Craft Brewing Co - Distillery
Bobs Farm, NSW

Set just across the road from the beautiful and Aboriginal-owned Worimi National Park north of Newcastle, Murray's Craft Brewing Co began as a micro-brewery before expanding four times and adding a distillery to make spirits that complement their beer, wine, and cider offerings. They balance traditional and contemporary techniques and botanicals in the production of their spirits.

Gaia Dry Gin 40.0%

BOTANICALS: Juniper, Coriander Seed, Angelica Root, Cassia, Lemon Peel, Orange, Almond, Native Pepperberry, Cardamom, White Pepper & Lime Zest

TASTING NOTES: Oriental spice notes with sweet citrus on the nose, cardamom and pepper heat with sweet orange and warming cassia on the palate, earthy spice and heated cinnamon linger to finish.

SERVING SUGGESTION: Enjoy with Fever-Tree Mediterranean Tonic Water.

Gaia Citrus Gin 40.0%

BOTANICALS: Juniper, Coriander Seed, Orange Zest, Lemon Myrtle, Lemon Zest, Grapefruit Zest & Makrut Lime Zest

TASTING NOTES: Makrut lime zest and coriander lead the nose, warming lemon and lime with toasted coriander on the palate, coriander and hints of lime leaf to finish.

SERVING SUGGESTION: Enjoy with Fever-Tree Mediterranean Tonic Water.

Gaia Savorous Gin 40.0%

BOTANICALS: Juniper, Smoked Juniper, Coriander Seed, Rosemary, Basil, Thyme, Grapefruit, Celery Seed, Bay Leaf, Lemon Apple, Olive & Cucumber

TASTING NOTES: Slightly smoky juniper with woody rosemary on the nose, initial baked rosemary with solid pine resin and savoury green herbs on the palate, oily rosemary lingers to finish.

SERVING SUGGESTION: Enjoy with Fever-Tree Mediterranean Tonic Water.

Black Forest Sweet Christmas Gin 38.0%

BOTANICALS: Juniper, Cherry, Cocoa & Others (aged in Oak Barrels)

TASTING NOTES: Tart cherry coated with chocolate on the nose, cacao and Morello cherry with concentrated vanilla and oak undertones on the palate, rich cherry and chewy tannin to finish.

SERVING SUGGESTION: Enjoy with Fever-Tree Ginger Ale.

Naught Distilling
Melbourne, VIC

Ensconced among the green spaces and art community of the outer Melbourne suburb of Eltham, Naught Distilling was co-founded by a former professional basketball player with the aim of being exceptional with a meticulous nature. They forefront texture in their gins with a mix of local and exotic ingredients, using organic wherever possible, and focus on showcasing them through cocktails.

Classic Dry Gin 44.0%

BOTANICALS: Juniper, Angelica Root, Cassia, Macadamia, Turmeric, Wattleseed, Lemon & Lime

TASTING NOTES: Bold juniper with wattleseed and hazelnut on the nose, burst of citrus with woody spice and earthy angelica on the palate, lingering citrus, juniper and pepper heat to finish.

SERVING SUGGESTION: Enjoy with Fever-Tree Aromatic Tonic Water.

Australian Dry Gin 41.7%

BOTANICALS: Juniper, Orange, Coriander Seed, Cassia, Star Anise, Native Pepperleaf, Macadamia, Wattle Seed, Angelica Root & Rosemary

TASTING NOTES: Strong juniper with coriander in support on the nose, oily juniper and coriander lead with pepperberry and earthy roots on the palate, a long macadamia and anise driven finish.

SERVING SUGGESTION: Enjoy with Fever-Tree Premium Indian Tonic Water.

Overproof Gin 57.4%

BOTANICALS: Juniper, Pink Grapefruit, Pink Lady Apple, Lime, Coriander Seed, Cassia, Cardamom, Native Pepperleaf, Macadamia, Wattle Seed & Angelica Root

TASTING NOTES: Juniper, grapefruit peel and a touch of cassia on the nose, juniper and coriander lead with supporting pepperberry and a touch of citrus on the palate, balanced oily cardamom to finish.

SERVING SUGGESTION: Enjoy with Fever-Tree Premium Indian Tonic Water.

Needle and Pin Spirits
Adelaide, SA

Distilling in the recently revitalised multi-ethnic Woodville inner-city suburb of Adelaide, Needle and Pin Spirits was established with a focus on gin and grappa using craft distilling and sustainable approaches. They use 'spent' wine from their family's and neighbours' vineyards as their base spirit with botanicals from local Riverland producers and 'seconds' citruses that would otherwise be rejected to keep their gin as local as possible.

Riverland Dry 40.0%

BOTANICALS: Juniper, Coriander Seed, Lemon Peel, Lime Peel, Orange Peel, Mandarin Peel, Grapefruit Peel, Lemon Flesh, Lime Flesh, Orange Flesh, Mandarin Flesh, Grapefruit Flesh, Bitter Almond, Olive Leaf, Saltbush, Angelica Root, Lavender & Raisin

TASTING NOTES: Oily citrus with hints of pine resin and green herbs on the nose, rosemary and pine lead with peppery spice building on the palate, lingering heat with orange blossom to finish.

SERVING SUGGESTION: Enjoy with Fever-Tree Mediterranean Tonic Water.

Sevílli Bathtub Style Gin 39.0%

BOTANICALS: Juniper, Coriander Seed, Raisin, Cinnamon, Seville Orange Flesh, Seville Orange Rind, Bitter Almond & Chamomile

TASTING NOTES: Orange with leafy green herbs and a touch of pine on the nose, freshly squeezed orange juice with a hint of pine and pepper on the palate, oily orange builds with a pepper emphasis to finish.

SERVING SUGGESTION: Enjoy with Fever-Tree Mediterranean Tonic Water.

Never Never Distilling Co.
McLaren Vale, SA

Located in McLaren Vale at the epicentre of South Australia's wine industry on the Fleurieu Peninsula, Never Never Distilling Co. is named for and inspired by the space beyond the horizon and between the stars, stepping into which is to seek adventure. They create their gins with a passion for classic drinks, including G&Ts and cocktails, deriving complexity in their gins through modern distilling techniques.

Triple Juniper Gin 43.0%

BOTANICALS: Juniper, Angelica Root, Orris Root, Lemon Peel, Lime Peel, Liquorice, Cinnamon & Native Pepperberry

TASTING NOTES: Pronounced juniper with a lime zest, pepper spice and orris on the nose, big juniper with warming pepperberry, tart citrus and earthy musk on the palate, juniper carries with lingering citrus and warming heat to finish.

SERVING SUGGESTION: Enjoy with Fever-Tree Mediterranean Tonic Water.

Southern Strength Gin 52.0%

BOTANICALS: Juniper, Angelica Root, Orris Root, Lemon Peel, Lime Peel, Liquorice, Cinnamon & Native Pepperberry

TASTING NOTES: Bright juniper with hints of spice and zesty notes on the nose, juniper leads with uplifting citrus, pepper and strong perfumed earthy tones on the palate, juniper lingers with pepperberry to finish.

SERVING SUGGESTION: Enjoy with Fever-Tree Mediterranean Tonic Water.

Juniper Freak Gin 58.0%

BOTANICALS: Juniper, Angelica Root, Orris Root, Lemon Peel, Lime Peel, Liquorice, Cinnamon & Native Pepperberry

TASTING NOTES: Robust juniper and resin with earthy undertones, resinous juniper with strong orris, warming pepper and citrus peel on the palate, warming juniper lingers with angelica to finish.

SERVING SUGGESTION: Enjoy with Fever-Tree Mediterranean Tonic Water.

Oyster Shell Gin 42.0%

BOTANICALS: Juniper, Oyster Shell, Marsh Grapefruit, Geraldton Wax, Wakame, Coastal Daisy-Bush, Saltbush & Round Leaf Mint

TASTING NOTES: Mineral sea breeze tones with striking waxflower on the nose, creamy lead with waxflower, minty freshness, and distinct savoury juniper on the palate, lingering waxflower and juniper to finish.

SERVING SUGGESTION: Enjoy with Fever-Tree Mediterranean Tonic Water.

Ginache 38.0%

BOTANICALS: Juniper, Angelica Root, Orris Root, Lemon Peel, Lime Peel, Liquorice, Cinnamon & Native Pepperberry (steeped in Grenache Grapes)

TASTING NOTES: Prominent juniper with liquorice and rich Grenache on the nose, liquorice with rich black cherry and tobacco on the palate, dry slightly chalky tannins with dark fruits to finish.

SERVING SUGGESTION: Enjoy with Fever-Tree Lemon Tonic Water.

New Norfolk Distillery
New Norfolk, TAS

Housed in a former hospital and asylum in New Norfolk at the heart of the picturesque Derwent Valley northeast of Hobart, New Norfolk Distillery are all about creating and nurturing rebellious spirits, rums, and liqueurs. They make their products with a Tasmanian focus for those seeking a twist on classic drinks, using Tasmanian mountain spring water with Australian and exotic botanicals.

Jovian Wilderness Dry Gin 46.5%

BOTANICALS: Juniper, Native Pepperberry, Hemp Hearts, Cardamom, Cinnamon, Liquorice & Lemon Myrtle

TASTING NOTES: Lemon myrtle, cinnamon and ginger-like character on the nose, soft dry pepper with bay leaf and floral hops on the palate, drying light heat and florals to finish.

SERVING SUGGESTION: Enjoy with Fever-Tree Mediterranean Tonic Water.

Newcastle Distilling Co.
Newcastle, NSW

Planted in the Newcastle suburb of Shortland near the wildlife sanctuary of Hunter Wetlands National Park, Newcastle Distilling Co. was started by a husband-and-wife duo and was originally branded as Catcher&Co before they moved to Newcastle to reconnect with their family and roots. They craft small batches using natural ingredients, believing that the passion that goes into each of their products ensures a premium experience for their customers.

Dry Gin 40.0%

BOTANICALS: Juniper, Lemon Myrtle, Liquorice, Angelica Root & Orris Root

TASTING NOTES: Musky baking spice with a touch of bay leaf on the nose, Indian spice notes with a bay leaf lead and slight nutty character on the palate, lingering baking spice to finish.

SERVING SUGGESTION: Enjoy with Fever-Tree Mediterranean Tonic Water.

Bathtub Gin 40.0%

BOTANICALS: Juniper, Lemon Myrtle, Aniseed, Cardamom, Peppercorn, Dandelion, Citrus Peel & Others

TASTING NOTES: Fruity lemon flesh with lemon myrtle and light herbs on the nose, candied ginger with cardamom and tarragon on the palate, lemon lingers to finish.

SERVING SUGGESTION: Enjoy with Fever-Tree Mediterranean Tonic Water.

Easy Street Collective Autumn Time 37.0%

BOTANICALS: Juniper, Cinnamon, Cassia, Blood Orange, Honey & Hazelnut

TASTING NOTES: Smoked paprika and cooked orange on the nose, white pepper and fresh lemon zest with rosemary and cardamom on the palate, hints of pepper with zesty lemon to finish.

SERVING SUGGESTION: Enjoy with Fever-Tree Mediterranean Tonic Water.

Easy Street Collective Spring Time Gin 37.0%

BOTANICALS: Juniper, Hibiscus, Lemongrass, Lavender & Rose

TASTING NOTES: Fresh stone fruit with light florals and passionfruit undertones on the nose, lavender with a touch of cinnamon and pear on the palate, hints of orange and lemongrass to finish.

SERVING SUGGESTION: Enjoy with Fever-Tree Mediterranean Tonic Water.

Easy Street Collective Summer Time 37.0%

BOTANICALS: Juniper, Lemon, Lime, Orange, Ruby Red Grapefruit, Cardamom & Ginger

TASTING NOTES: Cinnamon and ginger with fresh lime on the nose, oily layered citrus of orange, grapefruit and lemon on the palate, sharp fresh ginger juice with lingering citrus to finish.

SERVING SUGGESTION: Enjoy with Fever-Tree Mediterranean Tonic Water.

Easy Street Collective Winter Time 37.0%

BOTANICALS: Juniper, Clove, Cardamom, Cinnamon & Nutmeg

TASTING NOTES: Clove, anise and cinnamon drive the nose, opening to notes of dried fruit with clove and tarragon-like tones on the palate, orange oil and subtle spice linger to finish.

SERVING SUGGESTION: Enjoy with Fever-Tree Aromatic Tonic Water.

Strawberry Infusion Gin 40.0%

BOTANICALS: Juniper, Strawberry, Apple, Hibiscus, Rosehip, Orris Root, Angelica Root, Coriander Seed, Liquorice & Others

TASTING NOTES: Stewed strawberries with green leaves on the nose, stewed strawberries with warming spice, hibiscus and dry florals on the palate, dry tea and a peppery tingle to finish.

SERVING SUGGESTION: Enjoy with Fever-Tree Elderflower Tonic Water.

Newy Distillery
Newcastle, NSW

Anchored in the outer suburb of Edgeworth in laid-back and hipster-friendly Newcastle, Newy Distillery is family-owned, starting out in their household shed before expanding, and takes its name from the affectionate local moniker for the city. They are pledged to making high quality spirits with a creative flare, encouraging creativity, and creating unconventional drink experiences.

Signature Gin 40.0%

BOTANICALS: Juniper, Coriander Seed, Cassia, Almond, Orris Root, Grains of Paradise, Lemon, Orange & Lime

TASTING NOTES: Light citrus notes with cassia and earthy tones on the nose, perfumed orris, warming coriander and sweet orange supported by a juniper backbone on the palate, orris and orange sweetness to finish.

SERVING SUGGESTION: Enjoy with Fever-Tree Premium Indian Tonic Water.

Australiana Gin 40.0%

BOTANICALS: Juniper, Lemon Myrtle, Honey, Lavender, Eucalyptus, Strawberry Gum & Others

TASTING NOTES: Strawberry gum leads with honey and eucalyptus on the nose, striking florals with pronounced lemon myrtle and strawberry gum on the palate, dried lavender notes with lemon to finish.

SERVING SUGGESTION: Enjoy with Fever-Tree Refreshingly Light Indian Tonic Water.

Coal Miner Strength 55.5%

BOTANICALS: Juniper, Coriander Seed, Cassia, Almond, Orris Root, Grains of Paradise, Lemon, Orange & Lime

TASTING NOTES: Soft citrus with support from juniper and coriander on the nose, juniper leads with nutty creaminess and a touch of orris on the palate, lingering juniper warmth and violet from orris to finish.

SERVING SUGGESTION: Enjoy with Fever-Tree Refreshingly Light Indian Tonic Water.

Dry Gin 40.0%

BOTANICALS: Juniper, Coriander Seed, Cassia, Lemon Peel & Others

TASTING NOTES: Coriander and juniper lead with a hint of cassia on the nose, upfront juniper with supporting cassia, coriander, and bright citrus on the palate, perfumed earthiness with lingering cassia to finish.

SERVING SUGGESTION: Enjoy with Fever-Tree Premium Indian Tonic Water.

Passionfruit Gin 40.0%

BOTANICALS: Juniper, Coriander Seed, Cassia, Lemon Peel, Passionfruit & Others

TASTING NOTES: Creamy passionfruit leads the nose, dry citrus with dominant passionfruit and a touch of juniper on the palate, subtle spice with lingering passionfruit to finish.

SERVING SUGGESTION: Enjoy with Fever-Tree Refreshingly Light Indian Tonic Water.

Noble Bootleggers Distilling Co
Bendigo, VIC

Settled on the outskirts of the heritage architecture and vibrant food and wine scene of Bendigo, Noble Bootleggers Distilling Co is family-owned and operated with sustainability at the heart of everything they do. They have an ethos of creating exciting and innovative products with big, bold flavours, whilst focusing on traditional methods and quality ingredients.

Australian Contemporary Gin 40.0%

BOTANICALS: Juniper, Lemon Aspen, Lemon Verbena, Lemon Myrtle, Coriander Seed, Angelica Root, Vanilla & Others

TASTING NOTES: Lemon aspen and creamy vanilla notes on the nose, perfumed florals lemon and a touch dry cooking spice on the palate, florals sweeten slightly and subtle spice lingering to finish.

SERVING SUGGESTION: Enjoy with Fever-Tree Premium Indian Tonic Water.

Cherry Gin 40.0%

BOTANICALS: Juniper, Orris Root, Angelica Root, Wormwood, Rose Petal, Cherry & Others

TASTING NOTES: Fruity rocky road tones with rich florals and nutty characters on the nose, berry swirl ice cream notes with a touch of bitter wormwood and angelica on the palate, developing cherry with rose undertones to finish.

SERVING SUGGESTION: Enjoy with Fever-Tree Refreshingly Light Indian Tonic Water.

Christmas Pudding Gin 40.0%

BOTANICALS: Juniper, Coriander Seed, Orris Root, Liquorice, Cinnamon, Orange Peel & Others (macerated in Christmas Pudding for 3-4 months)

TASTING NOTES: Chocolate notes with nutty savoury spice on the nose, allspice to open with sweet dried raisin and warming pepper spice on the palate, warm sweet spiced fruits to finish.

SERVING SUGGESTION: Enjoy with Fever-Tree Ginger Ale.

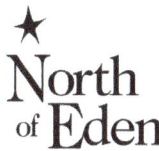

North of Eden
Stony Creek, NSW

Nestled in the rolling green hinterland of the pristine Sapphire Coast near the small township of Stony Creek, North of Eden is a tiny distillery with twin objectives of reflecting their area in their products and operating as sustainably as possible. They use old-school artisan methods and feature ingredients that either grow at the distillery or are foraged locally in their spirits.

The Classic 43.5%

BOTANICALS: Juniper, Coriander Seed, Orris Root, Angelica Root, Blood Orange, Grapefruit, Lemon & Finger Lime

TASTING NOTES: Striking citrus with supporting minty juniper and hints of almond on the nose, earthy spice with juniper and angelica on the palate, lingering pepper with a waxy finish.

SERVING SUGGESTION: Enjoy with Fever-Tree Mediterranean Tonic Water.

Oyster Shell Gin 43.5%

BOTANICALS: Juniper, Coriander Seed, Lemon, Lime, Kumquat, Oyster Shell, Saltbush, Hawthorn Leaf, Rose, Lemon Myrtle & Ginger

TASTING NOTES: Saltbush with pine resin and hints of lemon myrtle on the nose, dry saltbush with savoury green herbs, juniper and oily lemon on the palate, slightly mineral note with juniper and lemon to finish.

SERVING SUGGESTION: Enjoy with Fever-Tree Mediterranean Tonic Water.

The Admiral 57.0%

BOTANICALS: Juniper, Coriander Seed, Orris Root, Citrus, Ginger, Cinnamon & Kurrajong Seed

TASTING NOTES: Pronounced juniper with hints of sea breeze on the nose, juniper leads with notes of crushed green leaves and ocean spray on the palate, drying juniper with subtle sea breeze to finish.

SERVING SUGGESTION: Enjoy with Fever-Tree Mediterranean Tonic Water.

The Connoisseur 43.5%

BOTANICALS: Juniper, Coriander Seed, Citrus, Elderberry, Elderflower, Birch Leaf & Seaweed

TASTING NOTES: Juniper and eucalypt resin with hints of bitter almond on the nose, sharp pepperberry with supporting juniper and woody notes on the palate, drying juniper with lingering woody elements to finish.

SERVING SUGGESTION: Enjoy with Fever-Tree Premium Indian Tonic Water.

Nosferatu Distillery
Brisbane, QLD

Sheltered in the inner-city suburb of Bowen Hills just northeast of Brisbane's CBD, Nosferatu Distillery was born out of a love of Pimms, Campari, and Gin with a keen interest in the arts. They make gin laced with inspiration from film, art, literature, folklore, and culture using a triple citrus process, and designed to flow from one another like a four course meal.

Nosferatu Blood Orange Gin 40.4%

BOTANICALS: Juniper, Davidson Plum, Blood Orange Peel, Navel Orange, Dried Orange Peel, Roasted Fenugreek, Coriander Seed, Cardamom Seed, Wormwood & Angelica Root

TASTING NOTES: Davidson plums with hints of juniper and pronounced orange on the nose, juniper with plum, orange zest, and a slight roasted coffee note on the palate, herbal undertone with a lingering dry plum finish.

SERVING SUGGESTION: Enjoy with Fever-Tree Premium Indian Tonic Water.

Bunyip Sticky Gin 37.5%

BOTANICALS: Juniper, Lemon Peel, Coriander Seed, Cardamom, Grains of Paradise, Wormwood & Liquorice (blended with unfermented Pinot Gris Grape Juice)

TASTING NOTES: Poached pear with tart pineapple and baking spice on the nose, sweet lime blossom with pear and honey water on the palate, rich-sweet tones carrying from the palate to finish.

SERVING SUGGESTION: Enjoy with Fever-Tree Refreshingly Light Indian Tonic Water.

Giselle Pavlova Gin 37.5%

BOTANICALS: Juniper, Burnt Sugar, Double Cream Essence, Dried Orange Peel, Navel Orange, Blood Orange Peel, Vanilla, Coriander Seed, Wormwood & Angelica Root

TASTING NOTES: Caramel, banana and sweet florals on the nose, creamy banana with sweet strawberry and orange on the palate, confectionary-like sweetness to finish.

SERVING SUGGESTION: Enjoy with Fever-Tree Ginger Ale.

Mandrake Cucumber & Mint Gin 40.4%

BOTANICALS: Juniper, Cucumber, Mint, Fresh Lemon Peel, Lemon, Dried Lemon Peel, Coriander Seed, Liquorice, Wormwood & Angelica Root

TASTING NOTES: Lemon zest with cardamom, sweet cucumber and mint on the nose, initial burst of lemon and lime with cardamom and minty menthol heat on the palate, lasting mint with citrus lingering to finish.

SERVING SUGGESTION: Enjoy with Fever-Tree Mediterranean Tonic Water.

Old Kempton Distillery
Kempton, TAS

Occupying the historic Dysart House in the small, early colonial town of Kempton to the north of Hobart, Old Kempton Distillery aspires to create consistently remarkable small batch releases that tie in heavily with the history of their location. They use traditional hands-on methods of distilling in creating their range of spirits, including whisky, gin, and liqueurs.

Embezzler Gin 46.0%

BOTANICALS: Juniper, Coriander Seed, Orris Root, Chamomile, Lemon, Orange, Liquorice, Star Anise, Lime Leaf, Mint & Allspice

TASTING NOTES: Liquorice, mint and allspice form an aromatic nose, musky orris with lime citrus, liquorice and dry chamomile on the palate, lingering lime and soft anise to finish.

SERVING SUGGESTION: Enjoy with Fever-Tree Refreshingly Light Indian Tonic Water.

Barrel Aged Gin 46.0%

BOTANICALS: Juniper, Coriander Seed, Orris Root, Chamomile, Lemon, Orange, Liquorice, Star Anise, Lime Leaf, Mint, Allspice, Lemon Thyme, Pineapple, Mango & Kiwifruit (aged for 3-6 months in ex-Bourbon Casks)

TASTING NOTES: Pine notes with chamomile and allspice on the nose, lemon thyme and light dry woody notes with tropical hints on the palate, soft drying pine and woody character to finish.

SERVING SUGGESTION: Enjoy with Fever-Tree Premium Indian Tonic Water.

Six Shillings Gin 46.0%

BOTANICALS: Juniper, Coriander Seed, Chamomile, Lemon Thyme, Orange, Lemon, Pineapple, Mango & Kiwifruit

TASTING NOTES: Fresh oregano with dominant sweet citrus and tropical fruit notes on the nose, pineapple and mango lead with bitter florals on the palate, lingering oily lemon to finish.

SERVING SUGGESTION: Enjoy with Fever-Tree Mediterranean Tonic Water.

Original Spirit Co.
Somerville, VIC

Nestled between the bays on Victoria's Mornington Peninsula in the town of Somerville, Original Spirit Co. is a family-owned and operated distillery that prides itself on delivering gins for every palate with a focus on innovation and flavour. They achieve the colour and clarity of their gins through the use of premium natural ingredients with intensive blending and filtering.

Classic Dry 40.0%

BOTANICALS: Juniper, Coriander Seed, Angelica Root, Native Pepperberry, Lemon Peel & Orris Root

TASTING NOTES: Classic coriander and juniper with pepperberry and lemon peel on the nose, pepperberry, lemon zest and coriander continue well on the palate, orris lingers with pined juniper to finish.

SERVING SUGGESTION: Enjoy with Fever-Tree Mediterranean Tonic Water.

Single Barrel Reserve 48.0%

BOTANICALS: Juniper, Coriander Seed, Angelica Root, Native Pepperberry, Lemon Peel & Orris Root (aged for a minimum of 2 years in ex-Tawny Port Barrels)

TASTING NOTES: Distinct barky character with notes of caramel and tawny sweetness on the nose, sweetened tawny richness, vanilla, caramel and candied orange on the palate, mentholic mintiness to finish.

SERVING SUGGESTION: Enjoy neat or with Fever-Tree Ginger Ale.

Wild Sloe 30.0%

BOTANICALS: Juniper, Coriander Seed, Angelica Root, Native Pepperberry, Lemon Peel, Orris Root & Sloe Berry

TASTING NOTES: Juicy sloe with slight white pepper spice undertone on the nose, pleasantly tart with hints of cherry and honey on the palate, very elegant sweetness to finish.

SERVING SUGGESTION: Enjoy with Fever-Tree Lemon Tonic Water.

Otways Distillery
Forrest, VIC

Bundled away in the hinterland of the Otways' tranquil rainforests and scenery near Apollo Bay, Otways Distillery makes spirits that are a celebration of all they have in their part of Victoria. They use locally sourced and foraged ingredients to underpin the flavour profiles of their products, collaborating with locals to showcase the native and farmed botanicals and foods of the region.

Forrest Gin 42.0%

BOTANICALS: Juniper, Lemon Gum, River Mint, Rosemary & Lemon

TASTING NOTES: Lime leaf with saltbush and lemon verbena on the nose, lime leaf leads with eucalyptus, pine resin and forest florals on the palate, woody forest floor finish.

SERVING SUGGESTION: Enjoy with Fever-Tree Mediterranean Tonic Water.

Paradise Distillers
Gold Coast, QLD

Stationed in the Gold Coast's western suburb of Molendinar, Paradise Distillers began with a dream to create a range of beverages that suit their climate and individual palates. They work with local businesses where possible, taking inspiration from growing up on the Gold Coast and using Australian botanicals as a key element in their spirits.

Paradise Gin featuring Australian Kakadu Plum 40.0%

BOTANICALS: Juniper, Angelica Root, Pink Peppercorn, Cardamom & Orange Peel

TASTING NOTES: Sweet orange and musky juniper lead the nose, candied orange leads with pepper spice and soft angelica on the palate, juniper and citrus linger to finish.

SERVING SUGGESTION: Enjoy with Fever-Tree Premium Indian Tonic Water.

Pink Paradise Gin featuring Native Rosella Flower 40.0%

BOTANICALS: Juniper, Rosella Flower, Angelica Root, Pink Peppercorn, Cardamom & Grapefruit Peel

TASTING NOTES: Grapefruit with earthy florals and dusty pink peppercorn on the nose, pronounced angelica with cardamom and grapefruit on the palate, musky angelica with peppery heat to finish.

SERVING SUGGESTION: Enjoy with Fever-Tree Premium Indian Tonic Water.

Pietro Gallus Estate
Melbourne, VIC

Swaddled amongst the sprawling hills of Warrandyte on the north-eastern edge of Melbourne, Pietro Gallus Estate is a winery and distillery launched by a husband and wife team as a 'great Italian escape'. They celebrate traditional Italian techniques with a modern approach in creating their spirits, focusing on developing products that combine their heritage with local influence.

Crossover Gin 42.0%

BOTANICALS: Juniper, Coriander Seed, Angelica Root, Orris Root, Cassia, Orange, Cardamom, Thyme, Rosemary, Olive Leaf, Native Basil, Lemon Myrtle, Native Pepperberry, Aniseed Myrtle & Macadamia

TASTING NOTES: Zesty lemon with dried garden herbs on the nose, slightly creamy palate of anise, lemon myrtle and soft pepper, lingering lemon with delicate pepper heat to finish.

SERVING SUGGESTION: Enjoy with Fever-Tree Mediterranean Tonic Water.

Plan B Distillery
Hobart, TAS

Sitting in the shaded foothills of Mt Nelson in southern Hobart, Plan B Distillery was founded on a dream and the courage to follow it by two women who realised that a life well-lived might involve more than one journey. They recognise that everyone has different tastes and preferences, and these change, making an adaptable range of gins featuring local botanicals.

Pepper-Rose Gin 42.0%

BOTANICALS: Juniper, Coriander Seed, Cassia, Orris Root, Native Pepperberry & Rosehip

TASTING NOTES: Sweet rosehip and cinnamon with creamy blossoms on the nose, orange zest with oregano and a peppery heat on the palate, developing pepper with sweet fruit undertones to finish.

SERVING SUGGESTION: Enjoy with Fever-Tree Mediterranean Tonic Water.

Pepper-Spice Gin 57.0%

BOTANICALS: Juniper, Coriander Seed, Ginger, Chilli, Orris Root, Lemon Myrtle, Lemongrass, Native Pepperberry, Lime, Orange, Cardamom & Star Anise

TASTING NOTES: Dried Thai cooking spices with chilli and cardamom undertones on the nose, chilli spice and lemongrass lead with bursting orange zest on the palate, lingering lemon myrtle with baking spice and chilli heat to finish.

SERVING SUGGESTION: Enjoy with Fever-Tree Mediterranean Tonic Water.

Pepper-Zest Gin 42.0%

BOTANICALS: Juniper, Coriander Seed, Lemon, Cassia, Lemon Myrtle, Orange, Native Pepperberry & Lavender

TASTING NOTES: Pungent lavender with lemon curd and orange blossom on the nose, bursts of pepper with aniseed, coriander and bitter fennel on the palate, lingering pepper and lemon oil to finish.

SERVING SUGGESTION: Enjoy with Fever-Tree Mediterranean Tonic Water.

Mulberry Sloe Gin 25.0%

BOTANICALS: Juniper, Coriander Seed, Lemon, Orris Root, Cassia, Sloe Berry & Mulberry

TASTING NOTES: Well integrated mulberry with notes of sweet blackberry and rhubarb on the nose, jammy baked richness overlapping the subtle sloe, light marzipan and a soft peppery edge on the palate, grippy acidity and well-balanced sweetness to finish.

SERVING SUGGESTION: Enjoy with Fever-Tree Lemon Tonic Water.

Sloe Gin 25.0%

BOTANICALS: Juniper, Coriander Seed, Lemon, Orris Root, Cassia & Sloe Berry

TASTING NOTES: Dark overripe fruit with hints of cassia on the nose, persistent sloe character with sweet baking spice, hints of cherry and orris rounding the edges on the palate, bright acidity with a persistent sweetness to finish.

SERVING SUGGESTION: Enjoy with Fever-Tree Lemon Tonic Water.

Pokolbin Distillery
Pokolbin, NSW

Rooted in Pokolbin in the heart of the beautiful Hunter Valley outside of Newcastle, Pokolbin Distillery has both Polish and Australian roots, taking inspiration from a family story of passion and perseverance with distilling. They make their own wash from scratch using Australian ingredients to make their spirits along with naturally sourced ingredients inspired by their Polish heritage and native Australian botanicals.

Classic Dry Gin 40.0%

BOTANICALS: Juniper, Cardamom, Coriander Seed, Star Anise, Lemon Peel & Lemon Myrtle Leaf

TASTING NOTES: Musky earth notes and citrus with a hint of anise on the nose, upfront lemon myrtle with tingling spice heat and sweet orange on the palate, tingling spice continues with orange oil to finish.

SERVING SUGGESTION: Enjoy with Fever-Tree Mediterranean Tonic Water.

Bush Gin 40.0%

BOTANICALS: Juniper, Cardamom, Coriander Seed, Star Anise, Aniseed, Australian Bush Mint, Lemon Peel & Lemon Myrtle Leaf

TASTING NOTES: Resounding mint with subtle dry spice and mineral undertones on the nose, sweet mint tea with dry coriander and cardamom on the palate, lingering spice with honey water like sweetness to finish.

SERVING SUGGESTION: Enjoy with Fever-Tree Mediterranean Tonic Water.

Native Plum Finger Lime Gin 40.0%

BOTANICALS: Juniper, Davidson Plum, Finger Lime, Cardamom, Coriander Seed & Star Anise

TASTING NOTES: Hibiscus with musky florals and undertones of port wine on the nose, striking raspberry with musky florals and tart lime on the palate, dry earthy musk to finish.

SERVING SUGGESTION: Enjoy with Fever-Tree Refreshingly Light Indian Tonic Water.

Poor Toms Distillery

Sydney, NSW

Ensconced in the fun and friendly inner-city Marrickville suburb of Sydney, Poor Toms Distillery is named for the assumed identity of a character from Shakespeare's King Lear, reflecting a goal of drinking gin to transcend reality and dissolve the adornments of identity. They have taken on the mission of bringing real pleasure to people's lives with audacious and honest spirits.

Sydney Dry Gin 41.3%

BOTANICALS: Juniper, Granny Smith Apple, Strawberry Gum Leaf, Chamomile, Lemon Myrtle, Coriander Seed, Angelica Root, Cinnamon, Cardamom & Cubeb Pepper

TASTING NOTES: Fresh apple, stewed strawberry and peppery tones on the nose, crisp green apple and strawberry gum with support from sharp citrus and coriander on the palate, lingering lemon and fruity notes to finish.

SERVING SUGGESTION: Enjoy with Fever-Tree Refreshingly Light Indian Tonic Water.

Fool's Cut Gin 52.0%

BOTANICALS: Juniper, Coriander Seed, Angelica Root, Cinnamon, Cardamom, Cubeb Pepper, Chamomile, Liquorice & Grapefruit Peel

TASTING NOTES: Rich juniper with baking spice and pepper heat on the nose, robust coriander and earthy root tones with juniper and citrus peel on the palate, warming spice and lingering juniper to finish.

SERVING SUGGESTION: Enjoy with Fever-Tree Aromatic Tonic Water.

Strawberry Gin 40.0%

BOTANICALS: Juniper, Strawberry, Young Ginger, Hibiscus, Strawberry Gum Leaf, Cardamom, Cubeb Pepper, Lemon Myrtle & Chamomile

TASTING NOTES: Striking strawberry gum with undertones of stewed berries on the nose, burst of berry fruits with ginger spice and subtle juniper on the palate, lingering ginger heat with tart berry to finish.

SERVING SUGGESTION: Enjoy with Fever-Tree Wild Raspberry Tonic Water.

Portia Valley Wines
Adelaide, SA

Distilling in the recently revitalised multi-ethnic Woodville inner-city suburb of Adelaide, Portia Valley Wines is owned and operated by the Grigoriou family with vineyards at the top of the Monash Valley and Loveday. They use native Australian botanicals harnessed in a classic and traditional way to capture the aroma and flavour of the areas in which they are grown.

Native Australia Classic Dry Gin 40.0%

BOTANICALS: Juniper, Coriander Seed, Lemon Peel, Lemon, Lime Peel, Lime, Native Pepperberry, Rosemary, Angelica Root & Chamomile

TASTING NOTES: Pungent rosemary oil with hints of ginger and cassia on the nose, dry strawberry gum with fruity tones and garden herbs on the palate, lingering green leafy herbs to finish.

SERVING SUGGESTION: Enjoy with Fever-Tree Mediterranean Tonic Water.

Native Australia Lilly Pilly Gin 40.0%

BOTANICALS: Juniper, Coriander Seed, Orange Peel, Orange, Lime Peel, Lime, Lilly Pilly, Hibiscus, Angelica Root, Chamomile & Bitter Almond

TASTING NOTES: Hints of citrus with light delicate florals on the nose, upfront lilly pilly with a touch of clove and hints of tart fruit on the palate, dry with a textured acidity to finish.

SERVING SUGGESTION: Enjoy with Fever-Tree Elderflower Tonic Water.

Native Australia Saltbush & Lemon Myrtle Gin 40.0%

BOTANICALS: Juniper, Coriander Seed, Lemon Peel, Lemon, Mandarin Peel, Mandarin, Saltbush, Lemon Myrtle, Angelica Root, Cinnamon & Cardamom

TASTING NOTES: Green herbs with eucalypt and salty tones on the nose, burst of lemon myrtle with supporting black pepper and green herb characters on the palate, lingering lemon with savoury herbs to finish.

SERVING SUGGESTION: Enjoy with Fever-Tree Mediterranean Tonic Water.

Prohibition Liquor Co.
Adelaide, SA

Planted right in the heart of Adelaide's burgeoning city centre, Prohibition Liquor Co. was started by a couple of local lads with the dream of creating a world-class neat-drinking gin and takes their name from Australia's period of prohibition and keeping the spirit of its bootleggers alive. They combine that spirit with an artisan philosophy and focus on using fine botanicals to make premium products.

Prohibition Gin 42.0%

BOTANICALS: Juniper, Coriander Seed, Ginger, Pink Peppercorn, Blood Orange, Ruby Red Grapefruit, Lemon Myrtle, Green Tea, Vanilla & Lavender

TASTING NOTES: Juniper dominates with bright zingy lemon myrtle on the nose, upfront juniper and coriander with lemon zest on the palate, dry citrus with developing lavender tones from orris root to finish.

SERVING SUGGESTION: Enjoy with Fever-Tree Premium Indian Tonic Water.

Bathtub Cut Gin 69.0%

BOTANICALS: Juniper, Coriander Seed, Ginger, Orange Rind, Grapefruit, Orris Root, Cassia, Star Anise, Almond, Green Tea, Vanilla & Lavender

TASTING NOTES: Pronounced spice and herbal tones with juniper on the nose, bold juniper leads with ginger heat, supporting anise and a burst of citrus on the palate, tingling juniper settles with warming coriander to finish.

SERVING SUGGESTION: Enjoy with Fever-Tree Mediterranean Tonic Water.

Juniperus Gin 47.0%

BOTANICALS: Juniper, Cassia, Grains of Paradise, Lemon, Ruby Red Grapefruit, Navel Orange, Macadamia, Vanilla Bean, Coriander Seed, Angelica Root, Orris Root & Liquorice

TASTING NOTES: Bold juniper with coriander, citrus peel and pepper on the nose, warming juniper with spiced coriander and sweet orange peel on the palate, warming pepper with orris and orange to finish.

SERVING SUGGESTION: Enjoy with Fever-Tree Premium Indian Tonic Water.

Moonlight Gin 42.0%

BOTANICALS: Juniper, Red Juniper, Coriander Seed, Orris Root, Sandalwood Nut, Blood Lime, Lemon Peel, Grapefruit Peel, Black Goji Berry, Hibiscus, Butterfly Pea Flower, Pink Lady Apple, Clove, Lilac & Honeybush

TASTING NOTES: Dried currant with juniper and slightly woody spice on the nose, dry clove and bitter almond with fruity apple and rhubarb-like undertones on the palate, dry florals and pepper to finish.

SERVING SUGGESTION: Enjoy with Fever-Tree Refreshingly Light Indian Tonic Water.

Navy Strength Gin 58.0%

BOTANICALS: Juniper, Coriander Seed, Angelica Root, Macadamia, Ginger, Native Pepperberry, Ruby Red Grapefruit, Finger Lime, Desert Lime, Vanilla, Saltbush, Gunpowder Tea & Salt (Great Australian Bight)

TASTING NOTES: Pepperberry with zesty citrus, angelica and juniper on the nose, burst of juniper with pepperberry, fresh lemon and zingy coriander on the palate, lingering juniper and angelica to finish.

SERVING SUGGESTION: Enjoy with Fever-Tree Mediterranean Tonic Water.

Shiraz Barrel Gin 59.0%

BOTANICALS: Juniper, Coriander Seed, Ginger, Pink Peppercorn, Blood Orange, Ruby Red Grapefruit, Lemon Myrtle, Green Tea, Vanilla & Lavender (aged in Bourbon and Shiraz Oak Barrels)

TASTING NOTES: Bursting fresh citrus with hints of ginger and citrus tea on the nose, pleasant baking spice with lavender, oily citrus and buttery tones on the palate, drying spice and buttery barrel tones to finish.

SERVING SUGGESTION: Enjoy neat or with Fever-Tree Ginger Ale.

Puss & Mew Distillery

Melbourne, VIC

Positioned just off of Nunawading's bustling 'Mega Mile' in eastern Melbourne, Puss & Mew Distillery takes its name and inspiration from the story of an enterprising gin-slinger who created a vending machine to evade liquor licensing rules in 18th century Britain. They use the latest techniques and technologies in their processes with juniper and coriander as the absolute core foundation of their gins but diversity as a top consideration in their collection.

Signature Dry Gin 41.0%

BOTANICALS: Juniper, Coriander Seed, Angelica Root, Orris Root, Orange, Lemon, Lemon Myrtle, Strawberry Gum, Cardamom, Grains of Paradise & Vanilla Bean

TASTING NOTES: Strawberry gum with strong lemon zest and light pepper on the nose, lemon zest continues with cardamom and vanilla on the palate, lingering earthy orris and lasting vanilla to finish.

SERVING SUGGESTION: Enjoy with Fever-Tree Refreshingly Light Indian Tonic Water.

Honey Coconut Gin 41.0%

BOTANICALS: Juniper, Coriander Seed, Toasted Coconut, Cassia, Allspice, Honey, Nutmeg & Dried Fig

TASTING NOTES: Toasted coconut with distinct honey, cassia and allspice on the nose, sweet honey leads with spikes of cassia and allspice on the palate, spice lingers well to finish.

SERVING SUGGESTION: Enjoy with Fever-Tree Premium Indian Tonic Water.

Navy Strength Gin 58.0%

BOTANICALS: Juniper, Coriander Seed, Angelica Root, Orris Root, Orange, Lemon, Lemon Myrtle, Strawberry Gum, Cardamom, Grains of Paradise & Vanilla Bean

TASTING NOTES: Strawberry gum and zesty lemon myrtle lead the nose, bold lemon myrtle with warming citrus undertones on the palate, cardamom spice leads the finish.

SERVING SUGGESTION: Enjoy with Fever-Tree Mediterranean Tonic Water.

Spiced Turkish Delight Gin 41.0%

BOTANICALS: Juniper, Coriander Seed, Clove, Rose Petal, Orange, Vanilla, Cinnamon & Hibiscus

TASTING NOTES: Perfumed florals with candied orange peel and nutty spice on the nose, dried rose, cinnamon and orange peel lead the palate, drying finish with developing baking spice.

SERVING SUGGESTION: Enjoy with Fever-Tree Premium Indian Tonic Water.

Queenscliff Distillery
Queenscliff, VIC

Surrounded by water on three sides in the historic seaside town of Queenscliff at the entrance of Port Phillip, Queenscliff Distillery creates spirits that are inspired by the Bellarine Peninsula and reflect the beauty of their town. They support sustainable practices and local producers, using ethically sourced, local, and organic ingredients when possible to make their range of spirits in their partially solar and wind powered facilities.

Citrus Gin 42.0%

BOTANICALS: Juniper, Orange, Finger Lime, Lemon, Cinnamon & Ginger

TASTING NOTES: Juniper and pithy lime dominate the nose, juniper and lime continue with hints of cassia throughout the palate, persistent lime with lingering spice to finish.

SERVING SUGGESTION: Enjoy with Fever-Tree Premium Indian Tonic Water.

Botanical Gin 42.0%

BOTANICALS: Juniper, Lavender, Elderflower, Rosemary, Native Lemongrass & Angelica Root

TASTING NOTES: Striking lemon myrtle with strong mint and resinous pine oil on the nose, juniper leads with pepper heat, lemon myrtle and dry sea parsley on the palate, angelica and mineral ocean tones to finish.

SERVING SUGGESTION: Enjoy with Fever-Tree Mediterranean Tonic Water.

Navy Gin 57.0%

BOTANICALS: Juniper, Fennel Seed, Native Pepperberry, Cinnamon, Cardamom & Orange

TASTING NOTES: Juniper with angelica, cardamom, and a hint of cinnamon drive the nose, lively spice with sharp pepperberry on the palate, lingering spice and peppery heat to finish.

SERVING SUGGESTION: Enjoy with Fever-Tree Mediterranean Tonic Water.

Red Hen Spirits
Adelaide, SA

Seated right in the heart of Adelaide's burgeoning city centre, Red Hen Spirits is named for the redhen railcars that got its founders to and from school in their childhood. They specialise in making gin with a "say what's on the tin" mentality using local and native flora to craft small batches in a copper column still.

Dry Gin 42.0%

BOTANICALS: Juniper, Coriander Seed, Liquorice, Angelica Root, Cassia, Grains of Paradise, Cubeb Pepper, Lemon Rind, Muntrie, Almond, Rosemary, Celery Leaf & Orris Root

TASTING NOTES: Classic juniper with coriander, angelica and liquorice on the nose, angelica and juniper lead with pink peppercorn and celery on the palate, lingering green apple and rosemary to finish.

SERVING SUGGESTION: Enjoy with Fever-Tree Mediterranean Tonic Water.

Ultra Violet Gin 42.0%

BOTANICALS: Juniper, Coriander Seed, Cassia, Lingon Berry, Lemon Rind, Meadow Sweet, Black Peppercorn, Vanilla & Strawberry Gum (steeped in Butterfly Pea Flower)

TASTING NOTES: Dried citrus peel with touches of berry and soft florals on the nose, hints of vanilla with woody cinnamon, clove and developing florals on the palate, peppery heat with coriander seed to finish.

SERVING SUGGESTION: Enjoy with Fever-Tree Refreshingly Light Indian Tonic Water.

Republic of Fremantle
Fremantle, WA

Anchored in the lively port city of Fremantle on the southern side of the Swan River, Republic of Fremantle is a distillery that pays homage to Western Australia with a philosophy of instilling authenticity, individuality, and character into what they make. They produce their own base spirit from local Verdelho grapes to then create their flagship spirits, controlling the entire process from grape to glass.

Aromatic Gin 42.0%

BOTANICALS: Juniper, Coriander Seed, Lemongrass, Apricot, Lavender, Ginger, Grapefruit & Apple

TASTING NOTES: Bright honey-mead like spice leads the nose, zingy ginger and oily orange citrus on the palate, strong lasting citrus oil to finish.

SERVING SUGGESTION: Enjoy with Fever-Tree Mediterranean Tonic Water.

Full-Bodied Gin 42.0%

BOTANICALS: Juniper, Coriander Seed, Pink Peppercorn, Cranberry, Cinnamon, Clove, Fig & Rosemary

TASTING NOTES: Boyant red berry and a touch of oily herbs on the nose, light juniper with touches of fruit and light forest undertones on the palate, a strong peppery finish.

SERVING SUGGESTION: Enjoy with Fever-Tree Wild Raspberry Tonic Water.

Riverbourne Distillery
Jingera, NSW

Withdrawn amongst the forests of the Tallaganda National Park near Captains Flat in the Southern Tablelands, Riverbourne Distillery is run by a husband and wife team with a focus on handmade spirits and respect for tradition. They use natural spring water from the headwaters of the Molonglo River and mountainous environment to produce spirits with a flavour profile distinct to their region.

No.2 Gin A Shot in the Dark 42.0%

BOTANICALS: Juniper, Angelica Root, Liquorice, Ginger, Allspice & Lisbon Lemon Peel

TASTING NOTES: Allspice and ginger dominate the nose, ginger and allspice continue with light lemon zest and some earthiness on the palate, small touch of liquorice with woody-earth tones to finish.

SERVING SUGGESTION: Enjoy with Fever-Tree Aromatic Tonic Water.

Ruby Wednesday Distillery
Sydney, NSW

Based just down the road from the vibrant Cronulla beach in the southern Sydney suburb of Caringbah, Ruby Wednesday Distillery is named for a figure from their past that hosted a secret gin club during prohibition. They use the recipes from the 1920s along with indigenous Australian organic botanicals to craft their small batch gins.

Seasonal Citrus & Lemon Myrtle 43.0%

BOTANICALS: Juniper, Tangerine, Pomelo, Lemon Myrtle, Native Pepperberry & Others

TASTING NOTES: Pepperleaf backed by dried citrus peel and lemon myrtle on the nose, firm orange with pepper heat and chilli spice on the palate, a hint of menthol and lingering citrus to finish.

SERVING SUGGESTION: Enjoy with Fever-Tree Mediterranean Tonic Water.

Aniseed Myrtle & Star Anise 43.0%

BOTANICALS: Juniper, Aniseed Myrtle, Star Anise, Native Pepperberry & Others

TASTING NOTES: Fennel, star anise, and aniseed myrtle dominate the nose, burst of sweet anise supported by bitter fennel and sweet orange zest on the palate, developing anise spiced tones to finish.

SERVING SUGGESTION: Enjoy with Fever-Tree Mediterranean Tonic Water.

Harrison's Cut Barrel Aged 42.7%

BOTANICALS: Juniper & Others (aged in an American Oak Barrel)

TASTING NOTES: Bursting lemon myrtle with orange blossom on the nose, light lemon oil, woody baking spice and honey undertones on the palate, rich pine with lemon on the finish.

SERVING SUGGESTION: Enjoy neat or with Fever-Tree Ginger Ale.

Navy Strength 57.0%

BOTANICALS: Juniper, Citrus & Others

TASTING NOTES: Oily lemon balm with toasted nuts and cardamom on the nose, big oily lemon leads with peppery heat and mentholic cardamom on the palate, lingering lemon myrtle with spice heat to finish.

SERVING SUGGESTION: Enjoy with Fever-Tree Mediterranean Tonic Water.

Rose Petals & Strawberry Gum 43.0%

BOTANICALS: Juniper, Rose Petals, Strawberry Gum & Others

TASTING NOTES: Stewed strawberry and rhubarb with soft florals on the nose, initial hints of strawberry gum with rich florals of dried rose and jasmine on the palate, growing florals to finish.

SERVING SUGGESTION: Enjoy with Fever-Tree Elderflower Tonic Water.

S.A. Distilling Co.
Adelaide, SA

Produced under contract by Prohibition Liquor Co. in the heart of Adelaide's burgeoning city centre, S.A. Distilling Co. has a mission to showcase botanicals from all over South Australia and make gins that truly represent the region. They put South Australia throughout their products, from botanicals to local designers, printers, packagers, and Adelaide small businesses.

Heaps Good Gin 40.0%

BOTANICALS: Juniper, Orange, Finger Lime, Saltbush, Almond, Pink Peppercorn & Others

TASTING NOTES: Layered citrus with pronounced juniper and a sea breeze undertone on the nose, juniper with strong orange and hints of peppery spice on the palate, lingering citrus with peppery heat to finish.

SERVING SUGGESTION: Enjoy with Fever-Tree Premium Indian Tonic Water.

Native Pink Gin 40.0%

BOTANICALS: Boobialla, Native Currant, Muntrie, Lemon, Red Ruby Grapefruit, Quandong, Lemon Myrtle & Pink Grapefruit

TASTING NOTES: Bright lemon myrtle with fruity red currant on the nose, burst of lemon myrtle with undertones of red currant and strong candied grapefruit on the palate, lingering coriander to finish.

SERVING SUGGESTION: Enjoy with Fever-Tree Mediterranean Tonic Water.

Saint Felix Distillery
Melbourne, VIC

Tucked away in the southern Melbourne suburb of Mordialloc, Saint Felix Distillery focuses on fruit-based spirits that reflect a curiosity for worldly flavours and celebrate the cultural diversity that makes up Australia. They strive to find ingredients that push the boundaries of the distilling process, putting in research to uncover the best ways to champion each ingredient and pay respect to their origins, and using both traditional and innovative technologies.

Wild Forest Gin 42.0%

BOTANICALS: Juniper, Mastic, Orris Root, Cassia, Angelica Root, Coriander Seed, Ginger, Nutmeg, Lemon Myrtle, Bay Leaf, Green Cardamom, Black Peppercorn, Grains of Selim, Long Pepper, Rosemary & Lemon Peel

TASTING NOTES: Prominent pine with rosemary and undertones of bay leaf on the nose, pronounced green herbs with supporting juniper and touches of earth on the palate, sherbet-like lemon myrtle to finish.

SERVING SUGGESTION: Enjoy with Fever-Tree Mediterranean Tonic Water.

Sandy Gray Whisky Company
Spreyton, TAS

Sheltered in the small town of Spreyton just south of Devonport, Sandy Gray Whisky Company was started by two friends with a long association of playing music together and is named for one of their fathers. They distil their spirits in small quantities using premium Tasmanian barley and water from the Central Highlands in pursuit of their mission to create the finest possible spirits.

Sandy Gray Gin 46.0%

BOTANICALS: Juniper, Lime, Native Pepperberry, Cardamom, Cassia & Others

TASTING NOTES: Pine resin with eucalypt notes and pithy lime on the nose, pine led with woody spice and cardamom heat on the palate, subtle nutty notes with a touch of anise to finish.

SERVING SUGGESTION: Enjoy with Fever-Tree Premium Indian Tonic Water.

Seabourne Distillery
Noosaville, QLD

Founded in the relaxing riverside town of Noosaville on the north end of the Sunshine Coast, Seabourne Distillery was started by a local to celebrate the harmony forged between the land and sea, embracing the vibrant soul of Noosa. They make their small batch spirits with local botanicals, from both the land and sea, to capture the areas drifting flow.

Coastal Dry Gin 43.0%

BOTANICALS: Juniper, White Kunzea Flower, Sunrise Lime, River Mint, Native Pepperleaf & Sea Parsley

TASTING NOTES: Fresh oily lime with striking river mint on the nose, light brush of sea spray followed by a green leafy note supported by lemon on the palate, slightly mineral saltiness with fresh minty pepper to finish.

SERVING SUGGESTION: Enjoy with Fever-Tree Mediterranean Tonic Water.

Seppeltsfield Rd Distillers
Marananga, SA

Standing just west of Nuriootpa at the heart of the renowned Barossa Valley wine region, Seppeltsfield Rd Distillers was started by a husband and wife duo and named for the picturesque, palm-lined stretch of road on which it calls home. They are dedicated to producing gins that are bright, fresh, and exciting with a commitment to only using the highest quality ingredients.

Barossa Dry Gin 41.5%

BOTANICALS: Juniper, Coriander Seed, Angelica Root, Yellow Grapefruit, Lavender, Pink Peppercorn & Blue Cornflower

TASTING NOTES: Juniper and coriander lead the nose, initial citrus with classic juniper, angelica and warming coriander on the palate, developing florals with tingling pepper to finish.

SERVING SUGGESTION: Enjoy with Fever-Tree Premium Indian Tonic Water.

Barossa Shiraz Gin 38.5%

BOTANICALS: Juniper, Shiraz Grape, Coriander Seed, Angelica Root, Yellow Grapefruit, Orange, Lavender, Pink Peppercorn, Blue Cornflower, Chamomile, Elderflower, Cinnamon, Borage & Liquorice

TASTING NOTES: Muscatels and dried dark fruits with baking spice and lavender on the nose, sweet baked fruits with spiced pepper heat and a violet note on the palate, drying with a touch of sanded oak to finish.

SERVING SUGGESTION: Enjoy with Fever-Tree Lemon Tonic Water.

House Gin 41.5%

BOTANICALS: Juniper, Coriander Seed, Angelica Root, Yellow Grapefruit, Orange, Lavender, Pink Peppercorn, Blue Cornflower, Chamomile, Elderflower, Cinnamon, Borage & Liquorice

TASTING NOTES: Bright citrus with fresh florals and intermingling juniper on the nose, burst of juniper with chamomile tisane notes and zesty citrus on the palate, angelica and liquorice carry to finish.

SERVING SUGGESTION: Enjoy with Fever-Tree Elderflower Tonic Water.

Musician's Cut Gin 54.5%

BOTANICALS: Juniper, Coriander Seed, Angelica Root, Yellow Grapefruit, Orange, Pink Peppercorn, Liquorice, Lavender, Blue Cornflower, Chamomile, Elderflower, Cinnamon & Borage

TASTING NOTES: Lavender and clove with hints of grapefruit on the nose, pine resin with pink peppercorn and gentle anise on the palate, liquorice sweetness to finish.

SERVING SUGGESTION: Enjoy with Fever-Tree Premium Indian Tonic Water.

Native Ground Gin 42.0%

BOTANICALS: Juniper, Coriander Seed, Native Pepperberry, Peppermint Box, Finger Lime, Lemon Myrtle & Waxflower

TASTING NOTES: Coriander, lemon myrtle and hints of waxflower on the nose, subtle finger lime and waxflower with firm juniper on the palate, lemon oil with a touch of mint to finish.

SERVING SUGGESTION: Enjoy with Fever-Tree Mediterranean Tonic Water.

Savoury Allsorts Gin 41.5%

BOTANICALS: Juniper, Coriander Seed, Angelica Root, Lemon, Yellow Grapefruit, Star Anise, Liquorice, Marjoram, Thyme, Borage & Gentian Root

TASTING NOTES: Dry cooking spice with angelica and green herbs on the nose, pleasant juniper with woody spice, citrus and warming green herbs on the palate, sweet anise to finish.

SERVING SUGGESTION: Enjoy with Fever-Tree Mediterranean Tonic Water.

Settlers Spirits
McLaren Vale, SA

Established between McLaren Vale and McLaren Flat at the epicentre of South Australia's wine industry on the Fleurieu Peninsula, Settlers Spirits believes that botanicals are the natural world's language of joy and splendour. They respect this by hanging and steaming each botanical individually, to preserve and highlight each distinctive characteristic, combining botany and exploration with historical practices that have been given a modern twist.

Rare Dry Gin 43.0%

BOTANICALS: Juniper, Orange Peel, Lemon Myrtle & Native Pepperberry

TASTING NOTES: Lemon myrtle leads with eucalypt tones and pepper spice on the nose, confectionary lemon leads with pepper heat and eucalypt undertones on the palate, lingering sweet lemon with pepper heat to finish.

SERVING SUGGESTION: Enjoy with Fever-Tree Mediterranean Tonic Water.

Juniper 3 Ways 43.0%

BOTANICALS: Juniper & Blood Lime

TASTING NOTES: Distinctive juniper with supporting lime citrus on the nose, upfront strong juniper with delicate zest developing on the palate, lingering warming juniper with a touch of sweetness to finish.

SERVING SUGGESTION: Enjoy with Fever-Tree Premium Indian Tonic Water.

Yuzu Gin 43.0%

BOTANICALS: Juniper, Yuzu & Others

TASTING NOTES: Vibrant fresh yuzu flesh on the nose, layered yuzu showcasing zest, flesh and pith characters with a touch of juniper on the palate, lingering yuzu oil to finish.

SERVING SUGGESTION: Enjoy with Fever-Tree Refreshingly Light Indian Tonic Water.

Seven Seasons
Adelaide, SA

Conceived in the Larrakia country that covers the region around Darwin from Cox Peninsula to Gunn Point, Seven Seasons was founded by an indigenous food entrepreneur and named for the seasons of the Larrakia people. They are a sustainable family business that passes down the knowledge of positive aboriginal culture and traditional harvesting methods which are employed in the collection of native ingredients for their spirits.

Green Ant Gin 42.0%

BOTANICALS: Boobialla, Green Ant, Strawberry Gum, Lemon Myrtle & Native Pepperberry (includes suspended Green Ants)

TASTING NOTES: Jammy strawberry gum with light citrus tones and touches of eucalypt on the nose, sweet ginger and lemon with pleasant slightly sweet fruits on the palate, herbaceous green pepper to finish.

SERVING SUGGESTION: Enjoy with Fever-Tree Mediterranean Tonic Water.

Bush Apple Gin 42.0%

BOTANICALS: Boobialla, Bush Apple, Native Pepperberry, Lemon Myrtle & Finger Lime

TASTING NOTES: Fragrant hints of peach and nectarine with a nutty undertone on the nose, warm creamy stone fruits lead with eucalypt undertones and rosemary on the palate, fruity florals to finish.

SERVING SUGGESTION: Enjoy with Fever-Tree Mediterranean Tonic Water.

Sin Gin Distillery
Perth, WA

Situated at the heart of Western Australia's oldest wine region in the Swan Valley to Perth's northeast, Sin Gin Distillery is a nano-distillery, named for one of its co-founders, with integrity, ambition, and adaptability among their core values. They use local and international botanicals, in particular those that are local to Western Australia, in their range of spirits.

Original Sin 42.0%

BOTANICALS: Juniper, Cardamom Seed, Coriander Seed, Angelica Root, Calamus Root, Lemon Myrtle, Fenugreek Seed, Native Pepperberry, Orris Root, Pomegranate, Quandong, Strawberry Gum & Orange Peel

TASTING NOTES: Light citrus with juniper on the nose, hints of bright herbs with supporting juniper and classic spice on the palate, mellowing classic botanicals leads an oily finish.

SERVING SUGGESTION: Enjoy with Fever-Tree Mediterranean Tonic Water.

Perth Pink 40.0%

BOTANICALS: Juniper, Cardamom Seed, Coriander Seed, Angelica Root, Rosella Flower, Strawberry Gum & Lemon Myrtle

TASTING NOTES: Striking lemon myrtle amidst floral notes on the nose, native gum notes with continuing lemon myrtle on the palate, light florals to round out the finish.

SERVING SUGGESTION: Enjoy with Fever-Tree Mediterranean Tonic Water.

SIP Distillers
Melbourne, VIC

Secreted away in the urban sprawl of dynamic Melbourne, Sip Distillers was started by a brother and sister with a family connection to the Trojan War and who grew up on Greek mythology. They use Australian botanicals and Macedonian juniper in a vapour infusion process, and natural spring water to create their gin that pays homage to their ancestors.

Trogin Golden Apple Gin 40.0%

BOTANICALS: Juniper, Coriander Seed, Angelica Root, Liquorice, Orris Root, Lemon Myrtle, Star Anise & Apple

TASTING NOTES: Sour green apple leads with soft supporting florals on the nose, apple bursts open with perfumed orris and touches of heated spice on the palate, lingering orris with pepperberry and tingling coriander to finish.

SERVING SUGGESTION: Enjoy with Fever-Tree Refreshingly Light Indian Tonic Water.

SoHi Spirits
Bowral, NSW

Secluded in the charming Southern Highlands town of Bowral outside of Sydney, SoHi Spirits was started in pursuit of the good life with passions for gardening and gin, and named for the region. They use ingredients from growers in and around the Southern Highlands to capture the area's feeling along with the design of their bottle.

Garden Envy Gin 41.0%

BOTANICALS: Juniper, Rose, Lavender, Rosemary, Thyme, Orange Peel, Mint, Cress, Pink Peppercorn & Others

TASTING NOTES: Rosemary, lavender and oily thyme on the nose, citrus and lavender with developing thyme and rosemary on the palate, lingering notes of thyme, cinnamon, and clove to finish.

SERVING SUGGESTION: Enjoy with Fever-Tree Mediterranean Tonic Water.

South Coast Distillery
Wollongong, NSW

Set just south of Wollongong's vibrant centre in the suburb of Mount Saint Thomas, South Coast Distillery was born from a group of mates' tradition of 'Martini Thursdays' and the search for the perfect martini gin. They produce a range of different spirits with a focus on responsibility and sustainability by sourcing ingredients from Illawarra-based producers whenever possible.

Sublime Contemporary Gin 40.0%

BOTANICALS: Juniper, Coriander Seed, Caraway, Angelica Root, Cardamom, Dandelion Root, Grains of Paradise, Lemon Myrtle & Grapefruit Peel

TASTING NOTES: Candied citrus with cardamom and caraway on the nose, confectionery lime with cardamom, soft dandelion and a light sea breeze tone on the palate, warming citrus and spice to finish.

SERVING SUGGESTION: Enjoy with Fever-Tree Mediterranean Tonic Water.

Breakwater Navy Strength Gin 57.5%

BOTANICALS: Juniper, Coriander Seed, Caraway, Angelica Root, Cardamom, Dandelion Root, Grains of Paradise, Lemon Myrtle & Grapefruit Peel

TASTING NOTES: Green cardamom with caraway seed, pepper spice and dry citrus on the nose, sappy juniper with caraway seed and menthol spice on the palate, lingering spice with touches of juniper to finish.

SERVING SUGGESTION: Enjoy with Fever-Tree Mediterranean Tonic Water.

Five Islands Old Tom Gin 38.0%

BOTANICALS: Juniper, Coriander Seed, Caraway, Angelica Root, Cardamom, Dandelion Root, Grains of Paradise, Lemon Myrtle & Grapefruit (macerated in WuYi Mountain Oolong Tea)

TASTING NOTES: Caraway and dandelion lead the nose, sweet black tea with lavender, subtle pepper spice and pine undertones on the palate, sweet herbal tones to finish.

SERVING SUGGESTION: Enjoy with Fever-Tree Mediterranean Tonic Water.

Southern Wild Distillery
DASHER + FISHER
Tasmanian Gin

Devonport, TAS

Occupying a spot in the thriving centre of Devonport that acts as 'The Gateway to Tasmania' on the northern coast, Dasher + Fisher specialises in gins that speak of place and is named after two rivers that run from the snowmelt of Cradle Mountain through green meadows to the ocean. They use ingredients from dozens of family-run businesses across Tasmania with a desire to create spirits that embrace the seasons and all their beautiful imperfections.

Dasher + Fisher Ocean Gin 42.0%

BOTANICALS: Juniper, Wakame Seaweed, Chilli, Rose Petal, Nori, Jasmine & Others

TASTING NOTES: Chilli leads with a sea breeze and dried tea undertone on the nose, juniper, angelica and seaweed on the palate, rose undertones and angelica driven finish with a touch of sea breeze.

SERVING SUGGESTION: Enjoy with Fever-Tree Mediterranean Tonic Water.

Dasher + Fisher Sloe Gin 29.5%

BOTANICALS: Juniper, Sloe Berry & Others

TASTING NOTES: Ripe dark plum with black cherry on the nose, white pepper and cardamom spice with subtle sweetness on the palate, bright acidity and brambly finish.

SERVING SUGGESTION: Enjoy with Fever-Tree Lemon Tonic Water.

Spirit of Little Things
Perth, WA

Nestled in the eclectic and multicultural suburb of Subiaco in western Perth, Spirit of Little Things is a distillery passionate about producing small batch gins that are quintessentially Australian, to capture the essence of the sunburnt country. They focus on the exclusive use of Australian native botanicals in their core range with a bush to bottle process.

Signature Gin 40.0%

BOTANICALS: Juniper, Coriander Seed, Cardamom, Orange, Desert Lime, Star Anise & Cassia

TASTING NOTES: Strong orange with hints of gum and star anise on the nose, juniper with continuing orange and anise tones on the palate, lingering spice and citrus with light eucalypt notes to finish.

SERVING SUGGESTION: Enjoy with Fever-Tree Mediterranean Tonic Water.

Australian Botanical Gin 43.0%

BOTANICALS: Juniper, Native Thyme, Strawberry Gum, Lemon Myrtle & Finger Lime

TASTING NOTES: Oily lemon myrtle with eucalypt tones and hints of star anise on the nose, upfront river mint with lemon myrtle and drying pepper, on the palate, anise, pepper and lemon linger to finish.

SERVING SUGGESTION: Enjoy with Fever-Tree Mediterranean Tonic Water.

Australian Dry Gin 40.0%

BOTANICALS: Juniper, Coriander Seed, Orange, Aniseed Myrtle & Saltbush

TASTING NOTES: Pronounced river mint with pine needle and subtle liquorice on the nose, aniseed myrtle and star anise lead with angelica and dry thyme on the palate, oily orange to finish.

SERVING SUGGESTION: Enjoy with Fever-Tree Mediterranean Tonic Water.

Navy Strength Gin 58.0%

BOTANICALS: Juniper, Lemon Myrtle, Finger Lime, Native Thyme, Saltbush & Strawberry Gum

TASTING NOTES: Strawberry gum with river mint and touches of eucalypt on the nose, striking anise with strawberry gum and lemon myrtle on the palate, bitter nuttiness with driving pepper spice to finish.

SERVING SUGGESTION: Enjoy with Fever-Tree Mediterranean Tonic Water.

Tempranillo Gin 38.0%

BOTANICALS: Juniper, Saltbush & Others (macerated in Tempranillo Grape and then blended with Tempranillo Grape Juice)

TASTING NOTES: Buttery caramel with sea parsley and hints of menthol on the nose, slight leather with dried dark fruits and sea parsley on the palate, rich-chewy tannin with hints of saltiness to finish.

SERVING SUGGESTION: Enjoy with Fever-Tree Lemon Tonic Water.

Spring Bay Distillery
Spring Beach, TAS

Looking out at the tranquil Maria Island from the pretty Spring Beach on Tasmania's east coast, Spring Bay Distillery is the realisation of a dream for its co-owners with their long shared love of spirits. They use rainwater that is naturally salty from the sea in their products to add a subtle marine influence and ensure that they capture the oils from their spirit distillation while leaning heavily on tradition.

Spring Bay Gin 46.0%

BOTANICALS: Juniper, Coriander Seed, Cassia, Liquorice, Cardamom, Lemon Peel, Orris Root, Angelica Root, Wattleseed & Native Pepperberry

TASTING NOTES: Rich creamy nose with hints of green herbs on the nose, coriander with sweet juniper and peppery heat on the palate, tingling pepper with developing pine to finish.

SERVING SUGGESTION: Enjoy with Fever-Tree Mediterranean Tonic Water.

Pink Gin 40.0%

BOTANICALS: Juniper, Coriander Seed, Cassia, Liquorice, Cardamom, Lemon Peel, Orris Root, Angelica Root, Wattleseed, Native Pepperberry & Raspberry

TASTING NOTES: Bright raspberry and strawberry notes with rosella on the nose, creamy raspberry with cardamom and subtle lemon myrtle on the palate, lingering citrus and spice to finish.

SERVING SUGGESTION: Enjoy with Fever-Tree Wild Raspberry Tonic Water.

St Agnes Distillery
Renmark, SA

Sequestered away in flourishing Renmark at the heart of the Riverlands on the Murray River, St Agnes Distillery is one of the oldest craft distilleries in Australia, with a purpose of showing the world another face of Australian produce excellence. They make a range of premium spirits including brandy, whisky, and Australia's first fully certified organic gin.

Blind Tiger Organic Gin 42.7%

BOTANICALS: Juniper, Cassia, Coriander Seed, Angelica Root, Citrus Peel, Summer Savory & Liquorice

TASTING NOTES: Subtle juniper with light citrus and herbs on the nose, initial pine with liquorice root and tart lemon on the palate, subtle liquorice sweetness with lingering lemon to finish.

SERVING SUGGESTION: Enjoy with Fever-Tree Mediterranean Tonic Water.

Blind Tiger Organic Mandarin Gin 42.7%

BOTANICALS: Juniper, Cassia, Coriander Seed, Angelica Root, Citrus Peel, Summer Savory, Liquorice, Dancy Mandarin & Imperial Mandarin

TASTING NOTES: Mandarin, green pine and coriander on the nose, sweet mandarin with touches of juniper on the palate, sweet mandarin continues well with earthy undertone to finish.

SERVING SUGGESTION: Enjoy with Fever-Tree Mediterranean Tonic Water.

Stableviews Distillery
Springfield, WA

Housed on a family farm along the breath-taking Coral Coast near Dongara, Stableviews Distillery takes its name from the family farm and is a sister distillery to Illegal Tender Rum Co. with limited releases, one-off products, and seasonal spirits at the heart of their mantra. They make their own base spirit and use a medley of far-fetched and Australian botanicals to create their products.

Abrolhos Gin 40.0%

BOTANICALS: Juniper, Green Cardamom, Coriander Seed, Liquorice, Angelica Root, Cassia, Clove, Lemon Peel & Lime Peel (steeped in Grey Saltbush and Beaded Samphire)

TASTING NOTES: Cassia leads with lime zest on the nose, intense dry cooking spice and savoury notes on the palate, lingering spice and sweet lemon drive the finish.

SERVING SUGGESTION: Enjoy with Fever-Tree Premium Indian Tonic Water.

Strait Distillery
Beaconsfield, TAS

Located near the former gold mining town of Beaconsfield in the idyllic Tamar Valley north of Launceston, Strait Distillery is a luxury spirits company that prides itself on being a pioneer and supporter of innovation. They use locally grown and organic produce along with Tasmanian spring water in the creation of the range of spirits.

Strait 8 Dry 40.0%

BOTANICALS: Juniper & Others

TASTING NOTES: Juniper with floral lemon myrtle and pronounced lavender on the nose, mild pine with oily lemon and creamy rose blossoms on the palate, orange blossom and lavender building to finish.

SERVING SUGGESTION: Enjoy with Fever-Tree Elderflower Tonic Water.

Cameo Tasmanian Berry Gin 40.0%

BOTANICALS: Juniper, Raspberry, Strawberry, Blueberry & Others

TASTING NOTES: Distinct mixed berry jam on the nose, tart-fruity berries building and notes of sour cranberry juice on the palate, drying tannin to finish.

SERVING SUGGESTION: Enjoy with Fever-Tree Wild Raspberry Tonic Water.

Tasmanian Sloe Gin 40.0%

BOTANICALS: Juniper & Others (macerated in Sloe)

TASTING NOTES: Sloe berry with black cherries in syrup on the nose, rich sloe dominates with a sweet jamminess on the palate, dry and slightly chalky texture to finish.

SERVING SUGGESTION: Enjoy with Fever-Tree Lemon Tonic Water.

Tasmanian Strawberry Gin 40.0%

BOTANICALS: Juniper & Others (macerated in Strawberry)

TASTING NOTES: Stewed strawberry jamminess with a touch of baking spice on the nose, stewed strawberry with almond creaminess and fresh menthol on the palate, strawberry jam and herbaceous sweetness to finish.

SERVING SUGGESTION: Enjoy with Fever-Tree Wild Raspberry Tonic Water.

Styx Brewery and Distillery
Newcastle, NSW

Cloistered on either side by Throsby Creek and Hunter River in the suburb of Carrington next to the Port of Newcastle, Styx Brewery and Distillery was started by a scientist and a baker, naming it after the creek that runs through Newcastle and the link to the underworld in Greek mythology. They use foraged and locally sourced ingredients in the brews and spirits that pay homage to the Ferryman, Charon.

Achilles Gin 42.0%

BOTANICALS: Juniper, Lemon Myrtle, Strawberry Gum, Grapefruit, Makrut Lime, Orange & Others

TASTING NOTES: Pronounced strawberry gum, juicy citrus flesh and a light salty breeze on the nose, strawberry gum leads with sharp citrus peel on the palate, citrus continues with fruity florals to finish.

SERVING SUGGESTION: Enjoy with Fever-Tree Mediterranean Tonic Water.

Amato Small Batch Gin 42.0%

BOTANICALS: Juniper, Sencha Tea, Kumquat, Mandarin & Sancho Pepper

TASTING NOTES: Green tea with sweet mandarin and hints of sea breeze on the nose, savoury coastal notes with bitter tea leaves, mandarin oil and dry herbs on the palate, sea breeze with sweet citrus to finish..

SERVING SUGGESTION: Enjoy with Fever-Tree Aromatic Tonic Water.

Floral Small Batch Gin 42.0%

BOTANICALS: Juniper, Chrysanthemum, Chamomile, Sugar Plum, Sunrise Lime & Lavender

TASTING NOTES: Sweet chrysanthemum and daisy with bee pollen and sweet lemon thyme on the nose, striking florals with building bright citrus on the palate, lengthy lavender to finish.

SERVING SUGGESTION: Enjoy with Fever-Tree Elderflower Tonic Water.

Summerleas Distillery
Hobart, TAS

Huddled amongst the foothills of Kunanyi/Mt Wellington in the quiet southern Hobart suburb of Kingston, Summerleas Distillery is owned and operated by a 7th generation Tasmanian, taking its name from the local area and its distinct microclimate. They use Tasmanian and international ingredients to craft their range of small batch spirits with a one-shot distillation method while recycling, reusing, and re-circulating everything to avoid waste.

Dry Gin 43.0%

BOTANICALS: Juniper, Coriander Seed, Cardamom, Angelica Root, Orris Root & Tangerine

TASTING NOTES: Tangerine with musky orris, coriander and soft pine on the nose, leading violet note with cardamom, tangerine and juniper on the palate, earthy spice with supporting citrus to finish.

SERVING SUGGESTION: Enjoy with Fever-Tree Premium Indian Tonic Water.

Blackberry Gin 40.0%

BOTANICALS: Juniper, Coriander Seed, Cardamom Seed, Orange & Blackberry

TASTING NOTES: Coriander with cardamom spice and orange oil on the nose, upfront coriander with earthy spice and developing angelica on the palate, lingering dried fruits with florals to finish.

SERVING SUGGESTION: Enjoy with Fever-Tree Premium Indian Tonic Water.

Navy Gin 57.0%

BOTANICALS: Juniper, Coriander Seed, Cardamom, Angelica Root & Citrus Peel

TASTING NOTES: Coriander seed with white pepper and subtle citrus on the nose, oily lemon and lime with eucalyptus tones on the palate, oily citrus continues and mellows to finish.

SERVING SUGGESTION: Enjoy with Fever-Tree Mediterranean Tonic Water.

Sunny Hill Distillery
Arthurton, SA

Founded just outside Arthurton in the middle of the wonderful Yorke Peninsula near Adelaide, Sunny Hill Distillery is a farm-based, partially solar-powered, micro-distillery owned and operated by a husband and wife duo. They grow their own barley and wheat to use in making their vodka, base spirit, and whisky, along with rainwater, in a 'crop to drop' format for their spirits.

Dry Gin 45.0%

BOTANICALS: Juniper, Angelica Root, Orris Root, Coriander Seed, Cassia & Lemon Myrtle

TASTING NOTES: Baking spice and earthy musk open on the nose, perfumed violet with traces of resin and subtle spice developing on the palate, hints of earthy tones on the finish.

SERVING SUGGESTION: Enjoy with Fever-Tree Premium Indian Tonic Water.

Pink Gin 45.0%

BOTANICALS: Juniper, Raspberry, Strawberry Gum, Heritage Rose, Liquorice, Lemon Balm & Angelica Root

TASTING NOTES: Candied strawberry gum with sharp lemon on the nose, pronounced strawberry gum with developing rose florals and a touch of lemon on the palate, rose drives with drying strawberry gum to finish.

SERVING SUGGESTION: Enjoy with Fever-Tree Elderflower Tonic Water.

Sunset Gin
Mildura, VIC

Planted south of Mildura in the rich horticultural region of Sunraysia along the Murray River, Sunset Gin was conceived whilst drinking one sunny evening on a family vineyard committed to experimenting and finding new applications for there sultanas. They use sultanas from their vineyard and botanicals from their other farms to make gin that celebrates the region.

Golden Tommy 42.0%

BOTANICALS: Juniper, Sunmuscat Sultana, Orange, Almond, Lemon Myrtle, Native Pepperberry, Coriander Seed & Cardamom

TASTING NOTES: Slightly confectionery lemon with warming anise spice on the nose, warming pepper with bursting citrus and root spice on the palate, thick liquorice sweetness to finish.

SERVING SUGGESTION: Enjoy with Fever-Tree Premium Indian Tonic Water.

Sunshine & Sons
Woombye, QLD

Inaugurated in relaxed Woombye amongst the hinterland rainforest of the Sunshine Coast, Sunshine & Sons was born out of a bit of nostalgia, a why-not attitude, and a few lucky coincidences by four blokes in an empty shed. They make their pot-distilled spirits to evoke the allure and warmth of Queensland's subtropical coast while focusing on preserving the environment.

Original Dry Gin 43.0%

BOTANICALS: Juniper, Coriander Seed, Lemon Peel, Cinnamon, Lavender, Rose Petal, Pomegranate, Native Pepperberry & Orris Root

TASTING NOTES: Lavender, cinnamon and a hint of lemon on the nose, lemon and coriander with rose undertone on the palate, lingering violet with juniper to finish.

SERVING SUGGESTION: Enjoy with Fever-Tree Refreshingly Light Indian Tonic Water.

Barrel Aged Gin 43.0%

BOTANICALS: Juniper, Coriander Seed, Lemon Peel, Cinnamon, Lavender, Rose Petal, Pomegranate, Native Pepperberry & Orris Root (aged in ex-Sherry French Oak Barrels)

TASTING NOTES: Cedar spice over almond meal on the nose, notes of sweet baked cinnamon, angelica and sweet citrus oil on the palate, developing pine and lingering spice to finish.

SERVING SUGGESTION: Enjoy neat or with Fever-Tree Ginger Ale.

Pineapple Parfait Gin 38.0%

BOTANICALS: Juniper, Coriander Seed, Orris Root, Pineapple, Passionfruit, Strawberry, Coconut & Vanilla

TASTING NOTES: Juicy pineapple and tart passionfruit lead the nose, classic juniper and coriander with tart fruit notes and coconut on the palate, lingering tart passionfruit with subtle florals to finish.

SERVING SUGGESTION: Enjoy with Fever-Tree Refreshingly Light Indian Tonic Water.

Taka Gin Co
Melbourne, VIC

Positioned in the colourful Melbourne suburb of West Footscray, Taka Gin Co is an Indigenous owned and operated native fusion gin company that takes its name from the Gundijmara word for taste and focuses on blending Australian native botanicals in their spirits. They draw on knowledge from their founder's Indigenous heritage in combination with native ingredients and local suppliers to capture the taste and smell of Australia.

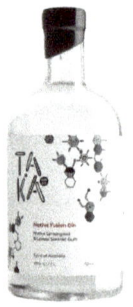

Native Fusion Gin 40.0%

BOTANICALS: Juniper, Coriander Seed, Angelica Root, Cassia, Finger Lime, Orris Root, Native Lemongrass, Lemon-Scented Gum Leaf & Desert Lime

TASTING NOTES: Striking lemongrass with lemon verbena and slight menthol note on the nose, cinnamon with desert lime and lemon verbena on the palate, mentholic finger lime lingers to finish.

SERVING SUGGESTION: Enjoy with Fever-Tree Mediterranean Tonic Water.

Tamborine Mountain Distillery
Tamborine Mountain, QLD

Stationed in Tamborine Mountain amongst the peaceful hinterland of the Gold Coast, Tamborine Mountain Distillery began as a family distillery on a renovated orchard before moving and expanding. They use a range of natural ingredients and native flora with multiple distillations and artisanal processes passed down through its founder's Russian and Ukrainian heritage to make their spirits.

Davidson Plum Gin 40.0%

BOTANICALS: Juniper, Coriander Seed, Lemon Peel, Orange Peel, Angelica Root & Davidson Plum

TASTING NOTES: Light plum fragrance with coriander and subtle citrus on the nose, plum and citrus lead with hints of coriander on the palate, mild sweetness and light spice to finish.

SERVING SUGGESTION: Enjoy with Fever-Tree Premium Indian Tonic Water.

Ginger & Rhubarb Gin 40.0%

BOTANICALS: Juniper, Coriander Seed, Lemon Peel, Orange Peel, Angelica Root, Ginger & Rhubarb

TASTING NOTES: Ginger and rhubarb lead with hints of creamy vanilla sweetness on the nose, upfront ginger with subtle rhubarb and touches of citrus on the palate, ginger and lemon linger well to finish.

SERVING SUGGESTION: Enjoy with Fever-Tree Ginger Ale.

Lilly Pilly Gin 40.0%

BOTANICALS: Juniper, Coriander Seed, Lemon Peel, Orange Peel, Angelica Root & Lilly Pilly

TASTING NOTES: Aromatic vanilla with coriander and subtle florals on the nose, creamy rhubarb with musky florals on the palate, developing tart fruit notes and florals to finish.

SERVING SUGGESTION: Enjoy with Fever-Tree Elderflower Tonic Water.

Tar Barrel Brewery & Distillery
Mornington, VIC

Anchored in the relaxed beachside town of Mornington on the east coast of Port Phillip, Tar Barrel Brewery & Distillery is named for a corner in nearby Red Hill where tar barrels were stored during road building on the Mornington Peninsula. They brew and distil with a philosophy of being local and using local, creating a range of craft beers, gin, whisky, and vodka.

Gunnamatta New World Dry Gin 40.0%

BOTANICALS: Juniper, Angelica Root, Lemon, Cardamom, Coriander Seed, Native Pepperberry, Orris Root, Wattleseed & Citra Hop

TASTING NOTES: Roasted wattleseed with heated pepperleaf on the nose, woody nuts with warming dark wattleseed on the palate, cardamom and orris rounding out the finish.

SERVING SUGGESTION: Enjoy with Fever-Tree Aromatic Tonic Water.

Cerberus Navy Gin 58.0%

BOTANICALS: Juniper, Angelica Root, Cascara, Coriander Seed, Gentian Root, Geraldton Wax, Grains of Paradise, Honey, Native Basil, Orris Root, Native Pepperberry, White Kunzea & Mosaic Hop

TASTING NOTES: Honey nougat with subtle geraldton wax, gentian and wormwood on the nose, strong dry spice with woody elements and cherry pith on the palate, liquorice root and angelica linger to finish.

SERVING SUGGESTION: Enjoy with Fever-Tree Premium Indian Tonic Water.

That Spirited Lot Distillers
Melbourne, VIC

Established in the scenic Seaford suburb of southern Melbourne, That Spirited Lot Distillers is independently owned and operated, and began as an idea between two brothers wanting to capture the love for flavours and travelling in a project together, then joined by two sisters. They specialise in producing one-shot pot and column distilled gins made from Australian grape spirit while maintaining environmentally sustainable production and waste management.

Ninch Dry Gin 43.0%

BOTANICALS: Juniper, Coriander Seed, Orris Root, Angelica Root, Ruby Red Grapefruit & Lemon Peel

TASTING NOTES: Zesty bright citrus with pine and earthy coriander on the nose, citrus and pine lead with earthy perfumed elements and fresh flowers on the palate, lingering orris and pine to finish.

SERVING SUGGESTION: Enjoy with Fever-Tree Premium Indian Tonic Water.

Hawker Market Gin 43.0%

BOTANICALS: Juniper, Makrut Lime, Ginger, Lemongrass, Toasted Coconut & Lime

TASTING NOTES: Dried ginger and lime leaf with hints of coconut on the nose, zesty freshness and coriander seed supporting sappy pine on the palate, developing fresh rosemary and marjoram to finish.

SERVING SUGGESTION: Enjoy with Fever-Tree Mediterranean Tonic Water.

Island Flower Gin 43.0%

BOTANICALS: Juniper, Coriander Seed, Dried Apple, Fig, Hibiscus, Lemon Peel & Others

TASTING NOTES: Crisp red apple with sweet florals and dried fig tones on the nose, baking spice with dried fruit, sweet hibiscus and coriander on the palate, warming clove and cinnamon to finish.

SERVING SUGGESTION: Enjoy with Fever-Tree Elderflower Tonic Water.

That House Pour 40.0%

BOTANICALS: Juniper, Coriander Seed, Angelica Root & Lemon Peel

TASTING NOTES: Warm coriander seed and resinous juniper on the nose, bold juniper with driving citrus and heated coriander on the plate, pine resin lingers with developing orris to finish.

SERVING SUGGESTION: Enjoy with Fever-Tree Premium Indian Tonic Water.

The Gram Bizarre Gin 40.0%

BOTANICALS: Juniper, Coriander Seed, Rose, Pistachio, Ginger & Lemon Peel

TASTING NOTES: Pronounced lemon with rose water and ginger undertones on the nose, bright pistachio nuttiness with fresh ginger on the palate, lingering lemon and green cardamom to finish.

SERVING SUGGESTION: Enjoy with Fever-Tree Mediterranean Tonic Water.

The Abel Gin Co.
Launceston, TAS

Huddled on the bank of the River Tamar in lively yet laid-back Launceston, The Abel Gin Co. was started by two women with a focus on producing quality gins designed to please and delight rather than confront or challenge while sharing the spirit of Tasmania. They only use freshly harvested botanicals, including those foraged from around Tasmania, to make their spirits.

Essence Gin 42.0%

BOTANICALS: Juniper, Coriander Seed, Angelica Root, Kunzea Leaf, Native Pepperberry, Seville Orange, Lisbon Lemon Zest & Citrus

TASTING NOTES: Strong orange peel with hints of green herbs on the nose, orange leads with a touch of juniper and pepper on the palate, citrus oil and spice lead the finish.

SERVING SUGGESTION: Enjoy with Fever-Tree Mediterranean Tonic Water.

Quintessence Gin 42.0%

BOTANICALS: Juniper, Coriander Seed, Damask Rose Petal, Smoky Tea Tree Blossom, Ruby Red Grapefruit, Lisbon Lemon Zest & Citrus

TASTING NOTES: Lemon and lime lead with pine resin and a slight mineral tone on the nose, sappy pine resin leads with nutty characteristics and mineral undertones on the palate, pine carries with hazelnut to finish.

SERVING SUGGESTION: Enjoy with Fever-Tree Mediterranean Tonic Water.

The Aisling Distillery
Griffith, NSW

Situated amongst the fresh produce and heritage of Griffith in the beautiful Riverina, The Aisling Distillery is family-run and started as a way to connect with their founder's Scottish heritage by making something from their past. They specialise in making small batch premium single malt whisky, rum, and gin with the aim of capturing the Riverina's beauty.

Pepperberry Classic Dry Gin 45.0%

BOTANICALS: Juniper, Native Pepperberry, Cinnamon & Allspice

TASTING NOTES: Pepper heat with cinnamon spice on the nose, pepper heat leads with cinnamon and allspice developing on the palate, tingling pepper spice to finish.

SERVING SUGGESTION: Enjoy with Fever-Tree Aromatic Tonic Water.

Murrumbidgee Dry Gin 45.0%

BOTANICALS: Juniper, Coriander Seed, Orange, Orris Root, Cassia & Angelica Root

TASTING NOTES: Oily orange peel on the nose, candied orange with a subtle green vegetal undertone and a hint of saltiness on the palate, zesty citrus with a fresh minty finish.

SERVING SUGGESTION: Enjoy with Fever-Tree Murrumbidgee Dry Gin.

Triple Juniper Gin Elderflower 42.5%

BOTANICALS: Juniper, Coriander Seed, Orange, Orris Root, Cassia, Angelica Root, Elderflower & Red Gum Honey

TASTING NOTES: Valencia oranges, earthy resin and hints of raisin on the nose, dusty green herbs with touches of honey and earthy musk on the palate, earthiness develops with juniper holding to finish.

SERVING SUGGESTION: Enjoy with Fever-Tree Premium Indian Tonic Water.

Triple Juniper Gin Elderflower 51.0%

BOTANICALS: Juniper, Coriander Seed, Orange, Orris Root, Cassia, Angelica Root, Elderflower & Red Gum Honey

TASTING NOTES: Spring time bouquet of florals with pronounced elderflower on the nose, initial honey with elderflower and angelica root on the palate, warming juniper and coriander to finish.

SERVING SUGGESTION: Enjoy with Fever-Tree Elderflower Tonic Water.

The Antipodes Gin Co.
Canberra, ACT

Settled in the northern Canberra suburb of Mitchell, The Antipodes Gin Co. is an ethical and sustainable spirits enterprise started by three close childhood friends that is certified organic and carbon neutral. They don't use any GMOs or ingredients that have been exposed to pesticides in their spirits while working alongside like-minded suppliers and farmers to share Australia's rarest flavours.

Antipodes Gin 45.0%

BOTANICALS: Juniper, Orange, Lemon Peel, Lemon Myrtle, Native Pepperberry & Others

TASTING NOTES: Lemon verbena leads the nose, lemon myrtle intertwined with orange peel followed by floral violet notes and subtle juniper on the palate, warming lemon to finish.

SERVING SUGGESTION: Enjoy with Fever-Tree Mediterranean Tonic Water.

Chai Gin 40.0%

BOTANICALS: Juniper, Ceylon Tea, Cinnamon, Chamomile, Fennel Seed, Native Pepperberry, Vanilla, Cardamom, Coriander Seed & Others

TASTING NOTES: Sweet baking spice leads the nose, fragrant fennel, cinnamon and dried tea leaves on the palate, creamy texture with pepperberry and tea notes lingering to finish.

SERVING SUGGESTION: Enjoy with Fever-Tree Aromatic Tonic Water.

Juniper3 40.0%

BOTANICALS: Juniper, Coriander Seed, Native Pepperberry & White Pepper

TASTING NOTES: Dried pinewood shavings with earthy juniper on the nose, pepperberry with green herbaceous characters and a lingering woody spice on the palate, hot pepper with wood shavings to finish.

SERVING SUGGESTION: Enjoy with Fever-Tree Premium Indian Tonic Water.

Oceanic Gin 40.0%

BOTANICALS: Juniper, Saltbush, Wakame Seaweed, Desert Lime, Geraldton Wax, Lemon Myrtle, Pink Peppercorn & Wasabi

TASTING NOTES: Salty juniper with native thyme and lemon aspen on the nose, slightly sweet saltbush with lime, pine resin and liquorice on the palate, developing saltbush with cinnamon and lemon oil to finish.

SERVING SUGGESTION: Enjoy with Fever-Tree Mediterranean Tonic Water.

Pink Gin 40.0%

BOTANICALS: Juniper, Blue Chamomile Flower, Kakadu Plum, Strawberry Gum, Grapefruit & Olida

TASTING NOTES: Wild native botanicals of lilly pilly and lemon myrtle on the nose, sweet summer fruits laid over wattleseed and a lightly sweet spice on the palate, peppery cinnamon twist to finish.

SERVING SUGGESTION: Enjoy with Fever-Tree Premium Indian Tonic Water.

The Craft & Co

THE CRAFT & CO — Melbourne, VIC

Seated in the hip Melbourne suburb of Collingwood, known for its music scene and converted warehouses, The Craft & Co is a distillery, brewery, and winery that prides itself on being one of the first micro-distilleries to open in Melbourne. They produce a wide range of spirits including liqueurs, grappa, amaro, limoncello, rum, whisky, and gin.

Collingwood Dry Gin 42.0%

BOTANICALS: Juniper, Coriander Seed, Angelica Root, Lemon Myrtle, Finger Lime, Orris Root & Blue Gum Eucalyptus

TASTING NOTES: Eucalyptus resin with supporting menthol on the nose, distinct juniper with dry spice, coriander seed and lemon myrtle on the palate, lasting zest with spice undertones to finish.

SERVING SUGGESTION: Enjoy with Fever-Tree Mediterranean Tonic Water.

Distiller's Cut Gin 48.0%

BOTANICALS: Juniper, Preserved Lemon, Coriander Seed, Orange Peel, Lemon Peel, Bitter Orange Peel, Grapefruit Peel, Lime Peel, Honey, Macadamia, Angelica Root, Aniseed Myrtle, Lemon Myrtle, Cassia, Cinnamon, Native Pepperleaf, Saltbush, Orris Root, Spearmint, Cardamom, Caraway Seed, Lavender, Fennel Seed, Tonka Bean & Nutmeg

TASTING NOTES: Eucalyptus with strong lemon myrtle and spice undertones on the nose, juniper leads with zesty citrus and growing herbal tones on the palate, developing hints of honey with citrus lingering to finish.

SERVING SUGGESTION: Enjoy with Fever-Tree Mediterranean Tonic Water.

Gingerbread Gin 40.0%

BOTANICALS: Juniper, Cinnamon, Nutmeg, Clove, Tonka Bean & Ginger

TASTING NOTES: Distinctive ginger with cinnamon, clove and nutmeg on the nose, sweet Christmas spice with dark Tonka bean notes on the palate, dry warming ginger and dark spice to finish.

SERVING SUGGESTION: Enjoy with Fever-Tree Ginger Ale.

Gingerbread Gin Liqueur 25.0%

BOTANICALS: Juniper, Cinnamon, Nutmeg, Clove, Tonka Bean & Ginger

TASTING NOTES: Striking Tonka bean with clove and ginger driving the nose, sweet Christmas spice leads with dark Tonka notes throughout the palate, spicy ginger and chocolate covered fruits to finish.

SERVING SUGGESTION: Enjoy with Fever-Tree Ginger Ale.

Navy Strength Gin 57.0%

BOTANICALS: Juniper, Paprika, Fennel Seed, Cumin, Black Peppercorn, Pink Peppercorn, Hazelnut, Almond, Sesame Seed & Others

TASTING NOTES: Fennel with almond and sesame drive the nose, sharp pepper spice with conifer supported by lengthy hazelnut and sesame on the palate, lasting almond nougat to finish.

SERVING SUGGESTION: Enjoy with Fever-Tree Premium Indian Tonic Water.

Old Tom Gin 45.0%

BOTANICALS: Juniper, Coriander Seed, Angelica Root, Lemon Myrtle, Finger Lime, Orris Root & Blue Gum Eucalyptus

TASTING NOTES: Woody sap with angelica, eucalyptus, and lime on the nose, woody orris with juniper, clove, and coriander on the palate, lemon myrtle and coriander linger to finish.

SERVING SUGGESTION: Enjoy with Fever-Tree Premium Indian Tonic Water.

The Derwent Distilling Co.
Dromedary, TAS

Sitting just outside the small town of Dromedary along the Derwent River to the northeast of Hobart, The Derwent Distilling Co. was started by a couple with lots of experience in the Tasmanian distilling industry who wanted to branch out and explore their own style. They prioritise local ingredients, supporting local businesses, and reducing their carbon footprint in the making of their spirits.

Last Sanctuary Organic Gin 45.0%

BOTANICALS: Juniper, Scented Paperbark, Coastal Tea Tree, Bull Kelp, Coriander Seed, Lemon, Lime & Others

TASTING NOTES: Aromatic oregano with basil, bay leaf, and woody notes on the nose, woody herbs with angelica and lemon balm on the palate, woody notes develop with a lemon undertone to finish.

SERVING SUGGESTION: Enjoy with Fever-Tree Mediterranean Tonic Water.

Last Sanctuary Pink Gin 45.0%

BOTANICALS: Juniper, Lychee, Damask Rose, Rhubarb, Chamomile, Coriander Seed, Cardamom & Others

TASTING NOTES: Rich creaminess with thyme and cinnamon on the nose, creamy rhubarb with hints of lemon myrtle and undertones of green herbs on the palate, drying herbs with touches of fruitiness to finish.

SERVING SUGGESTION: Enjoy with Fever-Tree Mediterranean Tonic Water.

The Melbourne Gin Company
Melbourne, VIC

Tucked away in the foothills of the Dandenong Ranges just outside of Melbourne, The Melbourne Gin Company was started by a winemaker seeking to doff his hat to London Dry Gin by merging his twin loves for gin martinis and his hometown. They make their gin in stills originally designed for making perfume with a non-chill filtered process and a twist of Melbourne.

Dry Gin 42.0%

BOTANICALS: Juniper, Coriander Seed, Grapefruit, Orange, Honey Myrtle, Orris Root, Angelica Root, Sandalwood, Macadamia, Cassia & Rosemary

TASTING NOTES: Rosemary and lifted citrus with a hint of fresh cut wood on the nose, upfront herbs and orris with harmonious zest and warming coriander on the palate, dry nutty linger with warming juniper to finish.

SERVING SUGGESTION: Enjoy with Fever-Tree Mediterranean Tonic Water.

Single Shot Gin 47.4%

BOTANICALS: Juniper, Bergamot, Orange, Angelica Root, Green Cardamom, Lavender & Leatherwood Honey

TASTING NOTES: Pronounced juniper and sharp orange with earthy undertones on the nose, juniper supported by lavende and coriander on the palate, lingering orange with light florals and strong cardamom to finish.

SERVING SUGGESTION: Enjoy with Fever-Tree Premium Indian Tonic Water.

The Splendid Gin
Cranbrook, TAS

Sequestered in the emerging viticulture region around Cranbrook on the central east coast of Tasmania, The Splendid Gin is a distillery that prides itself on innovation with a sole focus on gin and related gin mixers. They aim to produce high quality spirits that speak of the Tasmanian East Coast and its beauty using pure Tasmanian spring water and a triple distilled grape base spirit.

Purity and Obscurity 42.0%

BOTANICALS: Juniper, Coriander Seed, Lemon, Lime, Mandarin, Bergamot, Rosemary & Angelica Root

TASTING NOTES: Nutty with orange peel and a biscotti biscuit character on the nose, oily citrus peel with pepper spice and touches of woody elements on the palate, growing nuttiness with pine resin to finish.

SERVING SUGGESTION: Enjoy with Fever-Tree Aromatic Tonic Water.

Mesmeric Distiller's Strength 50.0%

BOTANICALS: Juniper, Coriander Seed, Lemon, Lime, Mandarin, Bergamot, Rosemary, Angelica Root & Navel Orange

TASTING NOTES: Subtle lime leaf with bergamot and pleasant pine on the nose, citrus and pine continue with pepper and creamy marzipan tones on the palate, sweet baking spice with orange to finish.

SERVING SUGGESTION: Enjoy with Fever-Tree Mediterranean Tonic Water.

Summer Cup 25.0%

BOTANICALS: Juniper, Coriander Seed, Lemon, Lime, Mandarin, Bergamot, Rosemary, Angelica Root, Roasted Dandelion Root, Native Pepperberry & Others

TASTING NOTES: Lemonade with orange curaçao character and orange sherbet like notes on the nose, bursting citrus with pepperberry and orange curaçao continuing on the palate, developing black tea tannins to finish.

SERVING SUGGESTION: Enjoy with Fever-Tree Ginger Ale.

the Still co. The Still Co.
Vine Vale, SA

Based just south of Nuriootpa at the heart of the renowned Barossa Valley wine region, The Still Co. is a distillery driven by a still to glass philosophy with a founding partner from a winemaking background but with a passion for distilling. They make their spirits with sustainably sourced botanicals grown both locally and globally.

London Dry Gin 40.0%

BOTANICALS: Juniper, Angelica Root, Coriander Seed, Orange Peel, Liquorice, Orris Root, Cassia & Almond

TASTING NOTES: Burst of juniper with lemon and cinnamon on the nose, dried cinnamon with warming citrus and firm juniper on the palate, lingering spice and citrus to finish.

SERVING SUGGESTION: Enjoy with Fever-Tree Premium Indian Tonic Water.

Barossa Shiraz Gin 40.0%

BOTANICALS: Juniper, Angelica Root, Orris Root, Black Peppercorn, Cardamom Seed, Ginger, Liquorice, Nutmeg, Cassia, Almond, Chamomile & Fennel Seed

TASTING NOTES: Watermelon shrub with balsamic like notes on the nose, white pepper with mulberry, young cherries and balsamic characters on the palate, drying tannins and a whisper of white pepper to finish.

SERVING SUGGESTION: Enjoy with Fever-Tree Lemon Tonic Water.

Blue Butterfly Gin 40.0%

BOTANICALS: Juniper, Angelica Root, Orris Root, Coriander Seed, Orange Peel, Lemon Peel, Lemon Myrtle, Cassia, Nutmeg, Almond, Chamomile & Butterfly Pea flower

TASTING NOTES: Earthy characters with dried flowers and subtle citrus on the nose, lemon myrtle leads with pepper and hints of baking spice supported by strong juniper on the palate, sweet florals and lemon to finish.

SERVING SUGGESTION: Enjoy with Fever-Tree Mediterranean Tonic Water.

The West Winds Distillery
Cowaramup, WA

Stationed in the quirky and picturesque town of Cowaramup in the South West of Western Australia, The West Winds Distillery maintains a vision of celebrating the unique botanicals and grains of Australia on the world stage with their spirits. They take inspiration from the Margaret River region and its high quality produce in their spirits.

Sabre London Dry Gin 40.0%

BOTANICALS: Juniper, Lemon, Lime, Lemon Myrtle & Wattleseed

TASTING NOTES: Tart lemon with hints of juniper and green herbs on the nose, burst of juniper with supporting citrus and subtle warming spice on the palate, warming citrus driven finish

SERVING SUGGESTION: Enjoy with Fever-Tree Premium Indian Tonic Water.

Broadside Navy Strength Gin 58.0%

BOTANICALS: Juniper, Coriander Seed, Bush Tomato & Sea Parsley (includes Margaret River Sea Water)

TASTING NOTES: Intense savoury notes of tomato leaf, sea parsley and coriander seed on the nose, salted lemon and pink peppercorn resin with hints of sea spray on the nose, strong spice driven finish.

SERVING SUGGESTION: Enjoy with Fever-Tree Mediterranean Tonic Water.

Cutlass New World Gin 50.0%

BOTANICALS: Juniper, Lemon, Lime, Cinnamon Myrtle & Bush Tomato

TASTING NOTES: Herbal drive with cinnamon myrtle and a hint of citrus on the nose, juniper and cinnamon myrtle morphing to savoury herbs on the palate, lingering savoury character with lemon and peppery heat to finish.

SERVING SUGGESTION: Enjoy with Fever-Tree Mediterranean Tonic Water.

Pinque Rosé Gin 37.5%

BOTANICALS: Juniper, Lemon Myrtle, Cabernet Sauvignon, Rose Petal, Vanilla Bean, Strawberry Gum & Orange Peel

TASTING NOTES: Unmistakable Provence rosé wine on the nose, opening to dried red fruits and an elegant garrigue freshness on the palate, a touch of raspberry and a light sweetness to finish.

SERVING SUGGESTION: Enjoy with Fever-Tree Refreshingly Light Indian Tonic Water.

Wild Plum Gin 39.0%

BOTANICALS: Juniper, Davidson Plum, Banksia Honey, Cabernet & Sloe Berry

TASTING NOTES: Pronounced juniper with light woody notes on the nose, jammy ripe plum fruitiness carrying a rich sweetness with notes of honey and cinnamon on the palate, tart fruits lead a drying finish.

SERVING SUGGESTION: Enjoy with Fever-Tree Lemon Tonic Water.

Three Little Birds Distillery
Adelaide, SA

Positioned just west of Adelaide's centre in the suburb of Miles End, Three Little Birds Distillery was created to celebrate Australia and takes its name from the rendition of a Bob Marley song by an indigenous singer, Philly, and their interview regarding it. They make their own base spirit, starting with the yeast, for use in their range of spirits and enjoy creating single-season gins with various fruits while supporting local wherever possible.

Signature Gin 43.0%

BOTANICALS: Juniper, Coriander Seed, Orris Root, Liquorice, Nutmeg, Cinnamon, Cardamom, Lime Zest, Lemon Myrtle, Strawberry Gum, Native Pepperberry, Geraldton Wax & Vanilla

TASTING NOTES: Complex geraldton wax with hints of lemon on the nose, bursting lemon zest with earthy perfumed musk on the palate, rich creamy honey tones with continuing earthy tones to finish.

SERVING SUGGESTION: Enjoy with Fever-Tree Mediterranean Tonic Water.

Bramble 34.0%

BOTANICALS: Juniper, Coriander Seed, Orris Root, Liquorice, Nutmeg, Cinnamon, Lime Zest, Lemon Myrtle, Strawberry Gum, Native Pepperberry, Geraldton Wax, Vanilla, Lemon Peel & Blackberry

TASTING NOTES: Pronounced lemon myrtle with lavender on the nose, sweet tropical fruits with candied ginger and hibiscus on the palate, hints of rosella and raspberry to finish.

SERVING SUGGESTION: Enjoy with Fever-Tree Mediterranean Tonic Water.

Shiraz Gin 35.0%

BOTANICALS: Juniper, Coriander Seed, Orris Root, Liquorice, Nutmeg, Cinnamon, Cardamom, Lime Zest, Lemon Myrtle, Strawberry Gum, Native Pepperberry, Geraldton Wax, Vanilla, Orange & Star Anise (combined with Jeanneret Wines Late-Harvest Single-Block Shiraz Grape)

TASTING NOTES: Chocolate coated orange rind with rich ripe dark fruit and baking spice on the nose, initial fruit sweetness with support from clove and apple on the palate, tannic finish.

SERVING SUGGESTION: Enjoy with Fever-Tree Refreshingly Light Indian Tonic Water.

Threefold Distilling
Adelaide, SA

Established in the south-western Glenelg East suburb of Adelaide among its many heritage homes, Threefold Distilling was started by three bartender friends over a few drinks with the goal of creating spirits that were complex, yet relatable and approachable. They design their spirits to match the moments they're enjoyed in, reverse engineering their recipes to suit once they have a moment in mind.

Aromatic Gin 42.0%

BOTANICALS: Juniper, Coriander Seed, Angelica Root, Wattleseed, Grapefruit, Orange, Lemon, Rosemary, Lavender, Pink Peppercorn & Native Pepperberry

TASTING NOTES: Sweet orange juice with rose undertones on the nose, pleasant lavender with wattleseed and tart grapefruit on the palate, pepper spice with lingering sweetness on the finish.

SERVING SUGGESTION: Enjoy with Fever-Tree Premium Indian Tonic Water.

GSM 38.4%

BOTANICALS: Juniper, Coriander Seed, Angelica Root, Wattleseed, Grapefruit, Orange, Lemon, Rosemary, Lavender, Pink Peppercorn & Native Pepperberry (includes Adelaide Hills Shiraz and McLaren Vale Mourvèdre)

TASTING NOTES: Sweet juicy blackcurrant juice on the nose, continuing juicy blackcurrant with dry tannins and herbaceous freshness on the palate, drying florals with a thick coating finish.

SERVING SUGGESTION: Enjoy with Fever-Tree Lemon Tonic Water.

Mediterranean Gin 43.0%

BOTANICALS: Juniper, Coriander Seed, Angelica Root, Celery Seed, Olive, Capers, Lemon, Rosemary, Bay Leaf, Thyme & Basil

TASTING NOTES: Complex bouquet of savoury garden herbs on the nose, unmistakable olive with developing green herbs, celery and thyme on the palate, lingering garden herbs with olive carrying into the finish.

SERVING SUGGESTION: Enjoy with Fever-Tree Mediterranean Tonic Water.

Summer Harvest Raspberry Gin 39.0%

BOTANICALS: Juniper, Coriander Seed, Angelica Root, Wattleseed, Grapefruit, Orange, Lemon, Rosemary, Lavender, Pink Peppercorn, Native Pepperberry & Raspberry

TASTING NOTES: Freeze-dried raspberry with sweet florals on the nose, dried fruit tea-like note with pithy grapefruit and herbal undertones on the palate, dried berry leads with hints of herbs to finish.

SERVING SUGGESTION: Enjoy with Fever-Tree Wild Raspberry Tonic Water.

Tinberry Distilling Co.
Adelaide, SA

Secreted away amongst the hustle and bustle of Adelaide, Tinberry Distilling Co. was started by three school mates reunited over a few drinks, with a focus on approachable spirits that can be shared and enjoyed on any occasion. They make their spirits using a self-made still while taking it as their responsibility to help their communities where and when they can through charity and carbon footprint reduction.

Signature Gin 42.0%

BOTANICALS: Juniper, Coriander Seed, Orris Root, Orange, Lemon, Lime, Lemon Myrtle, Cinnamon, Lavender, Clove & Star Anise

TASTING NOTES: Subtle juniper with anise and coriander on the nose, warming coriander rolls into lemon myrtle with developing florals and growing spice on the palate, star anise and dry juniper to finish.

SERVING SUGGESTION: Enjoy with Fever-Tree Premium Indian Tonic Water.

Tiny Bear Distillery
Melbourne, VIC

Situated in Melbourne's quiet eastern suburb of Knoxfield, Tiny Bear Distillery was started by a high school chemistry/science teacher taking their name from a combination of the fact they make small batches and another that they'll only divulge in person. They use raw ingredients and make their own base spirit from kale for all their products with sustainability at the forefront of their practices.

Doctor Gin 42.0%

BOTANICALS: Juniper, Coriander Seed, Angelica Root, Orris Root, Almond, Cinnamon, Liquorice, Hibiscus, Dill, Vietnamese Mint, Sage & Basil

TASTING NOTES: Bold base spirit characteristics with supporting spice on the nose, liquorice and cassia driven palate, spice heat and lingering angelica to finish.

SERVING SUGGESTION: Enjoy with Fever-Tree Premium Indian Tonic Water.

Gypsy Gin 43.0%

BOTANICALS: Juniper, Coriander Seed, Angelica Root, Orris Root, Almond, Lemon, Lime, Cucumber, Cardamom, Cumin, Sichuan Pepper, Black Peppercorn, Whole Pimento, Grains of Paradise, Clove & Ginger

TASTING NOTES: Sweet baking spice with ginger and musky earth on the nose, delicate grains of paradise with a hint of Sichuan heat and juniper undertones on the palate, lingering angelica and citrus to finish.

SERVING SUGGESTION: Enjoy with Fever-Tree Premium Indian Tonic Water.

Sailor Gin 58.0%

BOTANICALS: Juniper, Coriander Seed, Angelica Root, Orris Root, Orange, Cardamom & Clove

TASTING NOTES: Pronounced clove and cinnamon with orange rind on the nose, sweet orange peel with green cardamom and anise on the palate, lingering orange and a touch of grainy spice to finish.

SERVING SUGGESTION: Enjoy with Fever-Tree Premium Indian Tonic Water.

Tread Softly
Charlestown, NSW

Located in the town of Charlestown between Newcastle and Lake Macquarie, Tread Softly is an environmentally conscious wine brand that also releases a small number of gins. They focus on making lighter style gins with native botanicals while reducing their carbon footprint through efficient production practices and planting an Australian Native Tree for every six bottles sold.

Natural Botanicals Dry Gin 37.0%

BOTANICALS: Juniper, Finger Lime, Coriander Seed, Angelica Root, Pink Rose, Jasmine, Orris Root, Pink Peppercorn, Hibiscus, Lime Peel, Cinnamon, Lemon Myrtle & Nutmeg

TASTING NOTES: Floral apple with hints of dried fruits and citrus drive the nose, dried tea leaves with zesty lime and hints of cardamom on the palate, candied lemon notes to finish.

SERVING SUGGESTION: Enjoy with Fever-Tree Elderflower Tonic Water.

Delicate Botanicals Pink Gin 37.0%

BOTANICALS: Juniper, Finger Lime, Coriander Seed, Angelica Root, Pink Rose, Jasmine, Hibiscus, Chamomile Flower, Orris Root, Pink Peppercorn, Spearmint, Lemon Myrtle, Cinnamon, Nutmeg & Blue Gum

TASTING NOTES: Savoury lime peel with coriander and a slight sea breeze on the nose, lemon myrtle with cinnamon and pepper heat on the palate, dried tea leaves with developing lemon and pepper spice to finish.

SERVING SUGGESTION: Enjoy with Fever-Tree Refreshingly Light Indian Tonic Water.

Turner Stillhouse
Grindelwald, TAS

Set amongst the Swiss-style architecture in the small town of Grindelwald to the northeast of Launceston, Turner Stillhouse was started by an American with a family background in winemaking and distilling who married a Tasmanian from a multi-generational farming family and has cultivated an obsession with Tasmanian spirits and food ever since. They fuse the traditions of Tasmanian craft spirits with American influence to create their premium small batch spirits.

Three Cuts Gin - Founder's Release 42.0%

BOTANICALS: Juniper, Lime, Rose, Coriander Seed, Cinnamon, White Peppercorn & Others

TASTING NOTES: Juniper with spiced heat and rose florals on the nose, strong juniper lead with rose following well on the palate, subtle cinnamon with long lingering rose to finish.

SERVING SUGGESTION: Enjoy with Fever-Tree Refreshingly Light Indian Tonic Water.

Three Cuts Gin - Distiller's Release 42.0%

BOTANICALS: Juniper, Green Cardamom, Lime, Lemon, Coriander Seed, White Peppercorn, Rose & Others

TASTING NOTES: Pronounced cardamom with pepper heat and rose undertones on the nose, rose continues with zesty citrus, and pepper warmth supported by a juniper backbone on the palate, lime and rose linger to finish.

SERVING SUGGESTION: Enjoy with Fever-Tree Refreshingly Light Indian Tonic Water.

Three Cuts Gin - Chardonnay Barrel Rested 40.0%

BOTANICALS: Juniper, Lime, Rose, Coriander Seed, Cinnamon, White Peppercorn & Others (rested in ex-Tasmanian Chardonnay Barrels)

TASTING NOTES: Oaky notes with lime blossom and rosehip on the nose, tannins with cedar spice and light coriander seed on the palate, cinnamon throughout and lingering to finish.

SERVING SUGGESTION: Enjoy neat or with Fever-Tree Ginger Ale.

Three Cuts Gin - Pinot Barrel Rested 40.0%

BOTANICALS: Juniper, Lime, Rose, Coriander Seed, Cinnamon, White Peppercorn & Others (rested in ex-Tasmanian Pinot Noir Barrels)

TASTING NOTES: Swedish pine with hints of raspberry leaf and cinnamon on the nose, pronounced cinnamon with mild baking spice through the palate, notes of Swedish pine on the finish.

SERVING SUGGESTION: Enjoy neat or with Fever-Tree Ginger Ale.

Twenty Third Street Distillery
Renmark, SA

Sequestered away in flourishing Renmark at the heart of the Riverlands on the Murray River, Twenty Third Street Distillery is named for its location on the corner of Twenty Third Street and Renmark Avenue, and is all about creating great spirits and celebrating all creativity. They create their spirits with Australian ingredients, working to always have something intriguing and new around the corner.

Signature Gin 40.0%

BOTANICALS: Juniper, Coriander Seed, Lime, Mandarin & Angelica Root

TASTING NOTES: Clean slightly grassy note with mandarin and herbaceous undertones on the nose, mandarin flesh with angelica and coriander seed on the palate, earthy florals morph into lingering citrus to finish.

SERVING SUGGESTION: Enjoy with Fever-Tree Refreshingly Light Indian Tonic Water.

Red Citrus Gin 40.0%

BOTANICALS: Juniper, Blood Orange, Cara Cara Orange & Native Pepperberry

TASTING NOTES: Crushed blood orange flesh with a slight hint of pepper on the nose, initial fruity citrus burst followed by minty pepper on the palate, lingering blood orange with mint spice to finish.

SERVING SUGGESTION: Enjoy with Fever-Tree Blood Orange Soda.

Violet Gin 40.0%

BOTANICALS: Juniper, Finger Lime, Lemon Myrtle, Wattleseed & Others

TASTING NOTES: Floral lemon myrtle with hints of fruity leaves on the nose, confectionery lemon with finger lime developing to sweeter citrus on the palate, lingering lemonade to finish.

SERVING SUGGESTION: Enjoy with Fever-Tree Mediterranean Tonic Water.

Yuzu Gin 43.0%

BOTANICALS: Juniper, Yuzu, Buddha's Hand, Blood Orange & Navel Orange

TASTING NOTES: Candied citrus with touches of juniper on the nose, initial dry citrus with bursting yuzu flesh and hints of pepper on the palate, zesty mouth-coating yuzu with subtle spice to finish.

SERVING SUGGESTION: Enjoy with Fever-Tree Refreshingly Light Indian Tonic Water.

underground spirits canberra

Underground Spirits

Canberra, ACT

Seated in the large Canberra suburb of Kambah just south of the scenic Mount Taylor Nature Reserve, Underground Spirits was started by a self-styled 'ideas man' with a background as a fertility specialist and robotic surgeon, and a focus on the Australian spirit of innovation. They use a unique sub-zero, sub-micron, cryo-filtration process to eliminate impurities earlier than other distillation techniques in the making of their spirits.

Underground Spirits Gin 40.0%

BOTANICALS: Juniper, Angelica Root, Coriander Seed, Lemon Myrtle, River Mint, Native Pepperberry, Poppy Seed, Black Peppercorn, Basil & Cinnamon

TASTING NOTES: Cherry pit with thyme and hints of pine resin on the nose, nutty hazelnut and dark wattleseed notes with sharp lime on the palate, lengthy pepper to finish.

SERVING SUGGESTION: Enjoy with Fever-Tree Mediterranean Tonic Water.

Shiraz Gin with Tasmanian Pepperberries 40.0%

BOTANICALS: Juniper, Angelica Root, Coriander Seed, Lemon Myrtle, River Mint, Native Pepperberry, Poppy Seed, Black Peppercorn, Basil & Cinnamon (aged in ex-Shiraz Oak Barrels)

TASTING NOTES: Pine with green mulberry and cranberry on the nose, opening with toasted oak and subtle developing stone fruits on the palate, oaky finish with vanillin and dried apricot.

SERVING SUGGESTION: Enjoy with Fever-Tree Lemon Tonic Water.

Unexpected Guest Distillery
Sydney, NSW

Produced in Sydney, or just about anywhere actually, with their two copper stills mounted on the back of a 1972 Kombi, Unexpected Guest Distillery operates under the mantra that every bottle of gin is an unforgettable party. They name each of their gins after one of their 'unexpected guests' who rocks up and turns the whole night around, making each of them with quirky characteristics.

Bobby's London Dry Gin 40.0%
BOTANICALS: Juniper, Citrus, Pepper & Coriander Seed

TASTING NOTES: Crushed juniper with coriander seed on the nose, distinct coriander leads with wet juniper, citrus and pepper spice on the palate, persistent juniper, coriander and pepper to finish.

SERVING SUGGESTION: Enjoy with Fever-Tree Premium Indian Tonic Water.

Clementine's American Gin 40.0%
BOTANICALS: Juniper, Lavender, Orange & Vanilla

TASTING NOTES: Savoury vanilla and dried lavender on the nose, slightly sweet orange peel with developing dry florals on the palate, lasting dried flowers with hints of citrus peel to finish.

SERVING SUGGESTION: Enjoy with Fever-Tree Elderflower Tonic Water.

Disco Flamingo's Pink Gin 40.0%
BOTANICALS: Juniper, Orange & Lemon (steeped in Raspberry)

TASTING NOTES: Tart freeze-dried raspberries and baked plum on the nose, sweet raspberry jam-like notes with building lemon citrus in support on the palate, lingering raspberry jam sweetness to finish.

SERVING SUGGESTION: Enjoy with Fever-Tree Wild Raspberry Tonic Water.

Young Tom's Bathtub Gin 40.0%

BOTANICALS: Juniper, Lemon Myrtle, Orange, Almond & Vanilla

TASTING NOTES: Juniper leads with crushed wet green leaf undertones on the nose, spiced juniper with a gentle myrtle tingle on the palate, developing bitter orange peel with a creamy texture to finish.

SERVING SUGGESTION: Enjoy with Fever-Tree Premium Indian Tonic Water.

Wandering Distillery
Fremantle, WA

Sitting in the predominantly industrial suburb of O'Connor in lively Fremantle, Wandering Distillery is a family-owned nano-distillery that was born in Mount Eliza on the Mornington Peninsula before relocating, named for their distiller's wandering past and his English wife's hometown football team. They use organic botanicals wherever possible and local when available, including from their backyard, to make spirits that reflect their belief that every drink is a journey.

Signature Gin 43.0%

BOTANICALS: Juniper, Coriander Seed, Orange Peel, Lemon Myrtle, Cassia, Black Peppercorn, Rosemary & Angelica Root

TASTING NOTES: Oily rosemary with earthy root spice and supporting citrus on the nose, rosemary and coriander with supporting pepper heat and lemon myrtle on the palate, lingering citrus and crushed green leaves to finish.

SERVING SUGGESTION: Enjoy with Fever-Tree Mediterranean Tonic Water.

Naval Gazing Navy Strength Gin 57.6%

BOTANICALS: Juniper, Coriander Seed, Orange Peel, Lemon Myrtle, Cassia & Black Peppercorn

TASTING NOTES: Sweet lemon oil and a bright salty note on the nose, sharp zest with hot pepper spice rounding out to sweet citrus on the palate, lingering pepper with citrus peel to finish.

SERVING SUGGESTION: Enjoy with Fever-Tree Mediterranean Tonic Water.

Nomad Gin 42.0%

BOTANICALS: Juniper, Coriander Seed, Geraldton Wax, Samphire, Sea Parsley & Native Thyme

TASTING NOTES: Striking geraldton wax with a touch of sea breeze on the nose, juniper leads with waxy herbs and thyme on the palate, herbaceous minty heat from thyme and lingering geraldton wax to finish.

SERVING SUGGESTION: Enjoy with Fever-Tree Mediterranean Tonic Water.

Odyssey Gin 40.0%

BOTANICALS: Juniper, Coriander Seed, Lemon Myrtle, Finger Lime, Hemp Seed, Rosemary & Others

TASTING NOTES: Fragrant green herbs with bright citrus on the nose, oily rosemary with light lime zest and juniper on the palate, menthol spice carries with warming juniper to finish.

SERVING SUGGESTION: Enjoy with Fever-Tree Mediterranean Tonic Water.

Wild Flower Gin Distillery
Gold Coast, QLD

Nestled in the Varsity Lakes suburb of the Gold Coast near the tranquil Lake Orr, Wild Flower Gin Distillery takes its name from their use of wildflower honey and sometimes send out bee-friendly wildflower seed mixes with each bottle. They use honey from their founder/distiller's backyard bees that visit the wildflowers of Burleigh and add subtle, local flavours to their spirits.

Signature Gin 40.0%

BOTANICALS: Juniper, Coriander Seed, Angelica Root, Cassia, Lemon Peel, Honey & Smoked Cardamom

TASTING NOTES: Lifted juniper with a hint of lemon myrtle and a savoury fruit undertone on the nose, lemon myrtle leads with a hint of rhubarb and rising sweetness on the palate, sweet orange blossom lingers to finish.

SERVING SUGGESTION: Enjoy with Fever-Tree Mediterranean Tonic Water.

Pink Gin 40.0%

BOTANICALS: Juniper, Coriander Seed, Angelica Root, Cassia, Lemon Peel, Honey, Smoked Cardamom, Raspberry & Hibiscus

TASTING NOTES: Striking raspberry sweetness with perfumed floral tones on the nose, hibiscus with dried raspberry supporting on the palate, fruity tea-like tannin to finish.

SERVING SUGGESTION: Enjoy with Fever-Tree Wild Raspberry Tonic Water.

Wild Hibiscus Distilling Co
Sydney, NSW

Located in the McGrath's Hill suburb of northwest Sydney in the charming Hawkesbury Valley, Wild Hibiscus Distilling Co specialises in making brightly coloured all natural gins made for mixing. They use native and exotic botanicals grown on their own farms in the valley along with juniper from the Rhodope Mountains in Bulgaria, and others, loaded into oversized baskets to impart more flavour into their spirits.

Finger Lime Gin 40.0%

BOTANICALS: Juniper (Bulgaria), Makrut Lime, Tahitian Lime Leaf, Navelina Orange, Lemon, Vanilla, Coriander Seed & Cardamom (includes suspended Finger Lime Caviar)

TASTING NOTES: Pithy lime leads with delicate cardamom on the nose, zesty up front with supporting spice on the palate, mellowing cardamom with waxy lime to finish.

SERVING SUGGESTION: Enjoy with Fever-Tree Refreshingly Light Indian Tonic Water.

B'Lure Butterfly Pea & Elderflower Gin 40.0%

BOTANICALS: Juniper (Bulgaria), Butterfly Pea Flower, Elderflower, Honey, Lemon, Vanilla, Coriander Seed & Cardamom

TASTING NOTES: Warm melted honey tones with lemon and buttery notes on the nose, honeycomb with sweet elderflower and developing florals on the palate, creamy finish with lingering florals.

SERVING SUGGESTION: Enjoy with Fever-Tree Elderflower Tonic Water.

Flower & Ginger Gin 40.0%

BOTANICALS: Juniper (Bulgaria), Hibiscus Flower Juice (Cold Pressed), Ginger, Lemon, Vanilla, Coriander Seed & Cardamom

TASTING NOTES: Floral lead with supporting ginger undertones on the nose, sweet texture of hibiscus juice, hints of rose and sweet ginger on the palate, sweet lemon lingering well to finish.

SERVING SUGGESTION: Enjoy with Fever-Tree Elderflower Tonic Water.

WILD ROAD SPIRITS
Wild Road Spirits
Perth, WA

Ensconced in the industrial suburb of Welshpool in south-eastern Perth, Wild Road Spirits started as a couple of brothers in a small garage conceptualising products inspired by Australian contemporary flavours with a wild twist. They combine select botanicals with native Australian produce using methods walking the line between conventional and unconventional to make their spirits.

Citrus Mistress 42.0%

BOTANICALS: Juniper, Coriander Seed, Angelica Root, Orris Root, Grapefruit, Lime, Native Pepperberry, Rosemary & Sage

TASTING NOTES: Fragrant orange oil with undertones of orris root on the nose, fresh lime juice with hints of garden herbs and a slight almond tone on the palate, lime juice lingers to finish.

SERVING SUGGESTION: Enjoy with Fever-Tree Premium Indian Tonic Water.

D'ginn Du Sol 42.0%

BOTANICALS: Juniper, Coriander Seed, Angelica Root, Orris Root, Desert Lime, Sunrise Lime, Mandarin, Almond, Hazelnut, Wormwood, Nutmeg & Cinnamon

TASTING NOTES: Pronounced mandarin and lime with hints of florals on the nose, dry cooking spice with hints of coriander seed and cardamom on the palate, mandarin oil lingers well to finish.

SERVING SUGGESTION: Enjoy with Fever-Tree Mediterranean Tonic Water.

Gin Ne Sais Quoi 42.0%

BOTANICALS: Juniper, Coriander Seed, Angelica Root, Orris Root, Orange, Lemon Myrtle, Cinnamon, Nutmeg, Ginger & Clove

TASTING NOTES: Orange juice with hints of clove and ginger on the nose, strong warming nutmeg with spiced orange and developing angelica on the palate, hints of cardamom and warming orange to finish.

SERVING SUGGESTION: Enjoy with Fever-Tree Premium Indian Tonic Water.

Wild Wombat Spirits
Sydney, NSW

Based in northern Sydney near the Harbour Bridge, Wild Wombat Spirits has the outlaw character of Mr W., an anthropomorphic wombat, at their centre, with the mission to make great grog. They make a range of spirits, each with 'one helluva flavour', designed to convey rugged elegance in every sip and put a smile on your dial using Australian wheat base spirit and Australian spring water.

Wild Wombat Gin 42.0%

BOTANICALS: Juniper, Lemon Myrtle, Apple, Cassia, Orange, Coriander Seed, Angelica Root, Cinnamon, Clove, Nutmeg & Cardamom

TASTING NOTES: Pronounced base spirit notes with hints of light spice on the nose, subtle juniper with rich base notes continuing on the palate, butterscotch like note on the finish.

SERVING SUGGESTION: Enjoy with Fever-Tree Aromatic Tonic Water.

Wildbrumby Distillery
Crackenback, NSW

Situated in the heart of the Australian high country between Jindabyne and Thredbo, Wildbrumby Distillery is the highest distillery in Australia, only 22km from the highest peak, started with the dream of delivering a home-grown schnapps and taking inspiration from their surroundings. They use pristine alpine water, organically grown fruit, and native mountain botanicals with traditional methods learnt in Austria to make their range of spirits.

Wildbrumby Gin 40.0%

BOTANICALS: Juniper, Coriander Seed, Green Cardamom, Native Pepperberry, Pink Grapefruit & Kumquat

TASTING NOTES: Vibrant grapefruit zest with gentle spice and hints of juniper on the nose, light pepper with juniper, coriander and citrus on the palate, lingering cardamom warmth and lemon to finish.

SERVING SUGGESTION: Enjoy with Fever-Tree Premium Indian Tonic Water.

Rubus Patch Gin 40.0%

BOTANICALS: Juniper, Green Cardamom, Coriander Seed, Native Pepperberry, Raspberry, Rose Petal, Pink Peppercorn, Liquorice, Pink Grapefruit & Kumquat

TASTING NOTES: Bold pine with mountain pepper and rich florals on the nose, initial juniper with coriander, cardamom and a touch of pepper on the palate, lingering fruits and developing florals to finish.

SERVING SUGGESTION: Enjoy with Fever-Tree Elderflower Tonic Water.

Stallion Navy Strength Gin 57.0%

BOTANICALS: Juniper, Coriander Seed, Native Pepperberry, Cassia, Ginger, Black Tea, Green Cardamom, Pink Grapefruit, Kumquat, Orange & Raisin

TASTING NOTES: Pepper characters with dried tea notes and bitter citrus on the nose, cassia with pepperberry, saltbush and cardamom on the palate, strong black tea notes developing to finish.

SERVING SUGGESTION: Enjoy with Fever-Tree Mediterranean Tonic Water.

Willing Distillery
Darwin, NT

Planted in the Winnellie suburb of balmy and colourful Darwin, Willing Distillery is Australia's most northern commercial distillery and is driven by a desire to create a premium product that embodies and honours the best qualities of Northern Territory culture and the local natural environment. They use native Australian botanicals in their spirits while championing community and craft.

Darwin Dry Small Batch Gin 42.0%

BOTANICALS: Juniper & Others

TASTING NOTES: Striking cardamom with a pine needle and anise on the nose, anise and cardamom lead with strong pine and citrus pith on the palate, lingering pepper with a touch of liquorice to finish.

SERVING SUGGESTION: Enjoy with Fever-Tree Premium Indian Tonic Water.

Desert Lime Small Batch Gin 40.0%

BOTANICALS: Juniper, Desert Lime, Liquorice & Others

TASTING NOTES: Hints of liquorice and pronounced coriander on the nose, liquorice and coriander lead with support from juniper on the palate, warming citrus and pine to finish.

SERVING SUGGESTION: Enjoy with Fever-Tree Premium Indian Tonic Water.

Kakadu Plum & Quandong Small Batch Gin 40.0%

BOTANICALS: Juniper, Kakadu Plum, Quandong & Others

TASTING NOTES: Tart fruity notes and subtle herbal tones on the nose, pronounced plum with citrus and light spice on the palate, sweet spice and mellowing citrus to finish.

SERVING SUGGESTION: Enjoy with Fever-Tree Mediterranean Tonic Water.

Sweetheart's Navy Strength Gin 58.0%

BOTANICALS: Juniper, Cardamom, Cinnamon & Lemon Myrtle

TASTING NOTES: Bursting juniper with cardamom and cinnamon on the nose, cardamom and cinnamon continue with light juniper and anise on the palate, mentholic cardamom spice to finish.

SERVING SUGGESTION: Enjoy with Fever-Tree Aromatic Tonic Water.

Winding Road Distilling Co.
Tintenbar, NSW

Set amongst the scenic roads and hinterland of New South Wales' Far North Coast, Winding Road Distilling Co. is a family-run distillery founded with the aim of crafting premium small batch spirits that capture the natural beauty and abundance of the Northern Rivers region. They feature natural and local ingredients in their spirits influenced by Australian culture, the region, and their heritage.

Citrus and Sea Gin 44.0%

BOTANICALS: Juniper, Coriander Seed, Native Pepperberry, Whole Orange, Dried Orange Peel, Strawberry Gum Leaf, Native Pepperleaf, Angelica Root, Orris Root, Liquorice & Golden Kelp

TASTING NOTES: Pepperberry with citrus and a sea spray undertone on the nose, pepperberry leads with herbal undertones and drying strawberry gum on the palate, lingering strawberry gum on the finish.

SERVING SUGGESTION: Enjoy with Fever-Tree Mediterranean Tonic Water.

Winston Quinn Handcrafted Gin
Brisbane, QLD

Secreted away in charming and energetic Brisbane, Winston Quinn Handcrafted Gin is a small batch craft gin company named for its owner's two golden retrievers reflecting their tailor made process in their jeans-based naming convention. They draw on a vast range of botanicals and fresh produce, including locally sourced organic fruit, to create their range of spirits which are all naturally coloured.

Dry Cut Classic Dry Gin 40.0%

BOTANICALS: Juniper, Angelica Root, Coriander Seed, Lavender, Lemon Myrtle, Lemon Peel, Orange Peel & Violet Leaf

TASTING NOTES: Orange peel with bright lemon myrtle on the nose, pronounced lemon with supporting juniper and orange peel on the palate, oily citrus lingers to finish.

SERVING SUGGESTION: Enjoy with Fever-Tree Mediterranean Tonic Water.

Double Denim Navy Strength Gin 57.0%

BOTANICALS: Juniper, Angelica Root, Coriander Seed, Lavender, Lemon Myrtle, Lemon Peel, Orange Peel & Violet Leaf

TASTING NOTES: Striking orange with lemon myrtle and subtle juniper on the nose, oily lemon and pronounced violet on the palate, sweet orange and lemon myrtle to finish.

SERVING SUGGESTION: Enjoy with Fever-Tree Mediterranean Tonic Water.

Pink Fit Strawberry Gin 40.0%

BOTANICALS: Juniper, Strawberry, Orange Peel, Grapefruit Peel, Elderflower, Wild Apple, Hibiscus, Angelica Root, Coriander Seed & Lemon Myrtle

TASTING NOTES: Hibiscus, rose and geranium leaf with lemon on the nose, sweet baking spice with angelica, cucumber and leafy floral notes on the palate, warming clove and cinnamon to finish.

SERVING SUGGESTION: Enjoy with Fever-Tree Elderflower Tonic Water.

Skinny Jeans Blue Dry Gin 40.0%

BOTANICALS: Juniper, Butterfly Pea Flower, Lemon Peel, Orange Peel, Coriander Seed, Angelica Root, Lavender, Lemon Myrtle & Violet Leaf

TASTING NOTES: Lemon myrtle with pronounced lavender and hints of cucumber on the nose, refreshing lemon myrtle, light florals and dry coriander on the palate, lingering lemon to finish.

SERVING SUGGESTION: Enjoy with Fever-Tree Mediterranean Tonic Water.

Slim Crop Cucumber Gin 40.0%

BOTANICALS: Juniper, Cucumber, Lemon Peel, Angelica Root, Lemon Myrtle & Coriander Seed

TASTING NOTES: Cucumber water with floral honey sweetness on the nose, soft salted cucumber with hints of strawberry fruitiness on the palate, mentholic cardamom lingers to finish.

SERVING SUGGESTION: Enjoy with Fever-Tree Mediterranean Tonic Water.

Wolf Lane Distillery
Cairns, QLD

Housed in an early 1900s horse stable right in the centre of vibrant and tropical Cairns, Wolf Lane Distillery has a passion for creating spirits that pay homage to Tropical North Queensland and its selection of botanicals. They craft gins centred on locally sourced ingredients, supporting local farmers and growers that opt for sustainable and organic farming, both steeping dry botanicals and vapour infusing fresh ones.

Tropical Gin 42.5%

BOTANICALS: Juniper, Coriander Seed, Angelica Root, Cinnamon, Lemon Myrtle, Native Pepperberry, Cardamom, Macadamia, Ruby Red Grapefruit, Mango, Finger Lime, Lavender & Mint

TASTING NOTES: Cinnamon and cardamom with a minty aroma on the nose, tropical fruits with baking spice and tingling zest on the palate, gentle pine with musky earth notes to finish.

SERVING SUGGESTION: Enjoy with Fever-Tree Premium Indian Tonic Water.

Davidson Plum Gin 37.5%

BOTANICALS: Juniper, Coriander Seed, Angelica Root, Cinnamon, Lemon Myrtle, Native Pepperberry, Cardamom, Macadamia, Orange, Lavender, Mint & Davidson Plum

TASTING NOTES: Sharp citrus with fresh raspberry and cherry notes on the nose, crisp acidity with restrained sweetness on the palate, finishing with cinnamon and pepperberry spice.

SERVING SUGGESTION: Enjoy with Fever-Tree Lemon Tonic Water.

Navy Strength Gin 58.0%

BOTANICALS: Juniper, Coriander Seed, Angelica Root, Cinnamon, Lemon Myrtle, Native Pepperberry, Cardamom, Macadamia, Ruby Red Grapefruit, Mango, Finger Lime, Lavender & Mint

TASTING NOTES: Tropical fruits with dominant citrus on the nose, juniper and orange with creamy macadamia on the palate, sharp lemon peel and liquorice sweetness to finish.

SERVING SUGGESTION: Enjoy with Fever-Tree Premium Indian Tonic Water.

Yack Creek Distillery
Yackandandah, VIC

Sequestered away just outside the small tourist town of Yackandandah near the Stanley State Forest and steeped in the legacy of gold, Yack Creek Distillery was started by two friends with a passion for whisky and rum that has since expanded to vodka and gin. They make their own neutral spirits from Australian grain and molasses and use pristine water from the Yackandandah Creek that flows down from the Stanley Forest past their property.

Dry Gin 43.0%

BOTANICALS: Juniper, Cinnamon, Lemon Peel, Lime Peel, Mixed Peppercorn, Liquorice, Coriander Seed, Cardamom, Rosemary, Coconut, Elderflower & Star Anise

TASTING NOTES: Mossy character with woody cassia spice on the nose, crushed damp juniper with supporting cassia and lively star anise on the palate, liquorice sweetness to finish.

SERVING SUGGESTION: Enjoy with Fever-Tree Premium Indian Tonic Water.

Hibiscus Gin 43.0%

BOTANICALS: Juniper, Pink Grapefruit, Orris Root, Tea, Dried Hibiscus, Angelica Root, Cardamom & Coriander Seed

TASTING NOTES: Steeped tea notes with a touch of rhubarb on the nose, sweet hibiscus with grapefruit peel and lemon myrtle on the palate, light cardamom spice and lingering orris to finish.

SERVING SUGGESTION: Enjoy with Fever-Tree Premium Indian Tonic Water.

Lemon Myrtle Gin 43.0%

BOTANICALS: Juniper, Lemon Myrtle, Lemon Peel, Angelica Root, Orris Root, Coriander Seed & Pink Peppercorn

TASTING NOTES: Soft honey with lemon myrtle and hints of tea on the nose, upfront lemon myrtle with gentle ginger spice and soft honey on the palate, lingering lemon oil to finish.

SERVING SUGGESTION: Enjoy with Fever-Tree Premium Indian Tonic Water.

Livid Lime Gin 43.0%

BOTANICALS: Juniper, Coriander Seed, Lime Peel, Angelica Root, Ginger, Star Anise, Black Peppercorn & Allspice

TASTING NOTES: Ginger, star anise, allspice and woody characters on the nose, upfront pepper with rolling star anise and warm honey on the palate, earthy angelica to finish.

SERVING SUGGESTION: Enjoy with Fever-Tree Aromatic Tonic Water.

Navy Strength Gin 58.0%

BOTANICALS: Juniper, Cassia, Cinnamon, Liquorice, Orris Root, Pink Peppercorn, Black Peppercorn, Nutmeg, Star Anise, Coriander Seed & Rosemary

TASTING NOTES: Crushed juniper with cinnamon on the nose, juniper leads with cardamom and baking spice on the palate, lingering pepper with a touch of cinnamon to finish.

SERVING SUGGESTION: Enjoy with Fever-Tree Premium Indian Tonic Water.

Silk Road Gin 43.0%

BOTANICALS: Juniper, Coriander Seed, Cassia, Tea, Green Cardamom, Angelica Root, Jasmine & Ginger

TASTING NOTES: Gingerbread, cardamom and light menthol on the nose, steeped tea with warming cassia and ginger on the palate, light florals with a honeyed sweetness on the finish.

SERVING SUGGESTION: Enjoy with Fever-Tree Aromatic Tonic Water.

YOUNG HENRYS
Young Henrys Brewing and Distilling
Sydney, NSW

Positioned in the quirky and eclectic inner-city suburb of Newtown in Sydney, Young Henrys Brewing and Distilling was founded on the premise that the Australian beer scene should be more adventurous, innovative, and fun with the maxim to 'serve the people'. They blend techniques and flavours from both distillation and brewing, along with a love of Australian botanicals, and a focus on sustainability and ethical operations in the creation of their spirits.

Noble Cut New World Australian Gin 40.0%

BOTANICALS: Juniper, Angelica Root, Lemon Peel, Lemon Myrtle, Native Pepperberry & Enigma Hop Flower

TASTING NOTES: Sweet hops with blossoms and grassy sweet herbs on the nose, oily orange leads with soft fruity elements developing on the palate, a hint of pepper lingers to finish.

SERVING SUGGESTION: Enjoy with Fever-Tree Mediterranean Tonic Water.

Noble Cut Newtown Strength Gin 55.0%

BOTANICALS: Juniper, Angelica Root, Lemon Peel, Lemon Myrtle, Native Pepperberry & Enigma Hop Flower

TASTING NOTES: Confectionary lime character with hints of florals on the nose, building citrus with supporting florals, hints of juniper and pepper throughout the palate, strong citrus and floral tones linger to finish.

SERVING SUGGESTION: Enjoy with Fever-Tree Premium Indian Tonic Water.

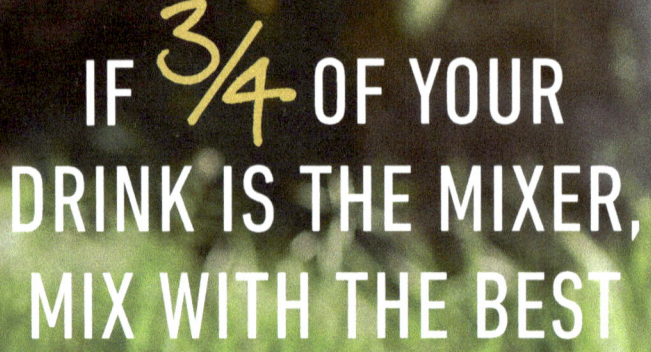

A SHORT HISTORY OF TONIC

NO CARBONATION, NO TONIC. NO TONIC, NO FEVER-TREE!
Does not bear thinking about. We have gin, we have ice and now we have carbonation. But what about tonic?

To find the answer to that question you only have to look at the name itself. You see, unlike gin, tonic really does have medicinal qualities to it. Or at least, quinine which is found in the bark of the Cinchona Tree from which Tonic is made does (and just as well too). In the 1600's, with the world plagued by malaria carrying mosquitos, a Jesuit monk called Agostino (Jesuits were considered the geniuses of the time) discovered that native Indians who would chew the Cinchona bark when they had fever would see their fever subside.

So, he wondered whether it could do the same with Malaria – and hey presto! The medicine was sent all over Europe and for the first time ever there was a way to prevent the epidemic spreading.

In the 1800s, we saw the first 'Indian Tonic Waters' created as the British soldiers stationed in India mixed their daily ration of quinine with 'a spoonful of sugar to help the medicine go down' along with some local spices and citrus. That little Cinchona bark pretty much changed the world. These enterprising soldiers and their counter parts in the Royal Navy couldn't resist mixing this medicinal mixture with their ration of gin. The humble G&T. This little concoction revolutionised the way people took their daily medicine and also when they took it. With the mosquitos choosing to come out as the sun went down, all over Europe people would raise a glass at sunset and enjoy a gin and tonic as a pleasantly social ritual.

In London, gin's reputation was on the rise. So much was gin's transformation that it inspired one London-based gentleman, an Erasmus Bond, to come up with the simple, yet wonderful idea of a pre-made tonic. In doing so, the social status of the drink had now been well and truly elevated.

DID YOU KNOW?
Under a UV light, the quinine in tonic water makes the water fluoresce a brilliant bright blue.

SIR WINSTON CHURCHILL SAID...
"Gin and tonic has saved more Englishmen's lives, and minds, than all the doctors in the Empire!"

HOW TO CREATE THE
PERFECT GIN & TONIC

It all began in 2003 with a meeting of minds and one simple premise: if three quarters of your G&T is the tonic, wouldn't you want it to be the best?

REIGNITING A LONG-FORGOTTEN AND NEGLECTED SECTOR OF THE DRINKS INDUSTRY

Our co-founders Charles and Tim, working in different parts of the drinks business, had both spotted that premium spirits were growing quickly, fuelled by consumers' increasing awareness of the provenance of what they ate and drank.

However, this growing interest in premium food and drink had seemed to neglect mixers, a crucial element of the drinks industry that remained flat. It struck them both as extraordinary that people were paying a good deal of money for a high-quality spirit, yet had no choice but drown it with a poor-quality mixer

CHARLES AND TIM SET OUT TO PUT QUALITY BACK INTO MIXERS

From the very beginning, Charles and Tim approached their business in a different way – there would be no compromise at Fever-Tree. Flavour and quality were of the utmost importance. This mindset led them on an 18-month adventure from the archives of the British Library to facing the wrong end of a Kalashnikov in the Democratic Republic of Congo and concluded with the launch of our Premium Indian Tonic Water in 2005, with the belief we still operate by today...

PIONEERING TO PRODUCE AN UNRIVALLED DRINKING EXPERIENCE AT EVERY OCCASION

Since we put the lid on our first bottle of our Premium Indian Tonic Water, we haven't wavered in our single-minded mission to bring quality, flavour and choice back to mixers. Innovation remains at the heart of Fever-Tree and we've developed an award winning range of tonic waters that perfectly complement the varied flavour categories of gin. We've found three incredibly diverse varieties of ginger that, together, create a remarkably deep, fresh and true taste, which we've used to make a selection of ginger ales and ginger beer. We have lemonades using the finest, naturally sourced ingredients and have recently launched our Soda

Collection – A brand-new range of three mouth-watering flavoured sodas, including Lime & Yuzu, Italian Blood Orange and Pink Grapefruit. Our story is about going to the ends of the earth in pursuit of the best and, the most exciting thing is, we've only just scratched the surface.

OUR MIXERS

We start with the idea that, if ¾ of your drink is the mixer, then you should use the best. We work with only the best naturally sourced ingredients from around the world and no artificial flavourings or sweeteners to create mixers that do justice to the world's finest spirits

PAIR YOUR FAVOURITE PREMIUM GINS WITH FEVER-TREE MIXERS

Gin is an often overlooked spirit, despite its incredibly rich diversity. Bursts of juicy citrus, deliciously savoury herb notes and crisp, floral flavours are just some of the immense range of characteristics this one spirit can contain. Fever-Tree has been on a relentless pioneering pursuit to create a selection of award-winning tonic waters, each one individually crafted to complement the diverse flavour profiles of gin. While made with gins in mind, our tonics pair equally as well.

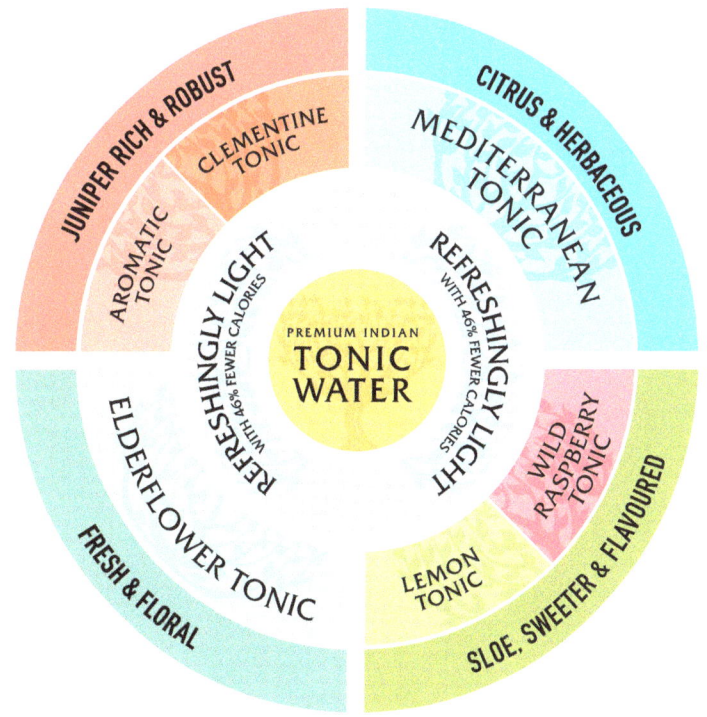

TONICS

PREMIUM INDIAN TONIC WATER

Available in Refreshingly Light with 46% fewer calories.

By blending subtle botanicals flavours with spring water and quinine of the highest quality from the fever trees of the Democratic Republic of the Congo, we have created a delicious tonic water with a uniquely refreshing taste and aroma.

MEDITERRANEAN TONIC WATER

Available in Refreshingly Light with 46% fewer calories.

By blending the essential oils from the flowers, fruits and herbs that we have gathered from around the Mediterranean shores with the quinine of the highest quality from the fever trees of the Democratic Republic of the Congo, we have created a delicious, delicate, floral tonic water.

ELDERFLOWER TONIC WATER

By blending the essential oils from handpicked English elderflowers with quinine of the highest quality from the fever trees of the Democratic Republic of the Congo, we have created a delicious, floral variation of our Indian Tonic Water.

AROMATIC TONIC WATER

By blending the gentle bitterness of South American angostura bark with aromatic botanicals such as cardamom, pimento berry and ginger, we've created a delicious, unique tonic water that can be enjoyed in a Pink G&T or as a sophisticated soft drink on its own.

LEMON TONIC WATER

By blending the finest Sicilian lemons with spring water and quinine of the highest quality from the fever trees of the Democratic Republic of the Congo, we have created a delicious lemon tonic water with an authentic refreshing taste and aroma.

WILD RASPBERRY TONIC WATER

Refreshingly Light with fewer calories.
By blending natural flavourings of juicy Scottish raspberries with sweet rhubarb, we've created a refreshingly fruity tonic water, reminiscent of summer. Simply mix with your favourite pink or London Dry Gin for a sweeter twist on a gin and tonic.

CLEMENTINE ORANGE TONIC WATER

By blending spring water with the essential oils of Spanish Clementine's, balanced with the gentle bitterness of our signature quinine. The sweet, juicy notes of the clementine's make it the perfect accompaniment to London dry gins, creating a delicious orange serve to be enjoyed all year round.

GINGERS & COLA

PREMIUM GINGER BEER

A brewed product that contains a unique blend of the finest gingers, subtle botanical flavours and spring water. Not too sweet on the palate and with a deep long lasting ginger character.

DRY GINGER ALE

By using a unique blend of naturally sourced gingers, subtle botanical flavours and spring water, we have created a delicious Ginger Ale with an authentic, refreshing taste and aroma. Perfectly balanced to enhance the flavour notes of the finest whiskies, bourbons and rums.

SPICED ORANGE GINGER ALE

A unique blend of our signature gingers, combined with sweet clementine and spicy cinnamon. The combination of ginger, citrus and spice has been crafted to complement the rich full bodied flavours found in the finest dark spirits, in particular Scotch, Cognacs & Rums.

DISTILLERS COLA

Our recipe is no secret. We are proud to use a selection of the finest naturally sourced ingredients including Caribbean kola nuts, Tahitian limes and a selection of distilled botanicals & spices including Jamaican pimento berry & Madagascan vanilla

SODAS

ITALIAN BLOOD ORANGE SODA

Juicy blood oranges from Sicily meet an iconic herbal blend to create our Italian Blood Orange Soda. This complex and sophisticated mixer pairs perfectly with Italian liqueurs, bitters and premium vodka.

LIME & YUZU SODA

Our Lime & Yuzu Soda is made with Tahiti lime from Mexico's fertile groves in addition to pressed juice from the wonderfully floral Japanese yuzu, to create a low-calorie soda that's perfect for mixing with premium vodka or tequila for a mouth wateringly zesty summer spritz.

PINK GRAPEFRUIT SODA

This delicious, low-calorie soda is made with real juice from hand-picked pink Florida grapefruits. Pairs perfectly with tequila or mezcal for a classic Paloma or with vodka for a refreshing, light spritz. Less than half the calories & sugar of traditional grapefruit juice or other grapefruit sodas.

PREMIUM SODA WATER

By using soft spring water, bicarbonate of soda and a high level of carbonation, we have created a delicious soda water with a delicate aroma. Perfect for bringing out the best flavours of the finest whiskies.

www.ingramcontent.com/pod-product-compliance
Lightning Source LLC
Chambersburg PA
CBHW062046290426
44109CB00027B/2753